Do We Need HR?

Do We Need HR?

Repositioning People Management for Success

Paul Sparrow
Professor of International HRM, Lancaster University Management School, UK

Martin Hird
Executive Director, Centre for Performance-led HR, Lancaster University, UK

and

Cary L. Cooper
Pro-Vice Chancellor (External Relations) and Professor of Organizational Psychology and Health, Lancaster University, UK

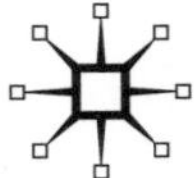

First published 2015 by
PALGRAVE MACMILLAN

Palgrave Macmillan in the UK is an imprint of Macmillan Publishers Limited, registered in England, company number 785998, of Houndmills, Basingstoke, Hampshire RG21 6XS.

Palgrave Macmillan in the US is a division of St Martin's Press LLC, 175 Fifth Avenue, New York, NY 10010.

Palgrave Macmillan is the global academic imprint of the above companies and has companies and representatives throughout the world.

Palgrave® and Macmillan® are registered trademarks in the United States, the United Kingdom, Europe and other countries.

ISBN 978–1–137–00232–7

This book is printed on paper suitable for recycling and made from fully managed and sustained forest sources. Logging, pulping and manufacturing processes are expected to conform to the environmental regulations of the country of origin.

A catalogue record for this book is available from the British Library.

A catalog record for this book is available from the Library of Congress.

Typeset by MPS Limited, Chennai, India.

Contents

List of Figures and Tables

Figures

Tables

Acknowledgements

We would like to thank the HR Directors of BAE Systems, Fujitsu, Hanson, IBM, Legal and General, McDonald's, Nestlé, the Nuclear Decommissioning Authority, Prudential, the Rank Group, Rolls Royce, Royal Bank of Scotland, Sellafield, Vodafone and the Welsh Government who have supported the Centre in this latest period of research. We also thank the CIPD for research support on two projects, and the hundreds of managers who we have interviewed as part of the research.

About the Authors

Paul Sparrow is the Director of the Centre for Performance-led HR and Professor of International Human Resource Management at Lancaster University Management School. He has worked as a Research Fellow at Aston University, Senior Research Fellow at Warwick University, Consultant/Principal Consultant at PA Consulting Group, Reader/Professor at Sheffield University and whilst at Manchester Business School, he took up the Ford Chair from 2002 to 2004 and was Director, Executive Education from 2002 to 2005. He has consulted with major multinationals, public sector organizations and intergovernmental agencies, and was an Expert Advisory Panel member to the UK Government's Sector Skills Development Agency. His research interests include cross-cultural and international HRM, HR strategy, cognition at work and changes in the employment relationship. He is co- and founding editor of the *Journal of Organizational Effectiveness: People and Performance* and is an Editorial Board Member on *Human Resource Management*, *British Journal of Management*, *Cross-Cultural Management: An International Journal*, *International Journal of Cross-Cultural Management*, *European Management Review* and *Career Development International*. From 2008 to 2012 he was voted amongst the Top 15 Most Influential HR Thinkers by *Human Resources* magazine.

Martin Hird is that rare thing: a senior executive whose experience has spanned both academia and industry. He is an honorary fellow of and was Executive Director at the Centre for Performance-led HR from 2005 to 2012. He was a co-author of *Leading HR* and has written extensively about organization design, HR delivery systems, talent management, leadership and executive coaching. After initial employment with the Dunlop Group, he entered higher education, becoming Dean of the Business Faculty at Humberside Polytechnic whilst also operating an OD/Development consultancy. He was HR Director at BAE Systems from 1988 to 2002, worked as an HR consultant to the McLaren Group from 2002 to 2004, and was Group Resourcing and Development Director at Royal Mail from 2003 to 2005. He brings the ideal blend of cutting-edge thinking in his field with the practical knowledge of what businesses need and what works. He has Master's in both Management Sciences and Employment Law and Industrial Relations. He has consulted extensively in the private sector and works with board-level executives.

Cary Cooper is a distinguished professor of organizational psychology and health. He is the author/editor of over 160 books (on occupational stress, women at work and industrial and organizational psychology) and over 100 chapters in books. He has written over 400 scholarly articles for academic journals and is a frequent contributor to national newspapers, TV and radio. He is also a co- and founding editor of the *Journal of Organizational Effectiveness: People and Performance*, founding editor of the *Journal of Organizational Behavior*, former editor-in-chief of the medical journal *Stress & Health* and co-editor of the *Journal of Organizational Effectiveness*. He is a Fellow of the British Psychological Society, the Royal Society of Arts, the Royal Society of Medicine, the Royal Society of Public Health, the British Academy of Management and an Academician of the Academy of Social Sciences. He is past President of the British Academy of Management, a Companion of the Chartered Management Institute and one of the first UK-based Fellows of the (American) Academy of Management (having also won the 1998 Distinguished Service Award for his contribution to management science from the Academy of Management).

chapter 1

Introduction: HR Looking out and Looking in

1.1 Where to start?

Our previous book, *Leading HR*,[1] was written principally for those with the responsibility of leading HR functions who wanted to have business influence. This book is written for those who have business influence and who want to understand the people and organizational challenges that this influence will create. We put people management into its rightful general management context. We have structured this book into eight chapters. After introducing its rationale in this chapter, we take seven contemporary themes – predominantly business-driven, but one purposefully driven by broader societal questions – and analyze the organizational and people management challenges that each creates.

Why have we written this book now? In our original work, back in 2010, we argued that rather than starting with defined structures and delivery models or prescriptions for high-performance work practices, and then trying to shoehorn these into the organization strategy, HR needed to be about "reversing the arrow." Its starting point needed to be an understanding of the organization's business model (and the alternative models that might also be debated), and its own analysis of the organizational implications and people management problems that such a model would create: the risks and opportunities to be managed, the journeys to initiate and the solutions to develop. To be able to do this, HR needed to bring to bear its own specialist skills and unique insights – be these coming from people with useful skills in labor economics, social policy, organizational psychology or any other educational background that could be identified with a particular skill, discipline and insight. It then had to trace the underlying strategic performance drivers that enabled the business model. These are the intermediate business outcomes that facilitate effective performance and it is these outcomes that we focus this book around – the need to be able to identify how you create innovation, customer centricity, lean management, collaborative and partnered performance. Each of these performance challenges in turn has been looked at and understood by a range of disciplines, such as operations management, marketing, services management, economics, strategy, and research and development (R&D). But HR leaders need to be able to "read" this general management literature and show how the delivery of each performance outcome is highly dependent on the people and management aspects of organization effectiveness. Armed with this business insight, they must then be able to deliver on two important conversations. They must understand how to build the strategic competence of the organization – which back in 2002[2] was defined as the ability to be agile, open to the environment and capable of picking up those weak signals indicative of the need for change, which must then be selected, filtered, stored, recalled and interpreted so that the organization can make wise decisions. However, to be able to influence the taking of wise decisions, the HR Director must have the personal capability and credibility to engage the Board on these issues, which meant having the rhetoric skills of business dialogue, but also being part of what we called a Golden Triangle between the Chief Executive Officer (CEO), the Chief Financial Officer (CFO) and the HR Director. This board engagement was not achieved with HR acting in a servant context, akin to the role of a consiglieri, but rather as an expert equipped with all the above understanding. We argued, in fact, that you could have all the best benchmarked HR practices that you could wish for, but if the HR function was not able to deliver on its business model insight, then these practices would come to naught. In order to demonstrate this business model insight, HR needed to be able to evidence performance drivers, to help build the strategic competence of the organization and to ensure that there was boardroom engagement with its own analysis of the strategy.

Only having once delivered on the above should we move into the more functional aspects of HR, and although this of course then triggers a very wide range of processes, there were two dominant strategies that needed to be put in place. The first was to be able to reconfigure the talent systems – deep and troubling questions were being asked of talent. The second was in essence to be able to market the strategy to employees (and indeed beyond to society) in ways that were meaningful and persuasive; in other words, to be able to show what it was that employees needed to engage with.

Only at the final stages of this reverse-engineered contribution to the organization, and only as an afterthought, should it then be possible to think about metrics that might be used to evaluate the performance of the HR function. And only then should decisions about how to organize and structure the delivery of HR be made.

1.2 Is this the world we created?

In our previous book we set out a challenging agenda. Much of this challenge remains today. Our prognosis for the future of HR functions was also disconcerting.

Much of the transactional work that had been farmed out to HR service providers was often carried out by these providers to questionable quality and, even when it was managed effectively, it still often presented HR functions with some difficult decisions. As HR service providers took on responsibility for more and more of the outsourced activities, these providers were driven by their own competitive and business development logics. In order to develop their own business, which operated across several client HR functions, the way in which they made technical and service investments was not always aligned with the interests of each and every HR function. They were scaling up their own activities, becoming fewer in number, and were creating what are called "multi-tower" solutions, combining service support for the likes of HR, information systems and finance. The increasing power of information technology and sophistication of e-enablement meant that these service providers were moving up the value-chain of services, adding more activities and expertise, and being able to provide these services direct to line managers if necessary. This expansion of services slowly encroached upon the activities of the internal HR function – transactional activities that most of course were more than happy to divest, though some sought to bring back, but nonetheless services which still had an impact upon the reputation of the internal function if they were not delivered effectively. Everyone has been on a learning curve. HR functions have asked questions about provider performance (typically around their reliability, skills levels, insight into the business, and the quality of their communication back to employees and managers). They have had to manage the expectations of staff around the use of technology portals as the main point of entry into a relationship with HR. They have had to deal with challenges around the lack of face-to-face contact and sense of depersonalization in this relationship. They have had to try and shape user behavior, manage how they take up self-service offerings and avoid managers following advice lines that are too narrow. Quality needed to be assured without fragmenting the service levels across business units or geographical lines. The speed of response was also critical and this was dependent on technology, systems performance and often massive investments in IT. This e-enablement of many HR processes naturally led to HR functions continuing to standardize their HR. Before the processes were standardized, we had to assume that they had first been optimized. Whether this was the case or not, the consequence was that e-enablement in practice cemented the way things had to be done, either discouraging HR functions from making too many adaptations and refinements to their processes on the basis of subsequent learning, or tempting them to think that tweaking processes was a useful endeavor.

It also put a breakpoint into the development of HR expertise between the lower end and more outsourcable delivery of transactional work (much of which does not require too much HR training) and the more specialized expert knowledge needed to design the HR processes required for things like resourcing, talent management and learning and development, compensation and benefits, engagement, organization development and international mobility, much of which is the bread and butter of line consulting firms. It placed an even bigger career break within the HR function – creating challenges in moving people across these siloed areas of expertise and then into more business-friendly and business-relevant HR activity. Working in these centers was not necessarily an attractive staff proposition, even though the centers represented an important piece of the jigsaw that made up a powerful HR function.

The next learning curve has been around the specialist (and supposedly more strategic) expertise that remained and was parceled up into "centers of expertise." But if truth be told, these still reflected the old "functions" of HR. Nearly every organization had the same centers of expertise in their structure, such as resourcing, talent management, organization development, and compensation and benefits. Faced with a set of common HR functions, line managers began to ask some challenging questions of HR functions:

- What was strategic about such functional knowledge, the strategists have asked?
- Why should freeing up time from transactional activity and punting it into these areas of expert knowledge make a function any more strategic?

- Were these centers just the arbitors of internal business processes (the processes around which HR was delivered for sure, but just processes nonetheless)?

Of course, standardizing around common centers of expertise meant that you could focus on "best practice" around many of these activities – such as assessment centers, selection, reward, the categorization of people on performance-potential matrices and so forth. But good process is only what was expected; no one rewards you just for carrying out your basic functional activity.

Again, the learning curve has seen HR spend time specifying how to parcel up its expertise, thinking about the clarity of the proposition and the governance of this expertise. It has created questions about the availability of expertise, as well as the level of skill and the level of business acumen needed within these centers:

- Did people in your expertise centers need as much business acumen as the people with business acumen working outside the centers, such as business partners?
- Were there questions about resource alignment and the need to think about the costs associated with any instability of expertise and demand, when to use the expertise and how to engage its services?

These questions reinforced the need to ensure quality assurance in terms of consistency of services (across countries and across internal business units). In turn, this needed HR functions to be clear about the boundaries between local and central operations, and between those working in central areas of expertise and the HR business partners. It made people think about role drift. It needed people to attend to the communication between centers of expertise and other elements of the delivery model, to think about the blend of expertise between those with functional expertise and generalist HR and business model expertise, and the division of labor within small teams.

Of course, all of the above hopefully was – and is if it is ongoing – invisible to line managers. It is not really their problem, although many continue to ask "where is HR?" Perhaps they now know that HR has been learning how to work its delivery model. What line managers do see is the role that acts as the main conduit between HR functions and the business. It is the HR business partners who tie HR into the bloodstream of the organization.

And here we have the Catch-22 problem. The better these people are (and there are some very good people in these roles), the more they are in demand, but the more they are in demand, the less they can be spread around, and the worse others think of them (or of those who are in less demand). The less they can be spread around, the more irate the leading line managers feel about there being a lack of aligned resources to their projects.

It has taken HR many years to build its cadre of business partners, and to get there, it has had to solve problems of capability (upskilling, building business acumen, cultural insight and relational skills), expectations (selling the proposition, educating the line about how to use this expertise and building the line capability to actually do it), aligning the resources behind the business partners (aligning them to the business, avoiding role overload and providing necessary support), regulating the relationships they have so that they can be aligned to potential differences between business unit and corporate agendas, thinking about the line management decisions over HR resources, avoiding role drift back into more reactive, operational or residual transactional work, and managing the boundaries between the business partner relationships and their connections back to work in centers of expertise and service centers.

Somehow, a delivery model intended to lower the maintenance costs of the HR–business relationship might feel a little high maintenance, but ultimately that is not the issue. The real challenge today is that the world has moved on since the last major paradigm for HR, and there seems to be a new set of challenges:

1. How do you ensure that your expertise remains innovative – how do you manage the proactivity of your experts and the balance of time between them exploring their expertise and knowledge and having it exploited?
2. Once HR functions find themselves starting to be "leaned," it becomes increasingly difficult to maintain all these areas of expertise – you could not justify the time usage and charges for the expertise.

However, as these centers are often the bedrock for building HR functional expertise, HR generalists need to be rotated through them in order to build their expertise. The more they serve as a temporary holding house for generalists-in-preparation, the more the leadership of such centers is at risk of being diluted, changed and networked away. Moreover:

- most of the problems for which organizations need HR support (that is, those that have a significant people element) are increasingly cross-functional, by which we mean that they not only involve but also need joint input from expertise from other disciplines, such as operations, internal communications, marketing and information systems; and

- the solution to these problems requires cross-functional (by which we now mean across the sub-functions of HR) expertise. No longer can people dedicated to organization design, employee engagement or talent management work as separate centers; they need to have their expertise "mixed and matched" and aligned much more flexibly with the business needs and with the major change projects of the day.

HR is now layering project and program expertise, and a broader organizational effectiveness capability, into its underlying architecture of transactional service centers, HR-process driven centers of expertise and its population of HR business partners.

1.3 Is it time to go back to the future?

In this book we lay out a range of developments taking place in the nature of organizations in response to a continuing set of business pressures, pressures that we argue are creating inexorable pressure for us to change and reposition the nature of human resource management (HRM). We bring to the fore the need to start from an understanding of the strategic performance drivers of organizations, and show how a number of these drivers create very significant people and organizational challenges.

The first business theme is that of innovation. In Chapter 2 we draw upon research on strategy, structure, technological leadership, organizational behavior and organizational psychology to identify the organizational agendas that the management of innovation brings. We lay out the radical changes to management models that it requires and the political decisions upon which it depends. We place innovation in the context of business model change and explain the importance of the organization design choices that have to be made in order to foster it. We address the need to build competence for open innovation, and the challenges of institutionalizing a culture and system of innovation. From these macro agendas, a series of micro-level people management issues follow. We look at the lessons for leadership, creating the right team climate and shaping the people through assessment.

In Chapter 3 we examine a second topical issue: the need to create more customer-centric organizations. We draw upon ideas from the fields of marketing and services management to explain how their thinking has moved us from ideas about the service-profit chain to the broader concept of customer centricity. This chapter takes us through six important building blocks: the need to manage mass customization, the involvement of consumers in the design process, the need to structure around the customer, to manage the empowerment of frontline staff, to democratize the customer's relationship with the business and to build the capability to filter massive datasets.

In Chapter 4 we examine the third business issue, which is lean management. We examine the operations management literature to lay out the range of process improvement approaches being used in organizations and focus specifically on lean thinking. We examine how the implementation issues have changed as the approach has been exported to non-traditional settings and examine the people issues at the heart of the philosophy, implementation failures and the actual process of implementation.

In Chapter 5 we examine the fourth and final business issue, which is the need for many organizations to work beyond the organization. We draw upon multidisciplinary research mainly from the fields of operations management, strategic management, marketing and organizational behavior to demonstrate the growth of a series of important inter-organizational relationships. We examine the importance of collaborative business models, open innovation and joint ventures, and the general shift towards collaborative organizational forms to identify three underlying challenges. These revolve around the management of risk, governance and building capability for a network of organizations. This shows that HR now increasingly has to be delivered across a broader network of organizations, such that we need organizations not just to design HR for themselves and their own workforce, but also for a number of other organizations with whom they now collaborate much more closely. In both instances, this raises questions about:

- who needs to know about and be skilled in HR?;
- who in HR needs to know about issues of organizational performance and the business context?

But there is a temptation to be driven by the Heathrow Business School view of this world, which has everyone asking what is the next big thing for HR? As Jeffrey Pfeffer once quipped about the talent debate, if everybody has to think outside the box, perhaps it is the box that needs fixing.

In this book we argue that the last 30 years has seen a necessary pull on HR functions to be concerned with what we call the *Looking in* agenda for the organization – how the function can contribute to and influence the strategic direction and discourse within the organization. This need is not going to go away; it continues with a vengeance. In addressing these strategic issues in the next four chapters, we shall take a forward, future-looking but essentially cross-functional and general management perspective. We are pleased that most of the references and endnotes in this book refer not to HR literature, but to work conducted in general management. We are also pleased that as we lay out the strategic pressures for innovation, customer centricity, productivity, lean management and collaborative business model delivery, it is clear that they all revolve around questions of people management, which should help tie in with the typical CEO concerns.

TYPICAL CEO CONCERNS

A range of consulting surveys into the issues that continue to concern CEOs show that although economic confidence has returned, a range of economic, policy and commercial risks still face organizations. The following signal their mindset:

- The 2014 Gartner CEO and Senior Executive Survey[3] found that 33 percent of respondents named growth as their top priority, mainly driven by technology and digital innovations; a quarter of the survey respondents say they now have a Chief Digital Officer. Adding in other Vice President and senior levels of digital leaders, and those respondents who plan to make an appointment either this year or next year, it appears that half of these companies will have a designated digital leader title by the end of 2015.
- In the 17th PricewaterhouseCoopers Annual CEO survey,[4] which is based on 1,344 interviews in 68 countries, 82 percent of UK CEOs think that the greatest disruptive impact on their businesses is expected to come from technological advances, with demographic shifts (69 percent) and shifts in global power (58 percent) also registering on their radar.
- The technical investments are in business analytics (44 percent globally, 62 percent in the US), socially enabled business processes, mobile customer engagement and cybersecurity, with attention focused on creating a digital ecosystem through investments in the hardware, software, services and communications infrastructure that make digitization possible.
- The forces reshaping business models across the four major markets of the US, China and Hong Kong, Japan and Germany follow a common priority – first product and service innovation, then increasing share in existing markets, followed by new geographical markets.

- A total of 52 percent of CEOs in the US are revamping their customer growth and retention strategies, moving away from stand-alone transactions towards an "always on" relationship.
- The global data show that the highest threats to growth are perceived to be a slowdown in high growth markets (73 percent). Of the top eight issues, three are people-related: the availability of skills (70 percent), rising labor costs in high-growth markets (58 percent) and lack of trust in business (52 percent).
- A total of 41 percent of US CEOs are currently changing and 52 percent are considering and planning change in their customer growth and retention strategies. The "doing" and "planning" figures for the other primary strategies (in order of "doing" importance) are 40 percent and 48 percent for technology investments, 38 percent and 54 percent for talent strategies, 38 percent and 48 percent for organizational structure and design, and 30 percent and 41 percent for supply chain.
- The theme of people and technology in this survey is strong. A total of 87 percent of CEOs report that their organizations are engaged in updating their talent strategy and 80 percent are revamping their technology investment strategies. Some 66 percent want governments to ensure financial sector stability, facilitating the creation of a globally skilled workforce, but only 27 percent think it important for governments to create jobs for 16–24 year olds.

It is evident from the above that our choice of the first four major business themes in this book – innovation (Chapter 2), customer centricity (Chapter 3), lean management (Chapter 4) and collaborative business models (Chapter 5), and our subsequent choice of engagement, well-being and fairness (Chapter 6), talent management (Chapter 7) and the importance thinking about the value of HRM (Chapter 8) – is timely. These themes of course arise not only as a response to what CEOs note as important – they also reflect what we see leaders of all the major directorates across organizations working on of their own accord.

However, we also argue in this book that we are returning to a *Looking out* agenda. Having fixated about its seat at the table and level of strategic influence for many years, a debate which either bemuses or bores the other functions, the HR function seems to have stopped looking out and stopped worrying about the trends that it can see are about to wash over the organization and its people management. Yes, everyone has their forward-looking scenario exercises or talks about the changing generations, and sometimes in doing so they wonder how much longer their existing HR processes might survive, but no one really seems to be thinking through how to reconnect the function with these external agendas. The agendas are quite fundamental. We have returned to a period of business history when the very nature of work is once more up for debate. The place of work and technology in society, the place of the family in organizations, work and technology, and the place of society in organizations are all once more in transition. After a 30-year period of economic liberalism, the financial crisis lit a slow-burning fuse, in which certainties about the future became a future of uncertainty, and the sense of paralysis has led to the paralysis of sense. Major questions about people management seem only one more crisis away.

In Chapter 6 we remind ourselves that there are now deep concerns over questions around employee engagement, organizational well-being and, perhaps most notably, fairness. We draw upon ideas from several fields of management, such as organizational psychology, economics, social policy, and legal and environmental studies, to identify five different perspectives (or what we call lenses) that should be used to think about questions of fairness. We link these to a number of contemporary social debates, such as those relating to executive and fair pay, the number of women on boards and the pensions problem, to encourage a broader consideration of the issues and solutions.

Before we look at these broader societal issues again, however, we think it important to explain why they are coming to the fore again. A number of programs relating to HR management that spanned the 1980s and 1990s – on the future of work and society, the link between corporate strategy change and HRM, and whether HRM was in crisis – still resonate today. As we were coming out of the competitive restructuring shock of the late 1970s, there were a number of macro-developments that were impacting the employment relationship and were serving to reshape HRM:[5]

- An exchange of free time for consumerism – although the futurists had said we could workshare, people were still choosing to invest their free time in work in return for the rewards of consumerism.
- The rise of the productive capacity of the household was changing and replacing the demand for employed services, as households replaced the need for paid service labor through the use of do-it-yourself tools and equipment (interestingly, now we both use our own highly productive capital equipment whilst also returning to the employment of household service labor).

- Long waves in technology, which were impacting the supply of technology as well as leading to a growth in joblessness (in terms of the maintenance of higher-paid and full-time jobs).
- Therefore, what was then seen as a pauperization of employment (in terms of pay, job design and job content, and security) was reflected in a pursuit of flexibility through the substitution of male full-time jobs for the growth of (female and low-paid) part-time work, creating peripheralized occupations that took the brunt of the consequences caused by economic downturns.

The Work and Society program concluded that in the mid-1980s we were facing seven fundamental challenges in the UK:

- A changing workforce (in terms of its demographics).
- The creation of a cadre of long-term unemployed.
- A young generation ill-equipped for the world of work.
- A workforce skill gap.
- An economy racked by regional and urban divisions.
- New technology fundamentally changing the design of work.
- New expectations and values at work.

We did not have PowerPoint in those days, but if we did, and you "cut and pasted" the bullet points on the slide and showed it today, would you notice the join? Have we managed to change anything in 30 years? With some minor tweaks to the language (and an update of the statistics), we could well point to the return of these broader societal issues, which have once again been made into legitimate points of discussion because of the global financial services crisis – sadly familiar and perennial issues then. In large part the persistence of these problems is why we have brought the themes of engagement, organizational health and well-being, and fairness into the book. We cover these topics in detail in Chapter 6.

A 30-YEAR UPDATE

The continued erosion of living standards: from 2010 to 2014, wages in the UK rose at a significantly slower rate than inflation, leading to an inevitable erosion of living standards. Only by April 2014 were inflation and wage increases running at about the same levels, and even then wages were still lower if the figures excluded those who received bonuses. However, in real terms, adjusting for inflation, wages were still at that point around eight percent lower than they had been in 2008. The projections made by the UK's Office for Budget Responsibility (OBR) show that although wages overtook inflation in 2014 and the gap will accelerate in the coming years, real wages will only reach their October 2008 level by the end of 2018. The financial services crisis will have led to a decade of lost earnings.

Wage inequalities: researchers from the Organisation for Economic Co-operation and Development (OECD) examined wages in 22 countries in 2011 and found that inequality had grown in 17 of them between the 1980s and the financial crisis of 2008. Chile, Mexico, Turkey and the US were the most unequal nations, but inequality had risen fastest in the UK, and even traditionally egalitarian countries such as Germany, Denmark and Sweden had experienced growing wealth disparity. Their 2014 analyses showed that the share of the richest one percent in terms of total pre-tax income (excluding capital gains, which would make the differences even starker) has increased in most OECD countries in the past three decades, ranging from seven percent in Denmark and the Netherlands up to almost 20 percent in the US. The increases have resulted from the top one percent taking a disproportionate share of overall income growth in this period: the top four countries being the Anglo-Saxon economies of Australia (the top one percent taking 20 percent of income growth), the UK (25 percent), Canada (37 percent) and the US (47 percent).[6]

The UK productivity challenge: economists argue that meaningful improvements in living standards can only achieved on the back of prior improvements in productivity. Between 1998 and 2007, productivity improvements in the UK ran at an annual rate of 2.5 percent. Yet, after years of stagnation and slow recovery from the global financial services crisis, productivity remains low (whether viewed in terms of output per hour worked or output per worker). Data from the Office for National Statistics showed that by March 2014, the annual improvement in productivity in output per worker was only 1.3 percent and 0.7 percent in output per hour worked. However, output per hour worked was still almost five percent below where it had been in the first quarter of 2008. Organizations not only kept employees on their books, which few would say was a bad thing to do, but also began to hire again. The price of this has been the storing-up of a productivity challenge. This seems to be a particularly British issue. The average productivity of the G7 major industrial nations (excluding Britain) is more than 20 percent higher than British (whole economy) productivity. Productivity has risen faster in competitor nations – in France, despite its own issues, productivity is well over 30 percent greater than in the UK.

The skills challenge: the 2013 UK Skills and Employment Survey shows that for the two decades from 1986 to 2006, the prevalence of over-qualification in the UK rose, but it fell between 2006 and 2012, and although mismatches remain high, for the first time, more jobs (rising from 20 percent in 2006 to 26 percent in 2012) needed a degree than needed no qualification at all (falling from 28 percent to 23 percent).[7] But at the same time, the Training in Britain Survey found that the proportion of British workers engaged annually in more than ten hours' training declined from 38 percent in 2006 to 34 percent in 2012, with average number of training hours per worker per year falling by 32 percent.

Having made the argument that HR needs to start looking out again to the broader societal issues that it has a responsibility to help resolve, we finally move into some traditional HR territory. In Chapter 7 we pick up on the talent management debate. We explain how HR captured the topic of talent management and lay out the issues in theory and in practice. We discuss the thinking and assumptions that underwrite four different approaches to talent management and use this functional area of HR to show that a much broader and integrated response is needed in HR.

Finally, in Chapter 8 we return to the general management literature. We draw principally on the strategic management literature to ask the ultimate question: what, then, is the value of HRM? We answer this question by using the example of talent management and the strategic management literature to lay out four value-generating processes around which a talent system should be designed. These include the activities necessary for value creation, value capture, value leverage and value protection.

1.4 Old questions, new contexts

Only once we have looked at HR from a general management perspective can we return to the strapline of this book: *Do We Need HR?* The title is intended to be provocative. We might also have asked: *Is HR What We Need?* This question has been asked before. Returning to the 1980s, researchers argued that we needed to see major changes in attitude inside organizations if we were to change the structures that were limiting our ability to create a form of HRM that would be more fit for purpose. To do this, we needed to develop a breed of HR professionals who had skills that enabled them to manage their function in a more strategic and societal context – another familiar theme for 30 years now. What did they need to know about?:

> The outer context includes the economic climate, business, social and political formations, and technological development within which companies must operate ... The inner context consists largely of intra-organizational features, namely: the structure (the formal framework of relationships); the culture (the beliefs, meanings, rationales, language, codes and rules); the politics (the internal distribution of power and key actors involved); the business direction (strategy, mission and perceived threats and opportunities); and the business outputs (the financial resources, products, and market performance).[8]

Long before talk of HR business partners and champions became popularized in the 1990s, the basic challenges were summarized as follows:

> Although the ability to link different areas of HRM content to variable contexts is a crucial area of human development in all organizations, the skills involved in relation to each area are traditional personnel management skills. The difference ... implicit in the way we interpret HRM – is in the ability to take and implement a strategic view of the whole range of personnel practices in relation to business activity as a whole ... [this is] an issue of ... needing to link together business, technical and HRM skills ... the problem is one of deciding the degree, or density, of business sophistication needed in the lower and specialized parts of the function, and the point at which a key individual or group of people should have a more composite HRM understanding. Moreover, such skills also need to be distributed throughout the organization and not just reside with the HRM professionals ... The problem, however, is not just the shortage of people with sufficient skills and competences. It is also one of recognizing the legitimacy of HRM. Putting capable personnel professionals into punishing environments is not a successful strategy.[9]

Given the problem of putting promising people into punishing environments, another book in 1996 – one that was ahead of its time[10] – argued that we needed to understand how to conduct "personnel management without personnel managers." It is important to recount some the arguments of these authors – they still resonate today and they serve in part to support the rationale for this book and our provocative question: "Do We Need HR?"

It was argued that there was a range of "managing withouts" that we had to cope with:

- top teams managing without strategic planning;
- managing change without traditional structures or owners of the change;
- managing without supervision; and
- managing without a complete full-time workforce.

All these changes carried with them both threats and opportunities:

- Sustainable competitive advantage was intimately linked to decisions about the input, throughout and output of people, and the ability of HR processes to manage this appropriately.
- However, given the rapidity and all-encompassing scope of change – the need to produce goods and services that were right first time, speedily, cheaply and flexibly (what we would today call the "agile organization") – was it an illusion to talk about sustainable competitive advantage?

Information was hard to hide from competitors, many organizational capabilities could be captured and emulated through reverse engineering, and there were few barriers to entry. The authors argued that the one resource that was hard to copy was an organization's human resources:

- The management of these resources – from the crafting of strategy, the creation of distinction cultures and the development of coherent employment philosophies – was something that top teams (and only top teams) could do.
- They had the responsibility to reconfigure the resource base of the firm – and that meant its structures, routines and processes.
- Whilst HR might be seen as a downstream activity that had to align the way in which people were managed more effectively or to help clear up the mess and improve the quality of strategic execution if these strategic choices were ill-considered, we needed the following:

> radically new organizational structures and forms, de-emphasizing formal planning systems, altering the traditional ownership structure

> of the firm, implementing a unitarist ideology between management and employees, empowering line managers to handle traditionally and historically specialized HRM activities, utilizing quality circles and self-managing teams, internalizing the quality ethos ... and creating new types of employment relationships involving a permeable core and ring strategy.[11]

It was argued even then that as organizations were being driven increasingly by "horizontal" and cross-functional issues, such as business process re-engineering, lean management and attention to quality, the continued quest by HR functions for strategic influence and their pursuit of vertical hierarchy meant that HR risked being seen by line managers as the "trash can" function. It risked becoming an opportunistic "collection of the incidental, peripheral and unrelated activities." It risked creating activities that would be perceived as an expensive and dispensable overhead – the conclusions arrived at even back in those days:

- In a world of shortened product life cycles, accelerating technology, information distribution networks and growing and uncountable variations in terms of consumer preferences, why would you want to maintain any functional specialisms, be that marketing or HR?
- Simply aligning your structure with customers would not bridge the gap between the espoused strategy and its execution; structural changes alone would not equip frontline staff with the necessary autonomy and responsibility.
- The empowerment and pursuit of a learning organization would mean getting employees to self-regulate between their own level of autonomy and the inter-dependencies they would accept or not. However, this choice brought with it risks of poor execution.
- Re-engineering processes and using these more horizontal thought processes to think about the structure of (or the need to take out) traditional functions would seem to make sense, but might introduce massive complexities.
- The only thing left, then, would be to design a more "intelligent" organization and then mobilize the commitment and energy of the workforce behind this.

These were good observations, made 20 years ago, and of course were never really implemented. The trends and shape of what was to come were already clear to us. But in reaching out to the fields of strategy and economics, we were left with what the authors saw as a Catch-22: you needed to take out hierarchy and traditional functions like HR, but then in managing that messy resource that we call people, you needed either multi-skilled and people-embracing line managers, or some kind of specialists who guided them.

This then, is the agenda that we pick up in this book:

- In what ways are the business and societal themes that we have chosen to focus on people-centric?
- What scope do they create for HR, if any?
- How do they suggest we might redesign and repurpose the function?

chapter 2

Innovation and People Management

2.1 Introduction

In the opening chapter we argued that to some extent we have been in a similar situation to that faced today, in that typically post-recession organizations find themselves following one of three pathways, and there is every reason to assume we shall see the same this time. The issues that drive HRM are those that characterize the industry dynamics of the surviving sectors. These reflect a "life cycle pattern" that falls into one of the following:[1]

- Managing a return to rapid growth, but through restrained resources. To a degree, this is picked up in Chapter 4 on lean management.
- Transitioning through a process of strategic retrenchment.
- Moving on to a path of strategic renewal through radical innovation.

In this chapter we pick on this last path, that of innovation. In doing so, we:

- outline the need for organizations to improve their management of innovation;
- define and explore a range of perspectives on innovation (at the macro-level and the micro-level);
- explain what is required in terms of organization, leadership and people management;
- raise questions as to whether HR functions are actually doing any of this;
- lay out the key role that HR needs to play in helping to orientate the organization and its people around an innovation mindset.

To do this we have to draw on research on strategy, structure, technological leadership, organizational behavior and organizational psychology.

When we read the popular literature on innovation, it argues that organizations will not be able to deliver innovative performance without there being big changes in the metrics they use – for example, moving from measuring return on capital to measuring things like profit per employee. It draws upon the principles of private equity, venture capital and research and development, and brings them into the culture of the organization. It talks about the necessary shifts being dependent on there being "mental revolutions" inside organizations, "major traumas" and "risks"[2] as we try to reinvent a more innovative form of management.

Indeed, in our own work, we have asked whether we are facing the potential for a slow-burn "mass extinction" event in the lives of organizations. We have used an evolutionary metaphor to paint this picture[3]. Every now and again, a perfect storm of climate change develops, with a series of waves breaking upon the shore, wave after wave, wiping out the ill-prepared. At several points in this book, and especially in this chapter, we shall refer to the continued fall-out from the recent credit crunch. In Chapter 3 we shall outline the potential for deep-seated and radical shifts in consumer behavior. In Chapter 4 we point to the deep impacts and pressures that attention to productivity, efficiency, effectiveness and lean management is bringing. In Chapter 5 we show how many business models are being disrupted and how many organizations are beginning to understand that they now operate increasingly as part of a highly integrated network economy, having to find new ways to co-create value. In Chapter 6 we shall signal the transfers of risk, responsibilities and accountabilities between economic markets, nation states and organizations.

The waves may only be short-lived or they may continue to roll in for a longer period of time, but regardless of their duration, the forces are strong enough to create a major shock to the system. Returning to the biological metaphor, not all species die at once; many hang on for several years afterwards, but from the moment that the first waves hit, they were already mortally wounded. Honed to perfection by the previous climate, their DNA does not have the adaptability to cope with the new climate. But at the same time, a host of species had been evolving quite nicely in the pre-shock world. They had already learned to adapt to the pre-credit crunch world that had equally powerful and impactful forces of deregulation, changing industry dynamics, demographics and business model change. Now suddenly they find that their DNA is even more ably fitted to the new world or is capable of making a rapid adaptation, and they flourish rapidly (innovate and adapt). Nothing new has happened. No new big ideas are needed to explain their destiny. Their DNA was known and they were always going to survive the impending climate change, but

the new competitive space and slow dying-off of many competitors future-proofed their survival.

Only history will tell how whether we are witnessing a climactic change that will radically accelerate organizational death rates. But the analogy of evolutionary change, of complex DNA patterns, of the ability to move into and exploit a new climate serves to capture much of the literature on innovation and it also illustrates the task facing HR:

- Can organizations analyze the many and complex components that represent your organization's DNA – the components that will lead it to innovate?
- Can organizations buy themselves enough time to allow its existing DNA to make the necessary adaptations?

We need to provide some definitions. Creativity, invention and generation of ideas are just the first part of the process that we review in this chapter. This has to be followed by innovation, which is the much deeper and more organizationally embedded capability that encompasses the application of novelty to produce things that are new and useful.[4] Innovation is a process that intentionally attempts to bring about benefits from change, taking what might have been a novel idea, but successfully managing it to a market introduction. It is the commercialization of invention, defined by experts in technical innovation as:

> a process of turning opportunity into new ideas and of putting these into widely used practice.[5]

It includes two key elements:

- capabilities that help apply and assess novel ideas; and
- the capability to implement.

As such, it requires a very different range of people strategies than those that just help in leading to general levels of creativity. This chapter draws upon key writing and ideas that look at innovation at two broad levels of analysis. If HR functions are to respond to the challenge of innovation, they have to tackle what is called a multi-layered problem. They need to marshal interventions at the macro-level, but also at the micro-level:

1. *Macro-level perspectives on innovation*: the challenge of business model innovation, the organizational and structural alternatives necessary to develop it and the challenges of institutionalizing an innovation culture.

2. *Micro-level perspectives on innovation*: the messages for leadership, creating a culture or climate for innovation at a team level, and shaping the people through the management and selection of individual talent.

We end by summarizing the various insights on innovation into six key component HR strategies that must be pursued and lay out the implications for the role of HR functions.

2.2 Macro-level HR strategies

2.2.1 Radical changes to the management model

For more than 20 years now, the increased demand for organizations to innovate has seen more attention being given to creativity and innovation, and the factors that shape them.[6]

The problem with innovation, then, is that it is what academics call a multi-layered problem. The solution requires strategies – including HR strategies – that touch upon and tie together a whole network of factors. Why is this? One of the earliest meta-analyses of the possible determinants and moderators of innovation showed that there are several different types of innovation in terms of scale and scope, each bringing with it a different set of challenges to manage.[7]

There is no one theory of innovation. There have been numerous studies carried out in economics, organizational theory, strategic management and marketing. There have been examinations of the role played by structure, climate and culture, group and organizational behavior, and individual psychology. Yet, across

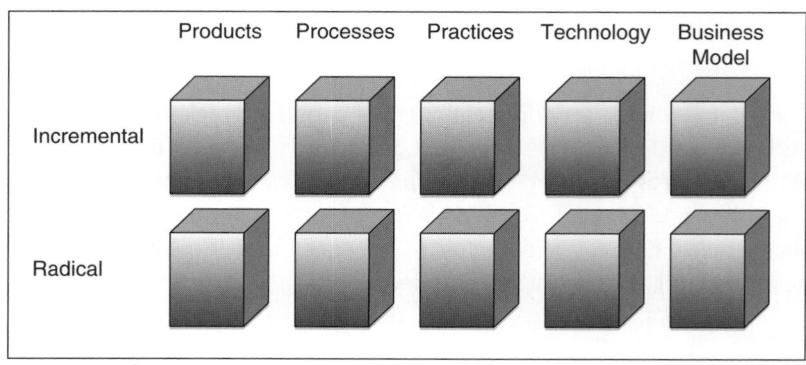

FIG 2.1 What type of innovation is being managed?

all these studies, there is no one set of antecedent variables that has emerged that differentiates between successful innovators and those that struggle. There are no simple maxims about the role of centralization, diversification, resource level and organizational size.

However, there are many who evangelize about innovation. Despite such sustained attention, early protagonists of innovation note that after decades of experimentation in the way in which we combine and transfer knowledge across talent, create the right incentives and eliminate other strategic distractions, both the natural condition of organizations and the nature of management is such that no organization has innovation or adaptability built into its DNA.[8] The argument runs as follows. Management has been designed to solve problems and do things with:

- perfect replicability;
- at ever-increasing scale; and
- steadily increasing efficiency.

In reality, then, the quest to shift organizations towards a more innovative culture will be more evolutionary than revolutionary. Whilst realizing the need for a radical shift in emphasis, they will wish to minimize risk by looking to alternative but already-existing management models from outside the world of major corporations and to the world of how experimentation is managed in the sciences:

> Companies must become as purposefully and creatively experimental in thinking about their management systems and processes as they already are in thinking about R&D or new product development.[9]

Management systems for innovation will be designed around principles that:

- set clear boundaries around different kinds of risk (we address the issue of risk in Chapter 5 on managing beyond the organization);
- test new ideas within boundaries;
- apply scarce resources through discretionary spending;
- refocus the management of talent (we discuss talent management in Chapter 7);
- place the voice of the user at the front of management processes (we pick up the topic of customer centricity in the next chapter).

Therefore, designing the organization for innovation is a task for the HR Director, the CFO and the Director of Planning, but its challenges require a totally new management model, and one with very different assumptions about:

- how to organize;
- lead;

- allocate resources;
- plan;
- recruit; and
- motivate.

The challenge has been expressed another way.[10] Organizational models for innovation have to:

- enable people to collaborate with each other at much lower cost;
- which means dramatically reducing both unproductive search and co-ordination costs.

This can be done by deploying such devices as talent marketplaces, knowledge marketplaces and formal networks, all of which make intangible assets flow more rapidly throughout the organization.

2.2.2 The political dimensions of innovation

The literature on the management of innovation shows that innovation tends to be managed under either a corporate or an entrepreneurship model. Both models stress the following challenges:

- resources and their deployment need to be mobile; and
- incentives have to be aligned so that those engaged in risky innovation have a chance of success.

This challenge is seen in the extreme in artistic organizations in sectors such as industrial design, entertainment, writing and advertising. The drive for creativity needs organizational models that:

1. help to advance incomplete ideas that are difficult to codify;
2. lower the risks associated with incorrectness; and
3. increase the rewards associated with novelty.

A number of political resource investments also have to be made. Organization development (OD) solutions have to be able to help manage four political risks or challenges that have to be managed in doing this.[11]

THE FOUR POLITICAL RISKS TO BE MANAGED BY OD SOLUTIONS

1. The speed of innovation is needs to be faster today than was previously the case. This makes learning how to reconcile the tension between creativity and control more difficult.

2. The more radical the innovation – sometimes the whole business model may need to be innovated – the more difficult is the route to commercialization, the higher the risk of failure and the more complex the challenges of managing appropriate organizational behavior.
3. The more that historical competence has to be destroyed, the higher the risk of conflict with powerful interests in the current business model – for example, existing sales and market positions may be cannibalized by the new operations, historical competence destroyed.
4. The riskier the resource allocations (in game theory this is called a constant sum game), the more uncertain are the claimed future revenue-earning escalators.

2.2.3 The drumbeat of business model change

In practice, organizations have choices. They might try and address innovation by doing the following:

- Exploiting and making better use of what they have (for example, by opportunistic development of new marketing channels or offering additional services that exploit new technical capabilities).
- Look for new (additional and stand-alone) revenue streams and business opportunities – broadening the portfolio of businesses that are run.
- Re-engineer and innovate the whole business model – replace the bulk of existing businesses and processes with a new value proposition.

THE ROLE OF INNOVATION IN CORPORATE STRATEGIES

Nestlé's internal R&D capability has driven most of the company's innovations. It has an internal network of 27 research, technology and development centers. In 2006 it introduced an open innovation model drawing upon an external network of universities, venture capital, small start-ups, biotech companies, large industrial suppliers and government bodies to co-create innovation. Much innovation is now driven by understanding the molecular and supramolecular (nanoscale) properties of food ingredients and nutrients. In the past, the main emphasis in the food industry was on product development from the perspective of raw materials. The emphasis is shifting towards defined product properties and benefits, which essentially reverses the way that food companies look at product development. They use both centralized models of R&D (to handle science-driven innovations that address the needs of all markets) and decentralized models (e.g., where innovations address localized food and consumer tastes). This means modifying the culture so that it understands and accepts the different types of innovation, and having leaders who can flex their leadership style to manage in both situations.

Vodafone has established a Joint Innovation Laboratory as a joint venture with Verizon Wireless, China Mobile and Softbank Mobile as a platform to develop mobile services and drive innovation and synergy in the industry, providing innovators with access to all four customer bases. Shared innovation is necessary now because of the importance of projects based on emerging technologies and market demand, such as in rapidly growing areas of mobile Internet services. The intention is that the global developer community and operators benefit by providing great content to their customers.

Shell spent $1.2 billion on R&D in 2009. Around ten percent of Shell's technical staff carry out R&D at technology centers located in 11 countries. These centers bring together engineers, geologists, physicists, chemists, mathematicians, biologists, anthropologists, environmental, financial and commercial experts. Three centers in Houston in the US and Amsterdam and Rijswijk in the Netherlands focus on innovation. Both upstream and downstream technology groups now operate on a single site to create synergies in the search for technologies to meet future energy demands. Shell is also famous for its GameChanger initiative – a cross-business innovation program (an open or distributed innovation group and center of innovation expertise) set up to identify, foster and sponsor the development of new breakthrough technologies in the context of the various technology futures for the oil industry. The ten percent of the R&D budget that goes to GameChanger initiatives incubates 30 percent of Shell's R&D projects.

BAE Systems draws upon R&D activities in a wide range of programs that include performance innovations, improvements to manufacturing techniques and technology to improve through-life support of products. Strategic R&D is particularly important in the Electronics, Intelligence & Support operating group, and the four global initiatives of Land, Security, Readiness & Sustainment and Unmanned Aircraft Systems. The company has launched an investment partnership aimed at small and medium-sized enterprises and academia to identify new technologies and help bring them to market.

Making innovation work, then, is highly dependent on a series of political judgments about:

- the investment of substantial resources from the organization;
- business ideas that might have resulted from the interplay of years of experience, but also from rapid insight amongst individuals;
- the intrinsic motivation of employees;
- marshaling the time and effort of multiple (often unconnected) people and groups;
- the management of uncertainty and risk; and
- the politics of persuasion.

Not surprisingly:

> The punishing thing about innovation ... is that the contest never ends. Create a new market, and other companies come flooding in ... Success requires being able to go beyond isolated wins to develop deep capabilities that allow companies to disarm disruptive threats and seize new growth opportunities repeatedly.[12]

However, responding to this challenge is so very important. Most innovations are sourced from within an organization's relevant business cluster – the industry, competitors and customers:

> through concentric growth or by moving to a new cluster altogether. Therefore, employees need to understand the dynamics of their cluster and be prepared to engage it.[13]

Within an innovation strategy, a range of component HR strategies have to be linked to the underlying business model, and all the competing drivers that we discuss in the following chapters for innovation, customer service, productivity, efficiency and effectiveness have to be woven together into a single fabric.

For economists, however, it is innovative business models that lie at the heart of things because they act as a dynamic force that disturbs the economic equilibrium.

THE CHALLENGE OF BUSINESS MODEL INNOVATION

Business model innovation refers to the creation, or reinvention, of a business itself – it results in an entirely different type of organization and way of competing. It has now become an area of separate strategic attention and a new field of study appears to be developing, applying theories of innovation to the creation of business models.[14] Researchers draw attention to the nature of disruptive innovation – where instead of technology being used to sustain and improve existing products and services (for example, improving the quality of CDs), disruptive technologies have to be marshalled to create a new customer paradigm that enables new entrants to capture market share and create new markets (for example, coming up with the iPod and creating services around the digital downloading of sound).

Business model innovation researchers argue that the solution to this challenge is to:

- create teams of innovators across a balanced portfolio of businesses;
- be clear about the strategic boundaries;[15]
- rather than removing these boundaries, articulate what are the "desirable," "discussable" and "unthinkable" strategic dimensions;
- introduce screening processes that reduce the level of uncertainty associated with innovative ventures;
- introduce structural support for innovative operations; and
- train employees to identify disruptive ideas.

Drawing upon such ideas, for example, IBM's financial analysts[16] argued that those organizations that put more emphasis on business model innovation experienced significantly better operating margin growth (over a five-year period) than did their peers. Their survey of CEOs found that they were

focusing 30 percent of their innovative efforts on business model innovation. In part this was because 40 percent feared that changes in a competitor's business model would radically change the landscape of their whole industry.

2.2.4 Understanding the structural models

In our previous book we noted that HR Directors must have a strong organization design and development capability, and it is the design aspect of this capability that becomes pre-eminent. This is especially true in relation to the different organizational models that may be chosen to manage innovation (see Table 2.1). Each design choice (competing model for innovation) brings unique organization development challenges, and the subsequent HR solutions (in terms of leadership, team climate and individual resourcing) flow from the preceding design choice.

TABLE 2.1 Alternative organization design solutions for innovation

Generic model	Key organization development issues
1. Building units that are specialized to the creative portion of the innovation problem (e.g., traditional skunk works).	Buffering these units from the dysfunctions of standard structures, processes and measurement systems.
2. Using fluid, lateral modes of co-ordination (teams) with joint decision-making rights at the front end (in time) of the innovation process.	Segment the innovation process in time from the rest of the organization by ensuring high personal and organizational flexibility before the subsequent emphasis on more codified and replicable business processes.
3. External venture capital model: acquiring and then internalizing the running of entrepreneurial start-up operations.	Segment the innovation process in time from the rest of the organization by setting up proto-governance structures with "incomplete" contracts (i.e., inbuilt flexibility) to accommodate the development path. Melding the incentive arrangements for newly internalized lead employees (agents) who can be overseen by governance arrangements that also protect the interests of the corporate owners (principals).
4. Internal venture capital/ entrepreneurial model (professional entrepreneur model). Building businesses that are born to be sold. Place investment bets in the units in return for offering a brokerage service to resources.	Alignment of the incentives between the entrepreneurs/innovators, the investors and the employees. Managing a rapid growth model and building a market-leading capability that may soon be overtaken by competitors/alternative innovations. Creation of "liquid" equity value (i.e., contractual arrangements) that ensure that the venture capitalists are prepared to invest in the necessary capability building activities, flexibility in organizational roles and loss of control over the innovation, *but* all in return for control over the timing of the sale.

(continued)

TABLE 2.1 Continued

Generic model	Key organization development issues
5. Internal professional services model.	Skill sets associated with the management of innovation (such as project management, business analysis and corporate performance management setting) made available and delivered to line businesses via a central center of excellence and business consulting unit. Central powers of control over the introduction of innovations exercised from the innovation business support service unit, but services also offered on a buy-in basis.
6. Innovation network model (sometimes also called distributed innovation). Could apply to a firm with several physical locations or to co-operation between a cluster of firms, e.g., partner SMEs that share business inputs and outputs to an innovation-driven business project (members brought together by a network trademark or reputation).	Leveraging the one-on-one interpersonal relationships between entrepreneurs and the development of co-operative capabilities. Knowledge transfer from the science to commercialization ends – industrial and business development competencies. Aligning the motives of independent of individual firm members, which may be information acquisition or involvement in a joint innovation. Injecting key brokering competences necessary to facilitate the development and reproduction of opportunism across the network.

The topic of innovation management through strategic networks of small and medium-sized enterprises began to receive attention in the mid-1990s with the advent of biotechnology organizations[17] and has since been applied to a wider range of industrial settings.[18] These type of networks have been found to perform best when they rely on bottom-up innovation processes. However, the larger the number of network members, the more important it becomes to have an administrative and co-ordination function to manage the configuration, formation and the governance of this network.

Common to all the options shown in Table 2.1 is the need to manage the following challenges.

FOUR CORE HR STRATEGIES

- *Structural and incentive system development*: all the examples involve the subtle use of incentive and contractual systems to engineer appropriate behavior between investors, innovators and employees.
- *The expansion of management skills in the unit*: for example, inventors/innovators tend to have a strong attachment to the technology or concept itself, which is not always viewed as means to an end. Most processes of innovation end before the phase of market entry is reached. Commercialization processes

generally require organization designs that shift resources to production and marketing, which has implications for those in other functions who invested resources in the innovation.

- *The need for competence destruction and reconfiguration of career systems*: most new innovations threaten old power structures, expertise is made obsolete, new career trajectories are initiated and problems of cultural fit are created as management skills and business models become redundant.
- *Understanding and putting in place the skill formation strategies that in turn build long-term organizational capability*: HR can work with line managers to build a deep understanding of the crucial skill ingredients for the new business models. We discuss a more strategic workforce planning approach to talent management in Chapter 7, under the guise of future proofing talent, which might include building and seeking advanced technological skills, creating hybrid skill or insight, or transforming or evolving existing skills or knowledge.

In managing these developments, the role of "organizational slack" – defined as excess resources that cushion the organization from environmental impacts and allow for discretionary allocations to innovative activity – has long been debated.

The evidence seems clear:

> financial resources are probably the most necessary, if not sufficient, element in ensuring the translation of creative ideas into new processes, products or services.[19]

However, this is not a message that the cost-cutting and productivity-seeking CFO might want to hear in tough economic times. As Chapter 4 makes clear, it is also an issue when organizations are overly driven by attention to lean management, but approach this lean thinking in a narrow-minded and cost-cutting way. This is because slack can also be seen as inefficiency. It has a curvilinear relationship with innovation performance – too little slack inhibits innovation, whilst too much shows diminishing returns.

2.2.5 Building competence across open innovation networks

Another macro-level issue is the need to build competence, often across open innovation networks. The field of innovation management argues that knowledge is now produced and exploited within networks that bring together multiple actors – from universities, industry and government – in very interactive ways. Open innovation focuses on bringing together different competences or technological capabilities both inside and outside of the organization to achieve some commercial ends.[20] In these open networks, often a large organization – such as Intel, IBM, BP, Lego or Nike – manages an open innovation in ways that develop enough gravitational force to attract additional knowledge providers to the network.

HR IMPLICATIONS OF BUILDING COMPETENCE IN OPEN INNOVATION NETWORKS

Open innovation models rely on:

- connecting people and technology from different organizations;
- individual-level learning;
- a capacity for the organization to transform its underlying structures;
- creating cultures that learn, i.e., cultures based on open-mindedness, knowledge-friendliness, reputation and trust;
- attention to intellectual property rights based on principles of non-disclosure;
- being part of a wider innovation ecosystem; and
- establishing learning communities that have a common purpose and common incentives for successful knowledge production and exploitation.

This is bringing greater complexity and inter-dependence between organizations, as well as a need to understand how best to manage this.[21] We shall discuss this development of more collaborative ways of working in detail in Chapter 5. However, at this point, we should note that the structural and HR challenge associated with each challenge is very different. Two areas of study have helped us to understand the management tasks involved in learning across networks:

1. Research into what are called knowledge-based inter-organizational collaborations (KBIOCs), in which organizations combine competences, share resources and distribute risks, running from minor incremental improvements right through to radical innovation. These arrangements may cross customers, competitors, suppliers, sub-contractors and partners.
2. Research into innovation, where researchers have documented a shift from linear and closed models of innovation to the more open and user-centric models that we see in many sectors today, often pursued as a result of higher levels of uncertainty, increased costs of R&D and shortened innovation cycles.

ORGANIZATIONS ARE BEING DRIVEN TOWARDS MORE COLLABORATIVE INNOVATION BY FOUR IMPERATIVES:

1. The "velocity" at which knowledge has to be applied across the partners has accelerated, making it important for partners to acquire and capitalize on knowledge in a short period of time.
2. There is a need to learn how to combine complementary knowledge across the partners – to exploit the sum of available knowledge – rather than to create new knowledge.
3. The partners all have a desire to exploit the available knowledge for commercial and monetary purposes, but also desire to create skills and develop new competencies as a consequence of the knowledge sharing.
4. There is an absence of any one single center of gravity in the collaborative arrangement. Partners are inter-dependent and equal in terms of power and authority.

There characteristics are believed to exist and to be important in a wide range of KBIOCs such as: knowledge supply-chain networks where knowledge integration and the interaction among partners needs to be managed; business networks, in which a constellation of firms is built up by a "central actor" in order to satisfy its business requirements; and research networks, which have the goal of creating new knowledge, with every partner carrying out the research activity without any leading company.

Managing these skills, knowledge and behaviors on a whole network basis means that there are now a wide range of competence-building responsibilities for the HR function.

THE NEW COMPETENCE-BUILDING RESPONSIBILITIES FOR THE HR FUNCTION

HR Directors have to ensure that they:[22]

1. establish the architecture that enables the emergence of the competences so that the organization can either build the core competences or deftly capture them from the network;
2. align the training and learning strategies, content and processes;
3. shift the focus of performance assessment accordingly;
4. develop a network strategy that makes clear what the strategic situation to be analyzed is, which members of the network to

be focused on, who and what determines the nature of the relationships, what part in the network each actor plays, and what leverage and steering potential each actor has;[23]

5. be clear about "networking pictures" (the views of the network held by participants in the network) and "network outcomes" (the actors to be involved; activities and resources);[24]
6. have people or units that act as systems integrators – ensuring that the systems and processes of the multiple collaborating organizations achieve the integration of knowledge across all parties involved;[25]
7. have a small number of powerful lead managers, who act as intrapreneurs, creating a strategic community both within and outside the organization, an organization within an organization (or set of partners), to forge connections and ensure that the communities work together;[26]
8. develop broader competence in managing inter-firm communication processes (called network competence) in order to support the development of a shared vision across network members and a shared sense of identity, through customer project teams, cross-departmental communication, secondment and co-location of key personnel;
9. manage the different types of knowledge that are shown to be important for all parties involved: know-how (common understanding of procedures), know-why (understanding of the principles involved), know-what (understanding of the customer's needs of the collaboration) and know-who (information about who knows what who knows what to do) knowledge;[27]
10. align performance targeting and management processes;[28]
11. absorb and embed themselves within their collaborators in order to be able to absorb and exploit knowledge[29] by establishing trusted relationships and aligning the various communities, networks and stakeholders that are brought together;
12. capitalize on a large number of intermediate organizations. These intermediary organizations act as enablers of knowledge, allwingall network members to benefit from additional sources of expertise beyond the immediate network, such as the social media, individual experts and freelancers.[30]

2.2.6 Institutionalizing a culture and a system of innovation

In discussing how organizations can institutionalize a culture of innovation, the paradox of creativity (invention, conceptual freedom) versus control (discipline, execution) has long been discussed.[31] The question is this: how do you manage the tension between these two legitimate forces? Research into how you institutionalize innovation so that it becomes just part of the culture is invariably case study-based. These accounts relate the practical mechanisms inside iconic organizations that have helped to build a reputation for innovation. 3M famously introduced a 15 percent rule whereby scientists were encouraged to spend 15 percent of their time on projects they liked. General Electric has also been lauded as an engine of innovation.

CREATING ORDER THROUGH ADAPTIVE RULES AT GENERAL ELECTRIC

General Electric (GE) has often been cited as being very adept at managing this need for paradox, successfully implementing simple rules that in practice generate effective levels of adaptive tension aimed at meeting key corporate goals. Its strategy has been described as pursuing two targets: the development of a corporate brain to manage innovation and the creation of a "boundaryless" organization where information is shared. This was achieved through the articulation and implementation of two clearly stated simple rules:

1. Organizational boundaries usually inhibit information from being shared. One of Jack Welch's main devices for stopping this was an "anti-hoarding" rule: anyone in GE who discovered a valuable idea or practice had to spread it through the rest of the company as quickly as possible or they faced being fired.
2. Business units had to be No. 1 or 2 in their industry or else they would be divested.

These rules were backed by strong incentives that made employees rich if they applied the rules effectively, but would get them fired if they broke the rules.

More recently, Google has also come to be seen as a benchmark for an innovative culture. What appear to be the rules of institutionalization there?

INSTITUTIONALIZING INNOVATION AT GOOGLE[32]

Google has become famous for developing an "innovation ecosystem" and for exercising "architectural control" over this system. Bala Iyer and Thomas Davenport have drawn attention to key elements of the organizational and cultural strategy that they argue are generalizable. The key for HR is to identify how certain aspects of people management – and symbolic practices – can reinforce an innovative business model:

> what truly sets Google apart from most businesses is its culture ... only some aspects are by other Internet-based businesses.[33]

The culture is one in which technocratic individuals prosper on the basis of their ideas and technological acumen – high value is based on ideas, technological acumen, intellect and opinions of employees.

The model hinges around owning the infrastructure for the product technology ecosystem and exercising architectural control over this system. This is based on a massive and scalable IT infrastructure, database management tools, an operating system enabling plug-and-play expansion of computer networks, and competitive product technology that enables "mashup innovation" (features capable of being added by third parties, such as independent software developers, open source community and Google engineers).

This in turn enables a "cloud" of flexible development resources that can be switched on or off, and a business model that enables them to earn revenue whilst adding value to the core product. The product development life cycle is accelerated because customers beta test, enabling parallel development and marketing.

Innovation is built into job design and soft and hard features of the HRM system are combined to support this:

- At a micro-level, there is a budget for innovation built into the allocation of employee time.
- Technical employees are allowed to spend 20 percent of time on technical projects of their own choosing.
- The performance management system exerts pressure to ensure that choices are made wisely.

- Management time is split 70 percent on core business, 20 percent on related but different projects and 10 percent on new business and products.
- Allocations are tightly managed but tradable over the year.

The culture supports both failure and chaos. A high level of risk tolerance and innovation go hand in hand. The CEO was quoted as saying: "let a thousand flowers bloom but please fail very quickly so you can try again." The Head of Personnel notes that "we like chaos. Creativity comes out of people bumping into each other and not knowing where to go."

Innovation was also supported by data and detail:

> [There is] ...extensive, aggressive use of data and testing to support ideas.

The culture was one in which the organization performs randomized and controlled experiments with multiple versions of product offerings (parallels exist in many retail and food organizations).

GIVING KNOWLEDGE MARKET VALUE

To make the culture work, Google has found ways of giving knowledge an internal market value. It becomes possible to artificially monetarize innovative bets:

- *Predictive markets*: there are 300 panels of employees to predict and assess things like customer demand for new products, product and competitor performance, and fun questions. These panels act as decision support tools. Executives have to be prepared to draw attention to what might to some of those already in power look like negative data.
- *An analytic and democratic approach to innovation*: ideas and predictions are voted upon – hence the creation of market value. The old concept of suggestion schemes has evolved into an idea management system. Employees email ideas for new products, processes and improvements. Every employee can comment on and rate the ideas of others.
- *External injections of ideas*: this market is supported by regular "tech talks" in which distinguished researchers from around the world present ideas – a commitment to continued learning and education.

All aspects of this culture are paternalistic and highly analytic. They also suggest:

> an unusually high level of recognition for the human dimensions of innovation.[34]

In exchange for privileged treatment, Google expects hard, almost excessive work. Employees are scored on 25 performance metrics, from how frequently they host tech talks to the variability (i.e., differentiated assessment) of their assessments of potential recruits.

Google's innovation culture is also characterized by a capability strategy that ensures:

- mastery of its core "nucleus businesses";
- patience in acquiring and learning how to run "electron projects or businesses."

According to the CEO back in 2007, the key to this strategy is:

> ubiquity first, revenues later … if you can build a sustainable eyeball business, you can always find clever ways to monetarize them.

The future business model will take care of itself. There are parallels with the models used at Apple and Amazon.

Only the foolish would believe that the answer is to copy these particular practices and to emulate them inside their own organization; it is not. But you can find the equivalent sorts of rules and principles that would work in your system.

Some people have tried to put some theory behind the examples such as 3M, General Electric and Google in order to explain what is really going on, and how to think about the rules that would work for a particular organization. It can be useful for HR Directors to know the way in which the strategists try and move the anecdotes in such case study examples into some more generalizable principles.

The most effective HR strategies help organizations get to the root sources of innovation. Otto Scharmer of MIT has postulated the Theory U of creativity.[35] He argues that expert systems software or scenario-planning methodologies are of help to organizations in understanding the near future, but are found wanting in the fast-emerging, often unpredictable scenarios typical of technology markets. The challenge is to devise creative solutions that also connect with a clear understanding of emerging future possibilities. He interviewed leaders considered to be adept at future-looking decision making that also involved great complexity. These included the traditional leadership skills of being able to absorb and correlate large amounts of diverse information and then to act quickly once a good idea was developed. Yet in between these stages, their methods were often highly unconventional. These leaders practised the art of what Scharmer calls "presencing" – creating the proper mental environment conducive to creativity and profound insight while sensing the hidden sources of idea generation.

Strategists are using (amongst a range of models) complexity theory to understand innovation – a theory that examines both the processes by which complex, irregular phenomena can achieve an appearance of order and the processes through which simple phenomena can become apparently driven by chance:

> the issue is not the search for simple causes to complex outcomes but to understand how simplicity emerges from complex interactions.[36]

2.3 Micro-level HR strategies

2.3.1 Lessons from leadership research

We know that leadership behavior and management style are critical to the innovation process. Employees have to be empowered, which means two things:

- being given sufficient autonomy and control over their work;
- but also being made comfortable with exercising more innovation – not feeling alone in the pursuit of innovation.

A review summarized the literature on leading creative efforts and explored the main models and approaches, concluding there is an:

> increasing amount of evidence suggesting that leadership [has] a profound influence on creativity and innovation.[37]

It identified the behaviors and modeled the core leader functions involved. This particular brand of leadership does not involve the competencies associated with the generalist or charismatic change leader.

The following sections have implications for the discussion of talent management in Chapter 7. Evidently, organizations need to ask the "talent for what?" question – the sorts of capabilities, potential and performances they need are different if they are looking for people to lead innovation as opposed to manage efficiencies.

LEADERS OF INNOVATION MUST PROVIDE:

1. *Substantial knowledge of the area in which they work*: technical expertise and creative problem-solving skills are highly predictive of follower creative performance. The technical knowledge also provides leaders with the power base to influence people, to represent the group, to communicate clearly and to identify the development needs of members.
2. *Mission definition perspective*: this enables project selection and the concretization of visions, provision of structure and goal orientation.
3. *Support for followers, seen in three ways*: support for ideas, for the work, and social support. An avoidance of negative feedback in the early stages of work.
4. *Skills of resource acquisition and resource distribution*: these have been shown to be more important than either structure or climate in predicting innovation.
5. *Structure*: the ability to induce structure where it was undefined. This is done in two ways: judgments about specialization, functional differentiation and professionalization of technical knowledge resources; and through internal and external communication.
6. *Evaluative feedback*: used to direct effort, timeliness in interventions and setting of output expectations.
7. *Organizational outreach*: a broad understanding of the organization, its strategy, long-term goals and tactics, sources of social support and product champions.

Studies that examine what leaders of creative effort think about show how they impact on the culture for innovation. They do this through:

- being driven by environmental scanning;
- strategy formation;
- mission definition;
- influencing how problems are structured;
- providing guidance for the generation of ideas;
- providing evaluative feedback;
- shaping planning and process management; and
- providing support and resources.

In short, leaders provide the parameters for idea creation and the context for information, but the two dimensions of leadership most related to innovative behavior are:

1. the quality of the relationship between subordinates and their leaders (this is called leader-member exchange or LMX). Low quality LMX is based on formal, impersonal exchanges whereas more mature interactions are characterised by trust, mutual liking, and respect. This LMX indirectly influences the climate - subordinates tend to generalise what they see in their supervisor behavior to the organization at large;
2. the expectations placed on the role of leaders. Research into innovation leadership shows that supervisors and subordinates engage in a mutual role development process and arrive at mutual understandings about three things: decision latitude; the level of influence, and the level of autonomy allowed.

The culture also places expectations on these innovation leadership roles. Research shows that the degree to which a supervisor expects a subordinate to be innovative is linked to the subordinate's actual innovative behavior. Experience also shows that:

- some leadership roles are prescribed by the organization or its technology (they are machine-driven by the culture);
- in some cultures managers lack the imagination to negotiate their subordinates' roles;
- the expectations that supervisors have for their subordinates shape the subordinates' expectations and motivations;
- performance expectations are communicated through the managers' behaviors/attitudes.

So there is a Pygmalion effect.

2.3.2 Creating the right team climate

A second micro-level factor is the creation of the right climate at team level. Research on team climate and innovation affirms two basic laws:

1. Individuals respond more to how they *perceive* the environment (climate) rather than to the environment per se!
2. Individuals *regulate their own behavior* in relation to these perceptions.

If an organization can manage perceptions, then it is well on the way to creating an innovative culture. Do teams generally perceive that there is a climate for innovation? The record is not good. Where are we actually at our most creative? This was summed up very nicely 15 years ago:

> In the bath. Walking the dog. On holiday. Looking at the fire. Walking in the mountains. While meditating. Swimming. Sailing. Fishing. In fact anywhere but work.[38]

A lot of attention, then, has been given to how organizations can make the work experience, and organizational life in general, more conducive to innovation.

THE ACID-TEST QUESTIONS FOR WHETHER THERE IS AN INNOVATION CULTURE[39]

Ask frontline employees the following questions:

1. How have you been trained as a business innovator? What investments has the organization made in teaching you how to innovate?
2. If you have a new idea, how much bureaucracy do you have to get through to get a small increment of experimental capital?
3. Are you actually being measured on your innovation performance or your team's innovation? Does it influence your remuneration?

If you substitute the idea of career reward and employability for compensation, then these questions apply to a wide range of organizations and not just the large corporates. In any event:

> when you ask these questions of first line employees, you quickly discover that in most companies there is still a big gap between the rhetoric of innovation and the reality.[40]

What can be done? The relevant research is captured under the umbrella topic of "climates for innovation." A central role of the organizational climate is to manage the team's attention to innovation rather than only letting the realization of crisis stimulate the necessary attention. In general terms, creativity and innovation is encouraged by climates that are:

- playful about ideas;
- supportive of risk taking;

- challenging; and
- tolerant of vigorous debate.

The values and beliefs of the organization impact key behaviors, such as collaboration, communication and risk. Innovation is then impeded by climates that emphasize formal rules, respect for traditional ways and clearly demarcated roles.

The word "climate" sits beneath these prescriptions. When applied to organizations, climate reflects the organization's expectations (as perceived by individuals) of behavior, the anticipated outcomes, and the feelings, attitudes and behaviors that characterize such an organizational life. Climate is defined as the shared perceptions of how things are done around here.

Research shows that it is the climate at team level that is most powerful and it is perceptions about this climate that are the most important. At this level the most important antecedents to creativity and innovation include:

- the quality of team leadership;
- problem-solving style;
- work group relations; and
- the type of jobs allocated (job design is important because discretion is positively associated with creativity).

EMPLOYEES MAKE JUDGMENTS OF THE CLIMATE BASED ON THE FOLLOWING ELEMENTS:

- Discussion content.
- Group objectives.
- Communications.
- Handling conflict.
- Decision making.
- Criticism.
- Expression of personal feelings.
- Task achievement/feedback.
- Leadership.
- Group sensitivity and review processes.
- Perceptions about the policies, practices and procedures.

Research asks three questions:

- What factors help or hinder innovation?
- What distinguishes highly innovative and less innovative teams?
- What practical measures can be recommended to facilitate innovation?[41]

FOUR KEY CLIMATE FACTORS

1. *Climate for excellence*: reflects each team member's commitment to high-quality standards, quality of decision making, critical appraisals, monitoring and clear task performance standards.
2. *Participative safety*: reflecting support for innovation through co-operation among team members, mutual assistance during the development of ideas and inter-personal interactions that result in group members feeling safe to propose and develop radical and risky new ideas.
3. *Vision*: how clearly defined, shared, attainable and valued are the team's objectives and vision?
4. *Task orientation*: commitment of the team to achieve the highest possible standards of task performance.

Of these factors, team climate researchers continue to find that climate for excellence drives the *quality* of innovation, whilst participative safety (also called support for innovation) drives the *quantity* of innovation.

2.3.3 Shaping the people

HR Directors are often naturally drawn to their familiar home territory, and many of the basic ingredients for an HR innovation strategy operate at the micro-level. They draw upon resourcing, training and organization development approaches.

THE TRADITIONAL INGREDIENTS OF AN HR INNOVATION STRATEGY

- Using selection and assessment processes to recruit creative and innovative individuals and allocating people to units and positions appropriately.

- Introducing procedures to encourage the generation of new ideas, e.g., brainstorming.
- Training leaders in the skills required for the successful management of the creative performance of their subordinates, i.e., holding leaders responsible for the management of the decision thinking environment of their teams.
- Changing the organization's own characteristics (structure, climate and culture) in ways that facilitate creativity and innovation.

The shaping of a few people can be a valuable tool in the company's armoury (again, this is an issue discussed in Chapter 7 in relation to talent management) and this raises questions about selecting and then developing individuals who are more entrepreneurial, innovative or creative. However, we must be clear what we are talking about when we use the word "innovation."

INNOVATION AT THE MICRO-LEVEL

Creativity and innovation are overlapping constructs. Different individual, social and organization level factors play a part in each.

The process of creativity is more concerned with invention and the generation of new and original ideas. This is based on subjective judgments being made that ideas that are generated can be deemed to possess some kind of novelty and are worthy of development. These judgments are typically made – and therefore need to be managed – at the individual and team levels. For psychologists,[42] creativity is then "the deliberate (required or voluntary) undertaking of behaviors designed to generate new ideas, processes, products and/or services in response to open or closed problems."

Models of creativity show that there are two separate HR strategies:

1. *Generating creativity-relevant skills*: once a creative idea has been generated, it needs to be protected, developed and sustained. Individuals therefore have to have *both* expert knowledge *and* creativity-relevant skills. The latter are used

so that people are tasked and led appropriately, operate in a motivational environment that has reinforcing norms and cohesiveness, and in the context of an organizational strategy that shapes the access to resources and culture accordingly. The former (expertise), of course, represents the lifeblood of any creativity. The range of technological and business model skills now necessary to create powerful new ideas is growing in depth and breadth. HR needs to have strategies that facilitate the development of such expertise.

2. *Engaging individuals so that they contribute their ideas*: often understated is the need to engage individuals so that they give their creative ideas in the first place. This issue comes up again in Chapter 4 on lean management. Employees understandably ask the following questions:

- Is creative action worth my while?
- What do I expect to happen (what is the level of effort needed to effect a change in this organization and will it lead to a useful effect)?
- Are there any positive benefits to me (employees make an instrumental judgment)?

Addressing these questions requires an HR strategy that is more concerned with managing general levels of motivation, making creative effort more explicit and central in job design, task and performance management systems, providing time resources and autonomy for resources, and removing or neutralizing the obvious counter-cultural blocks to this.

Attention has been drawn to a number of "roadblocks" that make it difficult to assess innovation at the individual level.[43] There is often a confusing terminology as to what it involves, or indeed where it comes from. Is it a single attribute or it a constellation of other factors that we have come to label as "being innovative?" Is it part of personality, a form of intelligence, more to do with knowledge or driven by motivation?[44] If it is part of intelligence,[45] then in what way? Is it just a subset of general intelligence, an aspect of genius, a particular set of cognitive abilities and way of thinking or a label of intelligence that we give to the people once we see they have done something really innovative? Is it more to do with knowledge? We know that there is an inverted-U relationship between knowledge and innovation – too much expertise or too little does not lead to innovation:

> Knowledge may provide the basic elements, the building blocks out of which are constructed new ideas, but in order for these blocks to be available, the mortar holding the old ideas together must not be too strong.[46]

These are not silly questions. If you want to assess innovation amongst individuals, you need to know the answers. The idea that entrepreneurs – and creative and innovative people – can be seen as isolated economic actors, under-socialized and immersed in processes quite different from other social phenomena, has been replaced by a new understanding. Social relations and the social context that surrounds those capable of innovation strongly influence levels of entrepreneurship, creativity and innovation. It is the social networks surrounding talented people that affect and influence actual economic performance and consequently the shape and form of subsequent innovation outcomes:

> Research on entrepreneurs has been moving away from dealing with the entrepreneur in isolation and instead looking to the consequences of embeddedness and the impact, implications and relevance of networks for entrepreneurship.[47]

As we make clear in Chapter 7 on talent management, it is not just having the appropriate human capital (skills, competencies, behaviors), but also having the appropriate social capital. This includes the:

- networks;
- sets of ties and connections;
- information;
- collaborative relationships formed by individuals within firms;
- relationships with other organizations; and
- resources that can be gathered through these networks.

Any attempt to shape and select key individuals through talent management processes has to be put into this context and a broad view of innovative talent must be taken:

- Is innovation a necessary condition to get into your organization's talent pools?
- Is it possible to assess this capability in a useful way?

2.3.4 Can we assess innovation at the individual level?

Finally, we look to research on individual differences to signal how organizations might make assessments of innovation amongst their talent. These researchers have been on a journey, initially focusing on creative thinking as a subset of general intelligence, then giving more attention to creative achievement, which meant giving attention to personality and motivation, and then thinking about the organizational context, which was more concerned with the final outcome of beneficial innovations.

WHERE DOES CREATIVE WORK TAKE PLACE? ONLY WHEN: [48]

- the task presents complex, ill-defined problems;
- successful performance depends on the generation of novel and useful solutions;
- work revolves around skills relating to problem definition and construction, information gathering, concept formation and concept combination, idea evaluation and refinement, and plan formation.

> Creative work is naturally person centric … and collaborative.[49]

For a resourcing strategy to be a viable option, we need to understand whether there might even be such a thing as the innovative and creative personality. The sub-text to this question is can HR help weight the odds by selecting more innovative people and placing them in the right parts of the organization before building the right infrastructure around those parts of the organization to help them prosper? The answer it seems is yes. This selection question was actually first addressed by researchers into entrepreneurialism (so substitute the idea of an entrepreneurial personality for an innovative one for a moment). Entrepreneurship researchers see innovation as being about the creation and pursuit of opportunities with a view to future capital accumulation. They share the perspective of many psychologists – that it is difficult to distinguish entrepreneurship and entrepreneurial climates from the role of entrepreneurial people. Entrepreneurship researchers also have long asked if there is such a thing as the entrepreneurial personality. Where innovation runs into a need for significant entrepreneurship, then the profiles of talent can start to look quite similar.

ENTREPRENEURS ARE PEOPLE WHO:

- perceive the potential of situations and gamble on their imagination;
- are alert to profit opportunities and the exploitation of these opportunities;
- need to demonstrate creative imagination in the face of uncertainty;
- have different horizons and envisioning space than do most top team members (a collapsed sense of time leading to a sense of urgency);
- can spot opportunities that might otherwise be overlooked, based on judgment skills;
- can combine intuitive holistic thinking (envisioning) with rational analytic skills;
- are aware of risks, but have attention tuned to economic value.

The investment analogy of "buy low and sell high" has been used to describe innovative individuals:

- They pursue ideas that are unknown or out of favour, but which have growth potential (buy low).
- They persist in the face of resistance until the idea is implemented (sell high).[50]

However, for psychologists, although innovation needs to be managed across all levels of the organization (through individual, team, strategic leadership and business processes), an entrepreneurial streak is an important part of the make-up of people who have innovation hard-wired into their personality and mindset. It is the *necessary condition* for innovation that has to come first from the spark or life force that resides within individuals and their ideas. Then, depending on the type of industry and organization, a choice is made as to whether the strategy is one of – a blend of – four streams of HR activity.

BLENDED HR STRATEGIES

- Managing large groups of creative people.
- Making the most of a few amongst many.

- Bringing the best out of what you already have, i.e., giving more attention to the leadership of others who are less creative but still have potential.
- The development of climates that bring all of these good things to the fore.

As an individual difference, innovation lies at the crossroads of personality and intelligence.[51] Constructs relating to an innovative personality can be reduced to four personality factors, some positively associated with innovation and some negatively. There are two positive associations:

- motivation to change (known to psychologists as TIE, i.e., typical intellectual engagement!); and
- challenging behavior (people driven by the motto that it is better to ask for forgiveness than to seek permission).

The negative factors are:

- consistency of work style (tackling work methodically); and
- adaptation (an incremental problem-solving style).

Linking intelligence to what are called the "Big Five" personality factors and an innovative personality shows that:

- innovation has little to do with intelligence (a small positive but insignificant correlation) – it is more clearly linked to personality;
- it is positively associated with openness to experience, and extraversion, and negatively associated with agreeableness and conscientiousness.

Conscientiousness is the one dimension of personality consistently linked to work performance and so is built into most selection systems whether by default or design. It is negatively related to innovation. Do we deselect the innovative? There are important lessons in this work on selection for innovation. However, most writers on innovation continue to caution that it is not just about shaping talent in this way:

> You can hire all the intrinsically talented people you want. There is a market for talent ... [but] the real challenge is making profits off those talented people ... combining talent and technology and organizational design to generate much higher profits per employee than was possible before.

TABLE 2.2 Six component HR strategies for innovation

Key factor in managing innovation	Component HR strategies
1. Organization models and structure	How will parts of the organization best be configured to generate innovation? How will the new and necessary interactions and appropriate flows of information be generated? How will the appropriate interpretive frames be put on that information?
2. Operational processes	How will operational processes impact upon the selection of ideas and the evaluation capability of the organization, i.e., the generation, development and implementation of ideas?
3. Organizational alignment	How will the dissemination of strategy impact decision-making quality with regard to innovations? How will the vision and goals of the organization to foster innovation be enacted (and not stymied) through appropriate control systems? How will the necessary level of organizational slack be afforded to the human, physical and financial assets?
4. Knowledge management	How will the utilization of knowledge in general and previous project insight be converted into organizational learning? How will HRM assist in the following knowledge requirements for innovation: the willingness to learn, the design and behavioral conduct of networks, and the maintenance and development of professional logics? How will interactions with customers and other value chain members within the competitive cluster be facilitated? How will key knowledge areas, e.g., market sensing (customer product and service preferences) and competitive awareness (industry trends and competitors' positioning efforts), be reflected in the talent system?
5. Management style and leadership	What are the responsibilities to be afforded to leadership that will impact employee motivations for innovation? How will leadership qualities be used to enable people to negotiate more autonomous roles (a pre-requisite for creativity and innovation)? What attitudes must be held by leaders towards innovative behaviors (versus important operational requirements) and how will they be used to generate appropriate employee behaviors?
6. Individual employees	How will the personal characteristics (individual differences) associated with innovative behavior be handled in the resourcing systems? How will the motivational behavior of employees be directed to impact innovative behavior?

> Talent is largely a commodity and can be bought anywhere. The challenge is to raise the return on human capital ... in terms of managing creative-thinking people.[52]

2.4 Conclusion: six component HR roles in innovation

To conclude, if HR is to respond to the challenge of innovation, it needs to move beyond some current (one could say outdated) accepted doctrines about innovative cultures, and develop a more sophisticated understanding of the challenges associated with managing innovative performance under a number of different organizational models.[53] In Table 2.2 we summarize six key factors involved in the management of innovation.

In this chapter we have argued that HR could indeed play a leading role in facilitating innovative organizations and people. We have charted out the contribution that they could make to the innovation journey by summarizing the ideas discussed and have laid out six component HR strategies. But as HR begins to tackle some of the more long-term and fundamental performance challenges that we outline throughout this book, beginning with this chapter on the challenge of innovation, this will bring new demands on the function.

The process of innovation is surprisingly people-centric, but to capitalize on this, we need HR functions that can advise on how the structure and incentive system must be developed, and how the organization can make use of incentives and contractual systems to engineer the right behaviors between investors, innovators and employees. HR have to become experts in organization design, with insights into how organizations might build innovation through skunk works, tightening the levels of control over time, using internal or external venture capital models, or developing innovation service units. It must help the organization expand the level of management skills within key business units as its innovations mature and shift resources from R&D, through production and marketing. It has to help the organization cope with the challenge of competence destruction and the reconfiguration of career systems that this will bring. New businesses based on innovative developments inside the broader organization threaten old power structures, make other forms of expertise obsolete, create new career trajectories and lead to problems of cultural fit. HR also has a role in helping the organization understand how it can secure access to future skills and how these new and important skills may be formed (we look at this challenge in Chapter 7). Finally, as organizations start to future-proof their talent systems, attention needs to shift to building long-term organizational capability.

If HR leaders are to contribute to the Board when the strategy is one that brings innovation to the fore, they and their function need to have an important set of skills and expertise. All of the HR solutions flow from the original organization design choice, so HR needs to be in at the start and to advise on this organization design. When it comes to the management of innovation, HR functions are facing an exciting future, but a challenging one, and it now needs a very specific type of expertise to be successful.

chapter 3

Customer Centricity and People Management

3.1 Introduction: from service-profit chain to customer centricity

We have chosen customer centricity as the second of our strategic performance drivers because we believe that senior HR leaders need to be fully aware of the concept in order to understand its relevance for their particular business. Most HR Directors have for several years now picked up on the service-profit chain to argue a link between employee engagement and performance. But as they work with the other functions – notably marketing and operations – on problems of customer centricity, they can see that they need to realign their own resources accordingly to deal with the people and organizational challenges that this performance driver entails.

In our previous book we argued there was a shift taking place within organizations and their relationship with their consumers and employees, and this was moving them from a position where once driven by brand, marketers and a set of promises, they were now assessed on what they actually did.[1] For consumers, the issue was moving away from being "about brand" towards being "about reputation." This naturally shifted the attention of HR towards employee engagement and employer advocacy.

Most HR professionals understand the basic tenets and assumptions of the original service-profit chain thinking. This theory, which argued that there is a clear link between employees' work experiences and financial performance in the service sector, with customer satisfaction acting as a critical intervening variable, was based on a series of associations and presumed causal links between the following:

- *Employee satisfaction and customer satisfaction*: the initial studies in the late 1990s reported correlations between customer satisfaction and a range of employee perceptions of the organization climate, reflected in attitudes such as satisfaction and commitment.[2] By the early 2000s, reviews by work psychologists[3] and empirical tests[4] confirmed that customer satisfaction and employee satisfaction were correlated.
- *Employee perceptions of the organization climate (especially its focus on service) and customer satisfaction levels*:[5] followed by an association between favourable climates and levels of employee satisfaction and commitment.[6]
- *Customer satisfaction and financial performance*: by the mid-1990s, marketing research argued that levels of customer satisfaction and intentions to purchase were linked,[7] although by the late 1990s, more mixed evidence began to emerge, with the link to intended purchases broadly supported,[8] but the link to actual purchases more uncertain.[9]

In the original work, Sears was described as having introduced a "change in the logic and culture of the business" by rebuilding the company around its customers and "developing a business model" (the employee-customer-profit model) that changed the way managers and employees thought and behaved.[10] We have previously used the example of McDonald's and its successful employee engagement strategy to show how many HR functions adopted service-profit chain thinking. Their engagement strategy also required that HR provision met a number of other important pre-conditions that together form the basis of a trust-based HR strategy, including: creating a baseline of positive employee engagement and involvement; putting in place a suite of flexible work policies; making investments in training and education, underpinned by a philosophy of social mobility; operating democratic planning feedback processes joined up to engaging social media; and e-enabling core HR processes in ways that enhance the management of the employer brand.[11] Interestingly, many years after this work, McDonald's remains in the Top 10 Best Workplaces in the UK in 2014, alongside brand organizations such as Capital One, Microsoft, eBay, Diageo, Pentland and Hyatt.

However, now the debate is not couched just in terms of customer satisfaction, but also in terms of what is called customer centricity. Back in 1980 Alvin Toffler quoted a prediction that:

> the most creative thing a person will do 20 years from now is to be a creative consumer … Namely, you'll be sitting there doing things like designing

> a suit of clothes for yourself or making modifications to a standard design, so that computers can cut one for you by laser, and sew it together by NC machine...[12]

Today a Chinese listed company reports being able to make 500 customized uniforms a day for policemen and service workers. Is this customer centricity? Customer centricity is said to involve:

> Describing an organization that is operated from a customer's point of view. Rather than developing new products and attempting to convince consumers to purchase them, a customer-centric firm develops products and services that customers need.[13]

Case studies abound on the topic, with organizations such as Intercontinental Hotels, Best Buy, Fiat, Amazon, Dell, Delta Airlines and projects like the London 2012 Olympics being used as examples of successful strategies. However, there remains a lot of confusion as to what the term really means.

We want to equip HR with the knowledge it needs to understand what customer centricity is, and is not, so that it can enter into the debate with the business. HR functions need to better debate the issue of customer centricity with the line, structure HR accordingly and then measure the value that HR adds, based on where the organization is on the spectrum of being product to customer-centric. HR functions need to work through a logical thought process about customer centricity so that they ask the following questions:

- Does the business model demand of the organization that it is customer-centric or not?
- If the answer is yes, how must HR align its internal customer focus with the organization's external customer focus?

Whilst service-profit chain thinking has been a good starting point for HR Directors in terms of linking their function to its internal customers (employees) and then through their employee's customer orientation to the organization's end customers, they now enter debates about customer centricity as another and more fundamental means of doing this. Customer centricity, then, is another idea that has stemmed primarily from marketing:

- What influence should customer centricity have on the strategy, business model and structure that organizations need to adopt in order to achieve business success?
- Should HR be aligned to internal customers or to end customers? Potentially it has to do both.

What is clear is that organizations now think much more broadly about the role of multiple stakeholders in the delivery of a service, and the cause-and-effect relationships across a whole network (we pick up the challenge of these much more collaborative business models in Chapter 5).

This chapter will show that the debates around customer centricity raise fundamental questions for HR Directors as to how they should think about their function in terms of the skills it needs, how resources are allocated and the value it adds.

3.2 Why is customer centricity being debated?

Despite the debate about the exact meaning and shape of customer centricity, which is outlined later in this chapter, the need for organizations to deal with increasingly radical changes to the way in which they deal with customers is becoming hard to ignore. The debate continues because there seems to be no decline or let-up in the levels of dissatisfaction, frustration and annoyance faced by a client, customer, consumer or "user" at poor degrees of service offered in many sectors of our economy, despite the enormous attention paid to the subject of customer relationships in organization strategy. With the advent of social networking and Web 2.0, there are now more places for people to complain publicly. It is therefore perhaps with a degree of "schadenfreude" that organizations are now turning to these very tools in the latest thinking about being customer-centric to provide them with real-time information on customer perceptions.

The concept of customer centricity entails much more than this – it is a logical and fundamental shift in organization strategy, structure and culture. By way of example, consider the impact of digital innovation and multi-channel retailing.

DIGITAL INNOVATION AND MULTI-CHANNEL RETAIL

The digital approach to retailing means the world is changing. Customers have more control, literally in their hands, with smartphones and apps. Organizations such as House of Fraser and Argos have all achieved commercial benefit from multi-channel shopping and click and collect schemes. Domino's Pizza has exploited digital innovation to develop what is seen as a multi-channel vision of distributed commerce across multiple touch points, managed from one single point. By 2012, 60 percent of its sales were online and £10 million of sales were made over iPhones, and by 2014, digital ordering represented 40 percent of its US sales. Developments span e-commerce, mobile-commerce, web analysis, testing, development and maintenance, social media, use of geo-locational social networks and in-store digital ordering. The growth of what is called the "packaged Internet" – where the fragmentation of digital channels across apps, smart TVs, tablets, e-readers, gaming devices and other emerging platforms are both eroding the dominance of websites but also requiring co-ordinated management of these touch points – is creating the opportunity for new service models. If you are going to change the design and feel of your services for customers, then you do the same for your staff.

An industry currently experiencing the impact of these developments is the fast food sector. It has a traditional service model, based on long tills, serving multiple customers and providing linear service. Food orders are cooked on projections of what is to be sold, with the constraints on capacity this entails. Although the industry is still highly fragmented – in the US the 50 largest companies account for about 20 percent of revenue – this quick service (QSR) business model, which first emerged in the 1960s and 1970s, represented a $191 billion dollar industry by 2013. It has long relied on a clear performance recipe, which meant that stores had to be managed on quality, service, cleanliness and value (QSCV). Organizations and brands (such as Subway, McDonald's, YUM, KFC, Pizza Hut, Taco Bell in the US, Café de Coral in Hong Kong, Greggs in the UK, or Seven & i Food Systems in Japan) operated in an environment where demand was driven by demographics, consumer tastes and personal income, and where the profitability of individual companies depended on efficient operations and high volume sales. They needed to think about speed, price and consistency. The growth of individualism, reflected in campaigns such as those undertaken by Burger King, led to new lines of products, such as breakfasts, salads and value meals based on price competition. Yet, the basic model remains one of competition driven by the quality of food served, rising commodity prices, market saturation and attractiveness of a franchise model.

However, this now competes with other models, such as what is called the fast casual service model (a full casual dining experience with a limited QSR service) and developments being triggered by the exploitation of data. The lines between casual dining, fast casual dining and quick service restaurants continue to blur, creating new opportunities for both customer engagement and the exploitation of business intelligence.[14] The fast casual model is based on customer-driven menu, commonly featuring a "build your own" offering, changes to the ordering and pick-up counter process. Adapting to the trend towards customization, alongside the assembly-line food production service, McDonald's has been beta-testing a "build-your-own-burger-with-an-iPad' model at the Laguna Niguel restaurant in southern California.[15]

The above example forms part of a general shift where choice will abound for organizations as they find their balance between the personalization potential offered by data with the level of uniformity that fulfils a brand promise. However, the future is one where data-gathering technologies such as low-cost sophisticated point-of-sale systems and data from social media mean that organizations can now rapidly adjust menu offerings based on information gathered about drive-thru customers, such as car make and model, number of passengers, items ordered or decision times.[16] They can tailor offerings "on the fly" for particular groups of customers at particular times. The industry is debating alternative business models, for example, where customers are assigned only one server to one customer with the server engaging in all aspects of the customer experience, including ordering, preparation, calling the customer by name (instead of by number) and hand-delivering his or her food.[17]

CUSTOMER CENTRICITY

Jez Langhorn, Senior Vice President Chief People Officer, McDonald's restaurants

Psychologists call it the "hedonic treadmill" and it's a primary driver of human progress and endeavour. It's also at the heart of what I believe will present some of the greatest challenges – and opportunities – for HR in the years ahead.

For a great example of the power of the hedonic treadmill, you only need to think about the smartphone in your pocket.

Forty years ago, telephones came with wires attached which meant that if you were out and about and wanted to make a call, you needed a phone box and a pocket full of change.

Thirty years ago the phone had gone mobile, but was expensive, unreliable and the size of a house brick.

Twenty years ago, the mobile phone had more than halved its size and *doubled* its functionality to include SMS text messaging as well as making calls.

Then along came the Blackberry and the iPhone.

At the time, every new innovation was heralded as a minor miracle of technology – the stuff of science fiction. Today if your mobile doesn't also include a high-quality digital camera, enough memory to store your entire record collection and more processing power than a 1980s mainframe computer, it's probably time to be thinking about an upgrade!

That's the hedonic treadmill. What was "miraculous" once is now, at best, merely "normal" and, at worst, laughable. So, as on a treadmill, if organizations want to maintain their position, they have to constantly keep moving forwards. And this doesn't just apply to technology providers – it applies to every organization that's providing goods or services.

Which, when you think about it, is pretty much every organization!

Meeting this unstoppable demand for continual improvement represents an enormous challenge for HR in two important ways.

First, HR needs a detailed understanding of the way in which the organization currently meets the needs of customers and those areas where there is an opportunity, through its people, to enhance the value the organization is delivering.

How this is achieved will clearly be different for every organization, but whether it's through superior skills, better service, greater innovation or deeper relationships, it's difficult to think of an organization where people – and therefore HR – don't have an enormous role to play in delivering this enhanced customer value.

Second, HR needs a detailed understanding of the way the organization creates value for its employees because, just like customers, their needs and expectations are subject to the influence of the hedonic treadmill.

And, once again, the way these needs and expectations are met will be different for every organization.

In short, HR's future success will be rooted in its ability to take customer centricity in organizations to a whole new level. Because I believe that putting the customer (whether that's the ultimate recipient of goods and services, or the employee as a recipient of value) at the heart of every decision the organization makes, and every initiative it implements, will be the defining factor in meeting the ever-increasing demands the hedonic treadmill will create in the future.

From an HR perspective, such shifts towards customer centricity need to trigger a range of important conversations. Those who are used to managing prior performance recipes – with the implicit reliance on specific resources and style of management – suddenly find that a new leadership and operational model is needed. Staff find themselves facing customers with very different need states and have to manage a range of interactions which in the above example would range from the traditional to the remotely ordered pick-up. A move from a less speed and transactional-driven service relationship to one in which more is known about the customer, and in which there is more face-to-face time, changes the sorts of skill, confidence and empathy levels that staff need. Customers can express dissatisfaction using social media immediately, so businesses have to get things right. To get customer centricity right, organizations have to start to work in a much more cross-functional way, linking up their marketing, innovation and IT, corporate communications, HRM and operations. This starts to change the way organizations need to structure themselves to support the strategy. Staff need to understand why this must be, and managers have to understand how to deliver performance in this new context. Customer centricity changes the relationship between the store environment and its service platforms, staff behaviors, the way customers are treated, the way in which teams should be organized to ensure that customer service is delivered, and even staffing patterns. This impacts the staff employee value proposition. In short, what appears to be an incremental shift in delivery channels ends up changing the whole "performance recipe."

3.3 What is customer centricity? Definitions and origins

To any HR specialist, from the above example, it becomes clear that once you start to think through the impact of personalization in service, this will have implications for store design, operations, customer service logics, brands and the role of customer intelligence. This in turn requires a significant change in the people management if the business change is to be successful. Those in operations or marketing might also see these implications – or they might not. Therefore, what becomes important is that there is a dialogue across functions about the implications of such business changes. Why? Because there is still much ambivalence about the topic of customer centricity:

- What do those in HR need to understand about this marketing-led performance driver?
- Which logics should be accepted?
- Which logics should be contested?

In the Centre for Performance-led HR's first review of the topic,[18] we asked whether this performance driver was a myth. Our first task then is to define customer centricity. To do this we need to briefly explore the history of the term and some of the latest ideas emerging on the topic. This will also entail a review of some of the strategic and structural implications of a customer-centric approach. We shall also consider what is becoming known as "social customer relationship management."

Back in the early 1980s, airlines were hailed as leading the way towards customer-orientated business strategies. Jan Carlzon, at the time CEO of Scandinavian Airlines (SAS), made a name for himself with his book *Moments of Truth*,[19] which contained a foreword by Tom Peters. He coined the term "moments of truth" to capture those experiential moments across the full customer surface of an organization in which the customer was in a particularly vulnerable state and the organization has an opportunity to impress or disappoint. He was famous for saying that SAS faced 50,000 moments of truth every day and that: "An individual without information can't take responsibility. An individual with information can't help but take responsibility." Reflecting on this:

> As new CEO of Scandinavian Airlines, SAS, in the early 1980s, Jan Carlzon found an industry where passengers – customers – were treated as disturbances and residuals in a system created for the administration of aircraft, pilots and flight attendants. His battle cry "Customer in Focus!" circled the globe and affected both business and governments. So customer centricity is not new.[20]

There are clearly still situations where leaders in an organization articulate a demanding change in strategy or paradigm that cannot be achieved through incremental change and that requires a fundamental change in culture, structure, systems and metrics.

Perhaps surprisingly, the term "customer-centric" is a new term, relatively speaking, dating back only to a decade ago.

Also in 2008, the elements of the "service-profit chain" were further elucidated,[21] describing the "propositions" in the chain that linked employee satisfaction, loyalty and productivity to customer loyalty in one direction and to company profitability in the other direction. Already these articles presaged one key aspect of customer centricity – the focus on employee empowerment and flexibility at the front line of service delivery.

THE PATH TO CUSTOMER CENTRICITY

It was in 2000 that an influential academic in the marketing field wrote a paper on the subject of customer-centric marketing[22] and the term thenceforth entered the vocabulary of popular management writers. On this path to customer centricity we have passed through many ideas. After the "moments of truth" movement, the importance given to thinking about customers continued throughout the 1990s and early 2000s. In the mid-1990s the concept of "one-to-one marketing" emerged – the idea that organizations should analyze the precise needs of every customer and deliver a product or service personally tailored to those needs. This presaged another concept contained in the customer-centricity movement: that of mass customization.[23] In short, there was growing awareness of topics such as customer satisfaction,[24] customer service,[25] customer loyalty,[26] quality as perceived by the customer,[27] the market-driven organization[28] and market-based learning.[29]

A more "service-dominant logic" or "customer orientation" was then suggested in the 2000s.[30] This argued that it was the actions of customers that led to value actually being realized – value is co-created by organizations and their customers. Marketing needed to create value independent of whether this was through goods or services. The manufacturer and supplier value chain might be based on mass manufacturing, whereas the customer value chain is much more individual and changeable. The word "service" should equate more with value, and this value is created both in production and the consumption process – rather then delivering value to the customer, it is about delivering value together with customers.[31] Finally, as the field of marketing extended into the study of business-to-business (B2B) activity, it began to see relationships as part of a whole network of connections. Increasingly organizations see themselves, their products and services as part of a many-to-many set of relationships – a network not just of customers and suppliers but also competitors, intermediaries, governments and customer-to-customer networks.[32] However, this path to customer centricity[33] has been portrayed by marketing researchers themselves (not HR academics) as very difficult for organizations to achieve and riven with problems caused by organization culture, structure, processes, leadership and performance metrics.

The true essence of the customer centricity paradigm therefore:

> lies not in how to sell products but rather on creating value for the customer, and, in the process, creating value for the firm.[34]

For many years now, marketing and management researchers have been trying to extend and align the different ideas that have been put forward about how organizations can have a "service-dominant logic." There are many concepts that are being discussed, some of which are not clearly understood or defined and others which show that the solution is complex.

These ideas are often linked back to the original ideas of Michael Porter[35] and his concept of the value chain. This painted a picture of value beginning with inputs of material, through manufacturing and assembly, and ending in activities such as marketing and after-sales support. This process was maintained by an organization's procurement, infrastructure, technology development and HRM. This was a very supplier-centric view of organizations, looking at value as created across the actions of the manufacturer rather than allowing for the fact that the consumer might also add value to a product or service.

Marketing management always stressed the mix between product or service, setting of price, promotion to make buyers choose the brand and distribution to the place where customers can easily get it. This more manipulative view of marketing was followed by growing attention to relationship marketing, where relationships and interactions, one-to-one marketing and the growth of customer relationship management (CRM) were all seen as important in creating long-term relationships with loyal customers. Customer-centric marketing was defined as "understanding and satisfying the needs, wants and resources of individual consumers or customers rather than those of mass markets or market segments."[36] Up to that point, organizations had placed the product at the start of the planning process; customer-centric marketing, on the other hand, places the customers' needs and wants at the start.

Alongside one-to-one marketing, organizations began to understand that if they were to create long-term win-win relationships between themselves as suppliers and their customers and other stakeholders, they needed to design these relationships so that the interactions between parties facilitated more co-operation, communication and dialogue – only then could all be satisfied. The danger still was that organizations could misuse relationship management and squeeze it into their marketing mix, still attempting to manage the customer relationships. The problem with this was that:

> suppliers should not manage customer relationships; they should interact with customers in relationships.[37]

This shift in focus is being driven by the low productivity of the marketing department, increasing diversity of the market, more well-informed and demanding customers and the advent of enabling technologies.

Marketing academics pointed to a consequence of this shift for organization structure and culture, as well as strategy. The customer-centric organization would be one in which all the activities of a firm – both customer-related and non-marketing functions – are aligned around customer value-adding work. The dominant "DNA" of the organization would have to shift from its technical or commercial origins (for example, engineering or technology) to become customer-centric, and the dominant leadership style would be crucial in adopting such a focus.

To summarize, customer centricity is therefore set aside from previous paradigms, it is argued, because it is concerned with the process of dual value creation.[38] This fundamental difference is often captured in stereotyping a product-centric versus a customer-centric approach – generally showing how these cultures run deep from structures, measurement and control systems to management philosophy.

A CUSTOMER-CENTRIC ORGANIZATION IS DIFFERENTIATED FROM A PRODUCT-CENTRIC IN TERMS OF:

- the differences involved in basic philosophy or mindset (from selling products to serving customers and seeking customer advantage);
- business orientation (from transactions to relationships);
- product positioning (from features and advantages to benefits and customer needs);
- organizational structures (from profit centers and product managers to customer segment centers and customer relationship managers);
- organizational focus (from new product development and market share to customer loyalty and employees as advocates);
- performance metrics (from product profitability to share of customer wallet and customer lifetime value);
- management criteria (portfolios of products to portfolio of customers); and
- customer knowledge (from customer data as a control mechanism to customer knowledge as a valuable asset).

3.4 Is it a myth or a movement? More critical views

The original definition and analysis of the customer-centric organization has been expanded by the industry of consulting and expert commentating that has proliferated over the years. In many cases (and this is an accusation frequently levelled at customer centricity), the term has merely become synonymous with timeless management fads around caring for the customer, service quality and the "customer is always right," hence the perception that the idea is more of a myth than a movement. When considering what has been written on customer centricity, it is clear that the term – like much management jargon – has become used as a catch-all for all types of customer service-oriented discourse, and to that extent, the term risks being devalued; less of a myth, therefore, and more an empty shell devoid of meaning. In part this is because it has to an extent been subsumed in the largely IT-driven CRM movement, which we will discuss later – possibly another source of criticism of customer centricity, as the customer was often perceived to be forgotten in the drive to install the latest enterprise software.[39]

The measurement of customer centricity (often based on customer perceptions of being understood, quality of staff, level of service, accessibility and relevant marketing), as opposed to customer distance, tends to place exemplar firms from sectors such as building societies, mobile phone operators, car insurers, supermarkets and traditional airlines in the lead, with many credit card, banks, low-cost airlines, power and utility companies faring badly.

We use the airline sector to convey how challenging drives towards customer centricity may be. One example our research captured is a typical initiative within an airline.

A CUSTOMER CENTRICITY INITIATIVE IN AN AIRLINE

The HR team was at the center of a customer centricity-driven change process. A cross-functional program (HR, internal communications and marketing) was implementing an integrated engagement program. The program put the brand at the center of the airline's customer-centricity effort. Five "brand behaviors" were identified to help people understand what customer centricity meant for the organization. These behaviors were introduced in every training course, in the performance management processes and in the internal communications. The airline saw itself as being very process-driven. The HR team therefore saw the need for mindset change as key to their customer-centricity project. The mindset needed was one that freed up and empowered the frontline employee to do a really good job for the customer.

Indeed, individually some airlines score high on customer centricity.

However, just how possible or not is the pursuit of customer centricity in this industry given the multi-party service experiences that passengers face in practice (again, we signal a forward link here to Chapter 5 on collaborative HR)?

THE AIR TRAVEL EXPERIENCE: CUSTOMER-CENTRIC OR CUSTOMER-DISTANT BY DESIGN?

Consolidation has long been expected in the airline industry. Hit by the global economic downturn and rising fuel costs, they seek scale, but know that excepting brand-loyal first-class passengers, travel is now a mainly commoditized market. Customer retention, re-attracting defected customers, attracting new customers and increasing the share of a customer's travel wallet all have value, but is a return to customer centricity possible?

The main moments of truth in the 1980s were when: you call to make a reservation to take a flight; you arrive at the airport and check your bags curbside; you go inside and pick up your ticket at the ticket counter; you are greeted at the gate; you are taken care of by the flight attendants onboard the aircraft; and you are greeted at your destination. This training program was exported to British Airways and Japan Airlines.

What a difference a few decades makes. Consider now how the fragmented industry structure makes it hard for an airline to cope with the delivery of a total service experience. Industry analysis shows that: "If airport management takes a strategic and holistic approach to customer service and airport branding, customer satisfaction with the airport experience can be significantly improved and airport net revenues can be tracked to show a direct relationship with increased customer satisfaction,"[40] yet, at the same time, "sometimes assure abominable service by their very design."

The problem is that whilst many are responsible for service delivery airport-wide (airport operators and the complex set of leases, permits and contracts they might have adopted, airlines, terminal operators, service contractors, government agencies for customs and immigration, concessionaires and retail tenants), customers still perceive the airport or airline as having principal agency, even if it does not. Brand perceptions crunch into the reality of standards, policies, procedures and systems as they operate across these agents. Customers judge facility condition and cleanliness; operational efficiency; employee behavior, appearance and knowledge; signage; airport and terminal planning and design; concessions; and construction impact on customers. Yet a customer-centric strategy requires a shared agenda, customer service standards and problem-solving capabilities across these parties, supported by co-ordinated systems and processes, co-operative marketing and communications, pan-organizational or pan-community customer service and performance management standards.

Imagine you are an airline (be it based on a stand-alone low-cost model or network models with its alliances and partners) with your many functions ranging from distribution, customer service, back office, operations, maintenance, repair and overhaul. Once more you are the target of – or darling of – the customer-centricity industry, being exhorted to fly high above market turbulence or be part of the customer travel lifecycle.[41] Your service performance sits in the center of the plethora of experiences over this life cycle, surrounded by successive rings of an airport on either side of the journey, and the transport arrangements to the airport, and even it seems the climate and behavior of volcanoes. Classic consulting prescriptions suggest suites of solutions: organizational realignments with associated cultural momentum programs; analytics to capture the needs, behavior and value of customers and the demography of their travel; tiered systems of customer advocacy, engagement and disengagement based on the problem context; information systems that combine vast amounts of data across multiple and disparate sources; loyalty and customer relationship based on the miles travelled, revenue or the breadth of products purchased; integrated marketing communications using data as the core driver of all marketing and customer-based activities; web-based self-service choices and social media to deliver offers appreciated by the customer; and tantalizing lounges and in-flight services.

As the above setting shows, the benefits inherent in individual initiatives within an airline may be clear, but in reality, in today's world flying is an embedded experience. We might ask the following questions:

- Do modern-day "moments of truth" experienced from the initial intention to travel through to the closing travel away from the final airport leave passengers with the view that this is a customer-centric experience?
- Are airlines now embedded in an industrial structure that by design makes it impossible to deliver an effective customer experience?

Academics therefore now talk of the need for balanced centricity. This view argues that customer centricity is just as biased and unbalanced as a supplier-centric view of the organization (it is a one-party view of centricity) – what has been called a quest that is little more than a "desk ideology." Whilst few would argue against the ability to understand the customer's situation and mindset (empathy) and make use of customer information, sometimes a customer-centric focus might be seen as incurring high costs but little gain in revenue. Sometimes thinking about patients, parents and students as customers reveals a fuzzy line between the obligations and rights of citizens versus their individual needs in a service relationship.

Often a network of customers now has to be considered, for example, in the pharmaceutical sector – a sector in which customer centricity is much discussed. With rising healthcare costs, decreasing growth rates, a decline in the number of innovative ingredients, the expiration of many patents and the increasing market power of producers of patent-free and generic drugs, differentiating on the basis of customer service becomes more attractive. The question of who is the customer is complex, with patients being consumers, insurance funds or health services the buyers and physicians the decision makers, with additional stakeholders, including pharmacists and pharmaceutical wholesalers and healthcare policy makers.[42]

What is needed is a two-party view that simultaneously zooms in on both suppliers and customers.[43] Customers form part of a larger context and network of relationships – one of a range of stakeholders who have a right to the satisfaction of their needs and wants. Customer service is generally created as a result of a whole network of contributors such as intermediaries, employees, the media, and the infrastructure of roads, electricity grids and broadband. It is evident that:

> Reality is complex and … a lot in marketing is built on beliefs and assumptions both in business and academe … Genuine customer centricity has never been implemented. There has been lots of rhetoric but little practice, more talk than walk. Perhaps, customer centricity cannot even be implemented? Can we indeed give one of many stakeholders priority? … Looking at the issue with customers' eyes: how intimate do they really want to get with suppliers?[44]

THE CAVEATS AND COUNTER-ARGUMENTS TO CUSTOMER CENTRICITY

- Not all elements are found in every customer-centric organization or are new ideas. Small organizations, and those at the high end of the luxury goods market, for example (low volume/high complexity offerings), have been tailoring solutions to clients for generations.

- This orientation may not be relevant for every organization.
- Customer-centric structures and the product-centric structures are not mutually exclusive, and both types can exist within a single organization.
- No organization is entirely product-centric or customer-centric in the way in which it structures itself and there will always be a group developing cutting-edge products in the most customer-centric organization.
- Likewise, understanding customers' needs and including this data in the design process for products (via focus groups, market research surveys and the like) are hardly new concepts.

However, even critical commentators reinforce the notion that there is now a "movement" towards customer centricity, that it is actually on the consumer side and that it is a movement that organizations are responding to too slowly:

> Yes, we do have a customer-centric movement going on – among customers. Irresistible global market forces are driving a gradual transition from past decades of sellers' markets to future decades of buyers' markets. As a result, customers are acting more empowered and emboldened and are continually upping their expectations of companies. More than just a "movement," this is a large rock rumbling downhill at increasing speed that imperils anything in its way.[45]

3.5 Six building blocks of customer centricity

So how should we think about customer centricity – whichever function we might be working in? We now filter out the commonplace and well-known commentary about structures and processes found in the marketing and customer service domains and concentrate on those elements which appear, in combination, to represent thinking of especial value to HR Directors planning how to support an organization moving to a customer-centric strategic orientation. There are several elements, or "building blocks," that recur and that we posit as the main characteristics of the customer-centric organization. We discuss each of these six recurring elements.

THE SIX BUILDING BLOCKS OF CUSTOMER CENTRICITY

1. Mass customization: finding the best possible proposition for a given customer.
2. Involvement of the consumer in the design process.
3. Structuring around the customer and not the product.
4. Enablement of frontline staff.
5. The democratization of customer relationships and knowledge.
6. The capability to filter massive data sets to add value to product and service offers (we discuss Big Data and HR analytics in Chapter 6).

3.5.1 Managing mass customization

The first building block is mass customization: finding the best possible proposition for a given customer. The move towards a customer-centric organization places mass customization at the heart of its strategy[46] by placing the demands of each customer at the center of value creation. The strategy is to find as many products as possible for its customer and to find ways of integrating those products. Pricing is driven more by the value to the customer rather than on the sum of products and services that constitute the offering. However, this must be achieved in a way that is cost-efficient – hence the idea of mass customization. This apparent oxymoron has been defined as "the technologies and systems to deliver goods and services that meet customers' needs at near mass production efficiency."[47] Therefore, one of the most straightforward ways of distinguishing the customer-centric organization – at least in theory – is to contrast it with its opposite, the product-centered organization.[48] In essence, the strategy of a product-centered organization is to find as many uses and outlets as possible for its product. It strives to deliver the best product with the most cutting-edge technology or set of features which opens the market up to new opportunities for future product placement. Its pricing is driven by market competition. Such changes are difficult to implement. Until the measurement systems become institutionalized, success is very dependent on the role and leadership of senior management in overriding the control systems if they tempt people to behave in a less than customer-centric way – to provide "air cover" for people in their part of the organization. Adherence to customer-centric behavior is driven by the quality of leadership. Thus, there are a number of challenges facing organizations as they "put upon" this layer of managers/leaders. Put bluntly, if you were to shift authority levels down to enable customer centricity, would it be safe to do so?

3.5.2 Managing the involvement of consumers in the design process

A second aspect of customer centricity is the involvement of the consumer in the design process. Why has this become important? Customers' needs and requirements are usually subjective and difficult to define precisely, even by the customers themselves. This makes them difficult to transfer into a concrete design specification for a customized product or service. By integrating the customer directly into the design of the product or service and using technology to simplify this, organizations are enabling the implicit specification of that product or service by the consumer. Technology also then enables the company to gain access to this "implicit" knowledge and make it explicit by transferring it into production processes or market research/future product development and specifications. Costs are reduced through lower investment into traditional market research and the more efficient use of consumer information (by having direct access to "implicit" knowledge). However, direct benefits should flow from increased customer satisfaction, loyalty and emotional engagement with the organization which has allowed their creativity to be unleashed. Social customer relationship management (S-CRM) represents some of the latest thinking in customer centricity. Early CRM initiatives focused the organization's efforts on a single customer view and one-to-one relationship management, and CRM initiatives quickly became associated with stripping out costs and efficiency drives. S-CRM involves the exploitation of the technology of social networking using a suite of tools for building a picture of an increasingly fragmented customer base. It merges two recent business changes: the orientation of CRM systems away from the purely technology-focused solutions towards the redevelopment of the business model to support customers; and the emergence of social network sites as a critical channel to the customer. The combination of these two trends puts the co-creation of value between the customer and the business at the heart of customer thinking:

> a collaborative value chain that engages the customer in the activities of the business sufficiently to provide each (the company and the customer) with what they need from the other to derive individual and mutually beneficial value.[49]

It is becoming an important tool in the shift to collaboration with the customer that might entail:

- collaboration on product development;
- customer involvement in internal process development;

- customers helping each other to resolve service problems;
- customers involved in long-term scenario planning.

At one level, it may be no more than learning to listen to the voice of the customer again, which has been lost – and the opportunity has merely re-presented itself through social networking, where customers have more opportunity to say what they think and have it recorded. S-CRM may just provide the tools to do the listening.[50] Is it just another way of communicating with the customer or something else? It has been described as "the new dynamic in building long-term, fruitful relationships for your company. It is a new way of approaching and cultivating customer relationships that's focused on people instead of tools, collaboration instead of control, and valuable experiences instead of transactions."[51] However, it is clear that organizations are slowly learning how to harness Web 2.0 technologies as a force for changing the relationship between the themselves and their customers – moving to more "customer-managed" services in which customers are engaged with the company in the development of propositions and provide real-time feedback on their experience to the business and to each other about their customer experience, modelled on the market leaders in "customer 2.0" such as eBay and Amazon.[52] If it has one major impact, it is that organizations have to be both clear about their true motives and authentic in the way they do this. Are they doing this because they want to understand their customers so that they can better serve them and benefit from what the customers want from them, or are they doing it so that they can sell more of their product or services to them? Customers are becoming increasingly sensitive to any lack of authenticity.

3.5.3 Structuring around the customer

The third building block is structuring around the customer and the product. Experts on Organization Design[53] have focused upon models and processes that support the development of customer-centric organization structures. Product-centric organizations are typically organized around product-focused profit center business units. These focus attention on product lines and information collected around those products. To reorient the organization's strategic plans, reviews and processes away from the product and towards the customer, organizations structure around customer segment profit centers. For Jay Galbraith,[54] culture plays a considerable role in underpinning a customer-centric organization. He identifies a key tension (or contrast) in the transaction with the customer. In the product-centric organization, the managers of the customer relationship are on the side of the seller, in that they are interested in pushing more features, better products or more products. In the customer-centric organization these people are more "on the side" of the customer, as their interest is in providing the best possible customized outcome for their particular customer. The contrasting strategies and "cultures" may of course exist in the same organization; banks, for example, may have a division dedicated to providing credit cards (a product-centered arm) and a division oriented towards providing financial and investment advice to high net worth customers (a customer-centered arm).

One initiative we have examined was a client first change process in a technology and professional service multinational.

SHIFTING TO A CLIENT FIRST CULTURE IN A TECHNOLOGY AND PROFESSIONAL SERVICES ORGANIZATION

The need to engender "client first" cultural behavior has been met by five strands of activity that have people management implications:

1. A co-ordinated realignment of resources across their clients structured around industry segments. This had three components: authority levels were balanced and pushed down to leaders; changes were made to control and business unit measurement systems; and issues of power and capability were addressed by making new appointments to affirm and formalize the new authorities needed.
2. Managing the role of leadership and developing the necessary leadership qualities. This had two components: new knowledge and skills were fed into the structure through a series of management development initiatives; and mobilizing their virtual networks and communities to pass on shared insights into the business model to ensure that leaders had the *same* level of complexity in and clarity of understanding of the business model being pursued, interpretation of mandates and levels of competence in pursuing a client first approach.
3. Providing the new cadre of leaders with the know-how to provide appropriate "air cover" to their teams to allow for local adaptation as circumstances see fit and make the most appropriate allocations of resources at the business unit level.
4. Providing formal communications in the change process and pursuing an employee engagement strategy at the corporate level.
5. Significant levels of work on process redesign in support of the client first model.

From such case studies it is clear that organizations have a hard-wired structural solution and set of connections that are intended to make them more customer-centric, but also a soft-wired requirement, which is a network, often a virtual network, of those who actually have the necessary resources to deal with the customer issues. What we often see in some of the initiatives we have examined is an exercise in having to equalize power and capability. Effectively what organizations have to say is now the people who are in charge of this (the customer-centric initiative) are on the same hierarchical level, so that all parties involved in the organization have the same complexity of understanding of the business model. The business model and the customer-centricity drivers generally tell you how the relationships must work in order that key roles are designed in such a way that they have equal power. A customer-centric approach therefore requires a deep understanding of the attitudes that drive customer buying behavior. However, achieving this "micro-segmentation" of the market often starts with changing the attitude of those members of your own organization who still think in classical terms either about the "product" or the "service" they offer.

3.5.4 Managing the empowerment of frontline staff

The fourth building block of customer centricity is the empowerment of frontline customer facing staff. This is likely to be nullified, or seriously undermined, if the rest of the organization is not brought into line to support them. Part of the problem is cultural, but the location of authority in the organization structure (as well as the structure itself) is also a critical factor in implementing a customer-centric strategy. Some have used the acronym of the "Highly Empowered and Resourced Operative"[55] to capture what frontline staff may need to look like. There are lots of symbolic stories used to provide examples: the Best Buy employee who replaced a customer's iPhone during the weekend after reading the customer's dissatisfaction with the product on a microblog by being engaged in monitoring the microblog in the first place, recognizing the potential damage to the organization's reputation (the customer had thousands of "followers" who were discovering his dissatisfaction) and having the authority to take a small but significant decision to solve the problem (and transform the negative publicity into positive). We have a picture of tech-savvy employees who may experiment with and use social network technology in close collaboration with managers and IT to provide instant decisions to customers. This of course may be light years away from the reality for the frontline employees of most organizations and even empowered employees must operate within defined and agreed boundaries and policies.

This has led to specifications of different levels of flexibility in frontline employees according to their customer strategy and characteristics of their client base in order to organize the degree of empowerment given to service employees[56] along the dimensions of complexity and variability of task and customer need, as outlined below. Generally, the longer, or more complex, the requirement is on each of these dimensions, the more empowerment is needed for frontline employees to deliver effective service.

FLEXIBLE LEVELS OF EMPOWERMENT FOR FRONTLINE STAFF

The major characteristics of *customer needs* complexity might be as follows:

- *Service product complexity*: the greater the product complexity (from the customer's perspective), the greater the need to empower employees.
- *Complexity/variability of the customer's needs*: the more complex or variable the needs of the customer, the greater need for empowerment.
- *Importance of speed of service*: the greater the importance of speed of service, the less appropriate the empowerment of contact employees as speed is often gained by standardizing service delivery routines.
- *Customization*: the greater the requirement for customization, the greater the need for empowerment.
- *The importance of service quality*: the higher the level of responsiveness, empathy and assurance (and hence the service quality) expected by the customer, the greater the need to empower contact employees.

The key dimensions of *task complexity* include:

- technology;
- creativity;
- product versus process focus;
- length of contact time; and
- the value added at the point of contact.

Organizations think along the lines of "scales of empowerment," drawing a distinction between an "empowered" frontline employee and an "enabled" one. What is the difference? It might be unrealistic to expect a relatively junior member of staff to make quite complex decisions, in real time and in contact with the customer, about what product and service offerings are best for that individual (and which also represent the best value for the organization) without clear guidance. The solution in such circumstance is to "enable" the employee by providing them with tools and scripts in order that they can see the relevance of offers to customer needs and can explain them to customers.

Another initiative we have examined was a "thinking like the customer" change process in a large financial services organization.

CUSTOMER CENTRICITY IN A FINANCIAL SERVICES ORGANIZATION

The organization ran a "thinking like the customer" change program. It looked at its customer relationship model in terms of attracting, engaging and deepening relationships, and specified its customer values as "first among equals." There was large-scale organizational redesign, moving to a matrix organization, structured around customers rather than products and services. The bank "replatformed" (a process of software migration, re-engineering, porting and technology upgrades) to provide the customer with a full choice and cross-product, cross-channel and cross-technology support. There was a culture change program aimed at encouraging employees to put the customer at the heart of things, rather than their manager. Large-scale process re-engineering work took place, using the customer as the starting point. To avoid being driven by "lean" only thinking (see the next chapter), it used a process called "Connect" to determine how decisions were made when changing processes. Each process change was viewed through the lens of four stakeholders: customers, colleagues, efficiency and effectiveness. The customer lens had priority, reprioritizing the criteria used to make the first decisions. The focus of corporate and business unit performance was changed through similar alterations to the balanced scorecard. Sales and profits went up in pilot branches. Efforts were also made to differentiate the frontline offering, which required: alterations to recruitment processes to understand the types of people it wanted to bring through the bank, rather than just recruiting for attitude; analysis of the skills needed for a customer-centric relationship; changes to the performance measurement system with the "how" being given equal weighting to the "what"; and changes in the reward processes. It believed the key was not just to change HR processes, but also to ensure they were embedded, a "People Journey" group was put in place, with representatives from every part of the organization. Individuals were also selected from what were called the "permafrost layer" – senior people managers who could stop things happening, but usually did so for very good reasons, because they could see the ramifications. Their insight was tapped in order to understand how to make the changes work.

3.5.5 Managing the democratization of customer relationships

The fifth building block is the democratization of customer relationships and knowledge. This has been characterized as the move from "information asymmetry" to "information democracy." S-CRM is often the means by which companies transform content into conversations and then into collaborative experiences.[57] Traditional customer relationships have been asymmetric. Information was scare and customers were relatively uninformed. Exchanges were scripted and one-directional, and marketing was, as noted earlier, driven by a command and control philosophy. Now the availability of information is leading to a much more democratic relationship. Information is ubiquitous, customers are more informed, exchanges become much more like conversations, and marketing is based on a "connect and collaborate" philosophy.

However, in order for customers to make intelligent decisions about how they are going to interact with an organization and to specify the value they want to receive from the service, there needs to be much more transparency, visibility and honesty. Yet, as noted at the beginning of this chapter, customers do not always know what is best for them. This is seen in the world of IT, where, for example, companies like Dell work on the model of "Customer is the King" and attempt to just do their bidding, whereas companies like Apple take it upon themselves to decide what is best for their customers and then develop a service model that they believe is able to deliver on this high promise, even though this might not go down well with a select community of high-end gadget users. But for a normal user who might not be very tech-savvy, the simplicity and user-friendliness of the devices (at the expense of controls that the company keeps) might not be such a bad thing. Organizations have choices as to how they will deal with the democratization of information and may find alternative ways of maintaining asymmetry. However, the choice has major implications for the type and quality of staff needed.

3.5.6 Building the capability to filter massive datasets

The sixth and final building block for customer centricity is the capability to filter massive data sets in order to add value to product and service offerings. In Chapter 1 we noted that investments in IT to enable the large-scale use of data are a major focus of CEO attention, and in Chapter 6 we shall discuss the topic of HR analytics in the context of the "Big Data" debate. At this point, however, we should note that the main factors holding back most organizations from taking up social customer relationship management are as follows:[58]

- The inability to link web activity to a specific individual customer.
- The lack of integration between different databases.
- Data limitations and lack of relevant information/actionable data from web analytics packages.
- Lack of time and resources to understand and analyze the data.
- Lack of skills and knowledge to understand the data.[59]

At the time, only a fifth of organizations surveyed were able to link the online channel to their internal back office systems; a further 28 percent had no capability for doing so. Many writers illustrate the technology-orientation of much of the work on S-CRM whilst also noting the structural and organizational challenges to the management of the massive amounts of data potentially created by the use of social networks: how do organizations ensure that people are both willing and able to assimilate, analyze and distribute information to the right places? This challenge triggers the need for five main capabilities:[60]

- Monitoring ("listening capabilities to filter out noise from the social sphere").
- Mapping ("linking social profiles to customer records to provide a holistic picture").
- Management ("tying data back to existing processes").
- Middleware ("tying the social world to the enterprise").
- Measurement ("benchmark on business objectives").

The Economist has laid out what such capabilities can enable. So, in the telecoms sector, software applications analyze a customer's social network rather than their own call records, allowing organizations to identify the really valuable customers in a much more sophisticated way (as well as those who simply spend more) and also to understand who to influence around them in order to, for example, encourage them to switch mobile phone operators. Bharti Airtel in India has achieved a substantial reduction in turnover by deploying such a system.[61]

3.6 Conclusions: implications for HR

In this book a central argument is that HR needs to understand the implications of important performance drivers if it is to make the wisest and most effective choices about the capabilities it needs and where it should invest its resources.

In distilling the rhetoric we have identified six building blocks, each of which has significant implications for the delivery of HR. The first four of these – mass customization, involvement of the consumer in the design process, structuring around the customer, and the enablement of frontline staff – do not really represent new territory. However, two of the building blocks – democratization of customer relationships and knowledge, and the capability to filter massive data sets to add value to product and service offers – represent quite novel challenges for organizations. Here HR will need to work with several other business functions to understand the people implications that are now faced.

Much of the HR support for customer centricity is to support cultural change, but interventions around the location of authority in the organization structure, as well as the structure itself, are also critical success factors in implementing a customer-centric strategy.

Which HR practices are either "mission critical" or otherwise support the different aspects of a customer-centric organization?

IMPLICATIONS FOR HR OF HELPING MAKE THE ORGANIZATION MORE CUSTOMER-CENTRIC

The following 29 activities become central to the successful pursuit of this performance driver:

1. A major communications program to put the organization's message over.
2. Culture change programs and exposure to alternative service models and mentalities.
3. Making the internal culture and organization design changes visible to the customer so that they see that changes are real.

4. Sourcing of senior talent capable of overview of industry dynamics – a "they (the customer) know best" versus "we know best" regulator.
5. Recruitment and resourcing of key data analytic skills and decisions on whether to develop new centers of expertise around this (see Chapter 6).
6. Transfer of knowledge and capability from these centers of expertise.
7. Resourcing/career progression and strategic planning activity focused on line management capabilities around creativity, innovation and consumer insight.
8. Technical and operational review of the implications of changes to systems and skills in key functions such as manufacturing, R&D, production and logistics, and delivery of major learning and development initiatives.
9. Organization development work with leadership teams to develop capabilities.
10. Alignment of the employer brand with the corporate brand to ensure fit and mutual insights between the organization and consumers involved in the design process.
11. Accommodation of broader stakeholder values around corporate social responsibility and ethics.
12. Ensuring two-way communication mechanisms to share knowledge and values between the organization and consumers involved in the design process.
13. Providing informal incentives to encourage customers to offer ideas.
14. Using informal mechanisms to ensure that there are shared values and task competence amongst the customer population, especially when they are communicating to others on the organization's behalf.
15. Providing contractual clarity over intellectual property rights and reputational issues between the organization and consumers involved in the design process.
16. Building employee "trust" in the judgments that their senior managers are going to make by ensuring task competence – that total understanding of how customer-centric solutions are actually all connected.

17. Ensuring internal information transparency and shared access rights to key databases.
18. Changes in the balance in corporate KPIs to the customer as stakeholder (from volume to customer value measurements) reflected down through business unit and individual performance management systems.
19. Organization design skills to identify the clusters of people whose interactions are driven by customer interfaces and the co-location of key decision-making authorities with these.
20. Changes to key control systems (financial, information system, etc.) and management processes designed to reinforce customer focus.
21. Analyzing whether the organization has got the appropriate authority and control levels established in its structures and job designs.
22. Being clear about the job design of frontline employees. Are they highly skilled and relatively independent and "empowered" or are they relatively junior and in need of "enablement" through scaffolding procedures and decision trees?
23. Ensuring that the appropriate skills are resourced and trained to fit this design at the frontline and team leader levels.
24. Contributing to the design of appropriate scaffolding and procedures to obtain the right balance of control and enablement for frontline staff.
25. Having an engagement strategy that builds employee identification with, internalization of and commitment to customer interests.
26. Capability building interventions that create the self-confidence, influencing and other self-efficacy skills in frontline staff.
27. Aligning any propositions offered by staff to customers (segmented staff profiles) with the level of customer sophistication, i.e., allowing the propositions to customers to have a different "touch and feel," or allowing the relationship to be more or less deep, thereby segmenting the service models. Of course, existing frontline staff might have been recruited to work in a different service model.
28. Making necessary job design changes and Organization Development (OD) interventions with frontline staff and

managers to ensure the appropriate balance of time and decision-making latitudes.

29. Ensuring sophisticated discussion and understanding of all these issues at each appropriate level of the organization – can they work this model?

Whoever said that linking HR to strategic performance would be easy? However, all of these people and organizational issues also need to be understood by any line manager wishing to deliver this performance driver successfully. They need HR as much as HR needs them.

Nevertheless, customer centricity has more strategic importance for HR, because, as with other performance drivers such as innovation and lean organization, it acts as a fundamental organizing and design principle that has implications for every HR process, be it recruitment, performance management or culture change. To the extent that customer centricity is a central part of the current or future business model, HR functions also need to look to their own structures to ask if their own expertise and business support activities can meet the challenge.

By equipping HR with the knowledge it needs to understand what customer centricity is, and is not, we hope that it can now enter into the debate with the business regarding the degree to which customer centricity should influence the company strategy, the business model and the consequent organization design. Therefore, HR leaders need to have a level of "mastery" of the concept in order that they can debate its relevance in relation to the particular business in which they are operating. A decision to move, in a substantial manner, towards customer centricity by a business will raise some fundamental questions for HR Directors in terms of the skills, capabilities and thinking required by members of the HR team to ensure that they add value to such a move.

THE HIGH-LEVEL IMPLICATIONS OF CUSTOMER CENTRICITY FOR HR

There are three high-level implications of our analysis of customer centricity for HR Directors:

1. Organizations that choose to adopt the strategic orientation of customer centricity are, by doing so, moving away from service-profit chain thinking which has been so predominant in driving HR strategy in many companies, but which is more appropriate for product-centric organizations.

2. HR departments in a customer-centric organization should not consider their own employees as their ultimate customers. Every department, including HR, needs to become customer-centric, having the end customer in mind.
3. In a shift towards customer centricity, certain HR practices become mission critical, and others supporting, in a way that might not be immediately obvious without a rigorous understanding of customer centricity as a strategic choice.

The shift towards being a more customer-centric organization generally involves all-encompassing changes in HR. This clearly presents a challenge to HR if it is acting merely as an internal service unit. We consider it valid to ask the following question: how do HR units incorporate these characteristics of customer centricity into their own strategy, structure, culture and processes?

chapter 4

Lean Management and Organizational Effectiveness

4.1 Introduction: lean and process improvement

In Chapter 1 we outlined the scale of the productivity challenge facing many countries. Productivity or efficiency can be thought about in different ways – how busy and utilized people and resources are – or, more constructively, how fast value can be delivered to customers. We have chosen lean management as the third of our strategic performance drivers because in a post-credit crunch world, it has gained renewed attention. The conditions that spawned the birth of lean management – a shortage in both capital and resources in Japan after the Second World War – have become features once more in the new context of an "age of austerity." Efficiency and effectiveness, coupled with attention to quality, are major drivers of change. Lean thinking has now been applied to a wide range of issues, spanning management, design and service delivery, and also business functions such as product development, logistics, service, sales, HR and production. Again, we need to look to expertise outside of HRM. Whilst the previous chapter took us into ideas and research from marketing and service management, this chapter takes us into work done mainly within operations management and management science.

Lean thinking addresses the productivity issue by focusing on value-adding work. Be it in engineering, designing a product, production or delivering customer service, value-adding work is defined as that that the customer cares about. This is why we address this performance driver having first dealt with customer centricity. Lean thinking argues that rather than simply locally optimizing and maximizing the utilization of employees or machines, a sustainable performance outcome requires competition based on the ability to adapt, avoiding inventory, working in very small units and removing bottlenecks to create faster throughput of value to customers. In lean thinking, sustainable performance is seen as the global system goal. This global goal concerns the flow of value to the customer without delay through the removal of non-value-adding activity (which is seen as a better definition than waste). This flow of value is in turn evaluated in terms of:

- the shortest lead time;
- best quality and value (to people and society);
- the most customer delight;
- at lowest cost;
- with high morale; and
- driven by safety.

Lean thinking was originally associated with product development and production systems at Toyota. The original name was the *Toyota Production System* (TPS), associated with its creator Taiichi Ohno, also known as *The Toyota Way*, or the less frequently used *Respect for Humanity System* or *The Thinking Way*. It emphasized a Toyota culture of mentoring people to think through and resolve root causes to problems, to help society and to humanize work.[1] Later, it was popularized by researchers at MIT who compared production at Toyota to mass production systems in their famous books *The Machine that Changed the World*[2] and *Lean Thinking*.[3]

Countless papers have tried to simplify and reduce the thinking down to easy-to-follow recipes. Countless experts have read and re-read original sources to argue what are the core principles and what are the secondary issues that might mislead or that if missed out might serve to later derail a lean initiative. Despite continued debate over the precise meaning and execution of lean management, it has:

> commonly been taken to involve techniques concerned with production, work organization, quality management, logistics, supply chain, customer satisfaction, efficient delivery and continuous improvement methods. In other words, the adoption of lean production implies integration in the use of operation (OM) and human resource management (HRM) practices.[4]

So what exactly is lean management and how does it sit alongside some other similar regimes? Attention to lean was triggered by the need for productivity. Between 1968 and 1978, US productivity increased by 23.6 percent, but Japan experienced a 89.1 percent increase.[5] To catch up, throughout the 1980s and 1990s, US and European companies began adapting the TPS in manufacturing under the title of just-in-time (JIT) to remain competitive with Japanese industry. They initiated the International Motor Vehicle Program (IMVP) benchmarking study.

Lean manufacturing extended the scope of the Toyota production philosophy by providing an enterprise-wide term that drew together the following key elements:[6]

- the product development process;
- the supplier management process;
- the customer management process; and
- the policy-focusing process for the whole enterprise.

Lean is therefore both a management philosophy and a practical operational perspective[7] that has come to be associated with sustainable and long-term performance. The work of Womack and colleagues[8] became influential in shaping ideas about lean management. For them, lean management thinking was based on a series of principles.

THE FIVE PRINCIPLES OF LEAN MANAGEMENT

- Specifying value through end customer needs.
- Identifying the value stream (the set of actions that transform a product or service) involved in bringing a product or service, from problem solving, information management through to physical transformation tasks.
- Ensuring this value flows by defining it, making it visible, reducing cycle times to a minimum, and standardizing around best practice in order to free up time for more creativity and innovation.
- Letting the customer pull processes, i.e., processes are produced on demand from customers.
- Pursuing perfection through developing a mindset across the enterprise so that the number of steps and the amount of time and information needed to serve the customer can fall continually.

To make its broad relevance clear, we need to outline how the thinking about lean management has developed and acknowledge some of its differences from other process improvement methodologies.

4.1.1 The range of process improvement approaches: Six Sigma versus lean

Although we shall use lean as the primary example throughout this chapter, arguably because it has become one of the most dominant[9] of the process

improvement methodologies, it is not the only system that has been popularized. There are also a number of competing or complementary systems that we need to briefly outline.

THE VARIETY OF METHODOLOGIES AVAILABLE FOR PROCESS IMPROVEMENT

There are a range of process improvement methodologies of which lean management is just one. These include:

- Six Sigma, Lean Management;
- Lean Six Sigma;
- Agile Management;
- Business Process Reengineering (BPR);
- Total Quality Management (TQM);
- JIT;
- Kaizen;
- Hoshin Planning;
- Poka-Yoka;
- Design of Experiments; and
- Process Excellence.

Closely related is the amalgam of tools under the Six Sigma movement. How are lean and Six Sigma different? In comparing the perspectives of leading academics and practitioners on Six Sigma and lean, the Centre for Research in Six Sigma and Process Excellence points out that both are quality/cost improvement approaches that focus on business processes and business needs as defined by the customer, use multi-disciplinary teams to address business problems, and use specified creative, technical and change management toolsets aimed at moving from operational chaos to operational excellence.[10]

SOME DIFFERENCES BETWEEN LEAN AND SIX SIGMA

Lean management is an inter-process improvement philosophy that:

- creates inter-process improvement, i.e. looks at links *between* one process and another;
- focuses on efficiency across sets of processes – minimal waste and elimination of non-value-added activities (called *muda*) – to improve speed and increase productivity;

- aims to produce products and services at the lowest cost and as fast as possible by promoting flow across processes;
- is based on qualitative models developed from years of experience, i.e., the formalization and codification of experience and judgment.
- generally requires the engagement of people at the grassroots level through creative and continuous improvement activities.

In contrast, Six Sigma is often seen as a system that creates intra-process improvement and:

- relies on advanced statistical insight *within* a particular process;
- focuses on the outputs from those processes that are seen as critical in the eyes of customers;
- is very reliant on a small number of analysts having advanced skills, but may not involve all people in improvement activities.

A former Toyota Plant and HR Manager differentiates the TPS from Six Sigma as follows:

> Lean six sigma is a compilation of tools and training focused on isolated projects to drive down unit cost ... The Toyota approach ... is far broader and far deeper. The starting point is the Toyota Way philosophy of respect for people and continuous improvement. The principle is developing quality people who continually improve processes ... The responsibility lies, not with black belt specialists, but with the leadership hierarchy that runs the operation and they are teachers and coaches.[11]

Six Sigma, originally championed by Motorola based on learning from one of its factories that was taken over by a Japanese firm, focuses on business improvement – minimal variation in the processes that might lead to poor quality. It was developed at Motorola through the efforts of Bill Smith, a reliability engineer, and was later championed through the work of Jack Welch, the then CEO of General Electric. It focuses on finding and eliminating causes of defects or mistakes in business processes through the use of statistical and non-statistical tools. Between 1992 and 2008, 417 referred journal articles, from various disciplines including business and management, operations management, information systems, technology, computer science, engineering, statistics and healthcare, referred to Six Sigma, growing from one per year in 1999 to around 80 per year from 2006 onwards.

The term "Six Sigma" refers to a statistical measure of defect rate within a system to a level of only 3.4 problems per million opportunities. This was made meaningful in the original work by Peter Pande at Motorola and GE through using two examples: if a post office was working at a 99 percent quality rating, for every 300,000 letters delivered, there would be 3,000 misdeliveries compared to only one misdelivery if it was operating at a Six Sigma level. If television stations operated at a 99 percent quality rating, there would be approximately 1.68 hours of dead airtime experienced per week in comparison to the 1.8 seconds experienced if it was working at Six Sigma levels.[12]

Organizations, which are rarely purists in terms of applying any philosophy, often find that in practice they end up:

> merging Lean and Six Sigma methods into a holistic systems approach to business process improvement with the methodologies blended using different levels of worker competence which are required to manage and improve work processes on a daily basis.[13]

When operations management experts analyze how organizations implement process improvement philosophies, they find that organizations have integrated lean principles with Six Sigma methodology.[14] Within a manufacturing environment, many organizations first adopt lean principles and then might attempt to use the more statistically complex Six Sigma.

In their attempts to provide empowerment, organizations often try to create a coherent approach to continuous improvement by integrating the two methodologies at the higher-level process analysis stages. They do this so that employees have true ownership of the process.

4.1.2 The export of lean thinking into other sectors

A number of organizations are well known for having implemented lean management. In addition to the likes of Toyota and General Motors, these include, for example, the new Jaguar S-Type production line, Unipart, Boeing, General Electric, 3M, Honeywell, Lockheed Martin, BAE Systems, the nuclear industry, Nestlé, Fujitsu, HM Revenue and Customs, Royal Mail, Shell, Legal and General, the Welsh Government and the National Health Service.

Early on in the movement, proponents argued that lean principles should be applied to the enterprise as a whole, under the "work smarter not harder" slogan.[15] Although it was originally applied to large manufacturing operations in high-volume, low-variety facilities, gaining early traction in automobiles and aerospace, by the 2000s, attention was being given to the viability of applying lean principles to "job-shop" companies, i.e., high-variety, low-volume work.[16] In recent years we have seen the application of lean principles beyond the traditional areas of manufacturing and engineering into other sectors and internal management functions. Its application into service industry settings has brought it more closely into the sphere of HRM.

Consultants argue that whilst most lean principles are very general and therefore exportable, such as a continuous improvement mindset or the use of manager-teachers who are work experts and act as mentors, other principles, such as long-term great engineers to long-term, great hands-on workers or new product development to new service, require minor translation.[17]

The application of lean management and related operational effectiveness methodologies such as Six Sigma has been reported in various other sectors – generally service and transactional industries – with increasing intensity in recent years.

We have looked at studies across a number of sectors. In each sector, case study research suggests that the pursuit of lean strategies is related to different drivers.

A BROADENED SET OF CONTEXTS FOR LEAN THINKING

- Call centers, where initiatives are driven by the need to streamline operations and reduce running costs of centers, avoid lost calls, allow customers to "pull" what they need from the call center, align resources to the more customer-centric aspects of operation, improve and diagnose the root causes of customer service support, and reduce employee stress.[18]
- The healthcare and health services sector, where initiatives are driven by drives for a reduction in processing or waiting time, an increase in quality through a reduction of errors, a reduction in costs or as part of generic culture change and improvement programs.[19]
- Software services, where initiatives are embedded in knowledge management.[20]
- National and local government, where initiatives are driven by government agendas, struggles with performance indicators, the introduction of new leadership or technology, threats of competition, demands for increased efficiency and the need for service expansion with limited resources.[21]
- Banks, insurance companies and related financial service providers, where initiatives are driven by pressures to reduce costs (operational inefficiencies are estimated to represent

approximately 20 percent or more of total banking industry costs), the desire to exploit market opportunities, and dissatisfied customers necessitating the design of new customer-orientated processes.[22]

- Human resource services, where initiatives are driven by the need to improve cycle times in key human resource processes such as recruitment and selection, to improve service quality, to deliver ongoing efficiencies and to strengthen internal and external customer orientation.[23]

The transfer of lean thinking to these other sectors began with the initial call for the industrialization of the service sector.[24] The generic challenges of transferring the learning about lean thinking from its previous application in manufacturing to the service industries have been examined by a number of writers.[25]

On the subject of the transfer from manufacturing to services, the following general observations have been made:[26]

- Manufacturers usually measure process performance and product quality, while this area is often overlooked in the service industry.
- The use of process models and flowcharts is quite common in manufacturing, but this tool is not used as much within service settings.
- A measurement system in terms of repeatability and reproducibility is explicitly defined in most manufacturing industries, whereas the lack of data quality and integrity is a problem in service industries.
- Uncontrollable factors such as human behavior (e.g., friendliness, eagerness to help) have a major influence on the quality of service processes and thus determine the quality of the service provided.

This shows:

> the importance of not only needing to include staff in the development of new ideas but also that maybe the concept of "standard work" does not "fit" in a public service, or even a service, environment where it may be important to respond to demand in a number of ways.[27]

On the translation of lean into customer service settings, we would note that lean management has much in common with the supplier value chain that was discussed in Chapter 3. Within the lean production literature, thinking has also begun to address the issue of lean consumption – what should happen at the customer end? This way of thinking about lean management recognizes that time is not free for customers. Waste can therefore be thought about by extending the thinking to notions of "customer respect." Waiting in line or being put on hold in a self-service telephone desk creates unnecessary waste and destroys value. In many offerings organizations and governments now pass requirements on to customers or citizens as if they were free labor.

What we see now is more organizations adding a customer value chain onto the end of their previous supplier-driven ways of thinking about lean management. Any organization that claimed that customer satisfaction was important would not be seen as authentic if it did not design its systems to do this. This requires that ideas about lean production be "translated" so that they can be applied to the customer consumption activities of the value chain.[28]

4.2 Why is lean management so people-centric?

4.2.1 People at the heart of the philosophy

The first way in which it becomes evident that lean management is closely intertwined with the management of people and organizational issues is by looking at the key principles on which the philosophy is based.

Lean involves several well-known but potentially mechanistic management tools, such as Kanban, root-cause analysis, removing waste or queue management. However, it is not the tools that are key – or some of the more ritualistic values and behaviors that are often prescribed – but rather the fundamental principles of "building people, then building products" by educating them to become skillful systems thinkers, harnessing their intellect and then building a culture of "challenge the status quo" or continuous improvement (called *Kaizen*):

> The essence of [the Toyota system] is that each individual employee is given the opportunity to find problems in his own way of working, to solve them and to make improvements.[29]

There are many different prescribed sets of "principles" or "pillars" as the thinking has been refined and exported across different organizational settings. However, at the highest level of abstraction, there are two pillars – respect for people and continuous improvement[30] – as is made clear in the following two quotes from Toyota senior managers:

> Respect is necessary to work with people. By "people" we mean employees, supply partners, and customers ... We don't mean just the end customer;

> on the assembly line the person at the next workstation is also your customer. That leads to teamwork. (Katsuaki Watanabe, Toyota CEO)[31]

> More important than the actual improvements that individuals contribute, the true value of continuous improvement is in creating an atmosphere of continuous learning and an environment that not only accepts, but actually embraces change. (Gary Convis, Toyota President)[32]

These two pillars are supported by a series of principles, many of which repeat the elements outlined above. We try to capture the essence of these below.

THE TWO PILLARS OF LEAN

1. **Respect for people:**
   - Do not create trouble for your customer (whoever consumes your work or decisions).
   - Develop people, then build products, making problems visible and then discovering how to improve them.
   - No wasteful work (no defects, wasted time, wishful thinking or overload).
   - Teams and individuals evolve their own practices and improvements.
   - Build partners with stable relationships – based on trust and responsibility for their activities.
2. **Kaizen or continuous improvement and challenging the status quo:**
   - Go See (called *genchi genbutsu*) by going to the place of real work – i.e., physical frontline place of value work where the hands-on value workers operate (called *gemba*) to find facts and build a consensus.
   - Out-learning the competition by generating more useful knowledge.
   - Using this knowledge, remembering it effectively and spreading it horizontally by letting knowledge unfold (called *yokoten*, similar to a community of practice).
   - Mastering standardized work to provide a baseline (set by the team itself and not a central benchmark) to improve against and to decide what is common-cause or special-cause variability.

- Stopping to find and fix the root causes of problems.
- Learning how to solve problems through hands-on experiments and then applying these experiments to new domains, making small step changes.
- Relentless efforts and small steps, incremental change (similar to the Plan-Do-Check-Act or Deming cycle).
- Retrospectives, frequent events to analyze and design activities.
- Decisions made slowly by consensus, thoroughly considering options, but implemented rapidly.
- 5 Whys analysis (asking why five times) to develop root cause analysis skills, using techniques such as fishbone (*Ishikawa*) diagrams.
- Value (activities the external customer would value paying for) and waste (all other activities which unnecessarily consume resources). The value ratio = total value time/total lead time and may be analyzed from concept to cash using value stream mapping (in development activities ratios may legitimately be as low as 5–7 percent).
- Eyes for waste, using taxonomies of non-value-adding activities (in production these might include the overproduction of solutions, waiting or delay, handoffs, extra processing of relearning or reinvention, partially completed work, task switching or motion between tasks, defects testing and correction, under-realizing potential, knowledge and information scatter and loss, and wishful thinking in plans, estimates and specifications.
- Improvement by removing waste activity, not adding new activities to heighten utilization, necessary temporary waste (given current capabilities and constraints) versus pure waste.
- Removing waste (investment without profit and hidden defects) by variability (called *mura*), e.g., varying cycle lengths, work packages, team sizes, delivery or request times, defects and overburden (called *muri*), e.g., arbitrary overtime, specialist bottlenecks).
- Work toward flow (lower batch sizes to lower the lake level and reveal the rocks, queue size, cycle time).

- Maximize pull systems (respond only to customer signals or downstream requests) and minimize push systems (inventory).
- Perfection challenge (to levels of skill, mastery, waste reduction and vision beyond the status quo).

It is clear from the factors involved in the pillars above that lean management is therefore an extremely people-centric strategy. At its heart, lean management revolves around the ability of managers to act as teachers, coaches and mentors of the thinking skills of the workforce. The practice of lean is rooted in the qualities or capabilities of the managers themselves and the philosophical integrity among senior management teams.

MANAGERS AS TEACHERS OF THINKING SKILLS OR COACHES AND MENTORS

- Managers have to be hands-on masters themselves of what they teach.
- "Walking the talk" – seen to mirror lean principles in their own actions and decisions.
- Teaching, not managing – training people to think for themselves (Toyota HR policies include analysis of how much time a manager spends teaching).
- However, not just letting people think for themselves, but directing the thinking through the use of structured reflection tools.

4.2.2 People issues at the heart of implementation failures

The second way in which it becomes evident that lean management is closely intertwined with the management of people and organizational issues is by looking at research on why initiatives fail. Lean management or Six Sigma programs may fail for slightly different reasons:

- Lean programs often fail to deliver bottom-line results because organizations start with the value stream-mapping initiatives, but lose energy and momentum before they progress to future stream maps or they fail to define value from the customer perspective.
- Six Sigma programs often suffer from attempts to develop highly analytical methodologies that require many years of statistical training and

development before they can be effectively applied. Whilst very reliant on advanced skills, they may not involve all people in improvement activities.

Research by operations management academics (not by potentially more self-interested HR academics, it should be noted) reveals the following key success factors for Six Sigma or for lean. It is surprising how people-centric the success factors revealed by these analyses are. In both systems, the two critical components for success are top leadership support and staff engagement. The pre-requisites for effective implementation are:

> top management commitment, cultural change in organizations, good communication down the hierarchy, new approaches to production and to servicing customers and a higher degree of training and education of employees.[33]

For lean, key factors, which are often observed in the breach rather than the observance, are:

- strong top management involvement and commitment;
- changing organizational culture;
- cross-functional teamworking;
- effective communication;
- organizational and IT infrastructure;
- training;
- project management skills; and
- linking and aligning Six Sigma to business strategy, corporate business objectives, customers, HRM, and suppliers.[34]

4.2.3 People issues at the heart of actual implementation

The third way in which it becomes evident that lean management is closely intertwined with the management of people and organizational issues is by looking at the existing research on the pursuit of lean management. There is evidence that – putting to one side for a moment the risks of poor implementation noted above – lean management can produce financial and non-financial benefits.[35] The landmark manufacturing case studies – a selective sample of the better rather than poorer implementations of lean of course – suggested that short-term gains in employee engagement can be dramatic, although they may not always be sustained. In one of the best-known case studies, reflecting back on the Toyota/General Motors (GM) experience at their New United Motor Manufacturing Inc. (NUMMI) plants:

> The union and workers didn't just accept Toyota's system, they embraced it with passion. The absenteeism that had regularly reached 20% or more? It

> immediately fell to a steady 2%. The quality that had been GM's worst? In just one year, it became GM's best ... what changed the culture at NUMMI wasn't an abstract notion of "employee involvement" or "a learning organization" or even "culture" at all. What changed the culture was giving employees the means by which they could successfully do their jobs ... In turn, this was based on an attitude to problems based on "the ability to focus on solving problems without pointing fingers and looking to place the blame on someone."[36]

Of course, the nature of such benefits has long been contested. Evidence on the impact of lean management can be difficult to assess given the often adversarial or ideological research designs that may be used – be this advocacy of particular positions held about employment relations and work organization or advocacy of preferred business process improvement methods.

Early research examining lean manufacturing argued that it leads to work intensification and represents "management by stress."[37] Reflecting on the "lean is mean" debate, it has been observed that:

> The view that lean is pro-company, not pro-employee, has some validity, and cannot be dismissed. For example, it is said that employees feel a sense of insecurity, perceiving lean as a redundancy threat ... that management avoid accountability when problems arise, letting it filter downwards onto the lower levels of hierarchy ... [but this] is to miss the fundamental underpinning of empowerment and cultural change, resulting from a failure by management to approach lean with the correct goals. Lean requires and relies on a review of organizational values, which in itself is key to sustainability of lean. Without this we see an adverse affect on morale, increasing levels of worker unhappiness and withdrawal, ultimately leading to operational failures.[38]

More recently, the "lean is mean" debate has begun to take a more circumspect position. It has picked up on three issues:

- the opportunities and threats encountered given the pursuit of lean principles in sectors beyond manufacturing;
- the role of line managers and the quality of implementation in determining the nature and direction (positive or negative) of employee outcomes;
- the mediating role of choices made about job design.

The outcomes do indeed depend on the quality and integrity of implementation by managers. A study of 1,391 worker responses at 21 sites in four UK industry sectors measured whether the implementation of ten key lean practices was successful or not and the impact on employee stress. The findings were as follows:[39]

- There was a non-linear relationship between implementation and stress involving three stages – an initial zone of low but increasing stress as implementation proceeded at low levels – then a leveling off of stress in a middle stage until it reached an inflection point – and finally decreasing stress as there was further advanced implementation.
- Commitment and dissatisfaction reflected a mirror image of this curvilinear relationship – it starts high, falls to low and then recovers.
- Lean production is not inherently stressful and worker well-being is not deterministic; it depends heavily on management choices in designing and operating lean systems.
- At a high level of implementation, positive outcomes achieved by continuous improvement projects, improved quality, more orderly workplaces and more predictable workflows compensated for the stress and high intensity of the initial work and potential repetitiveness.

From an employee relations perspective, work organization is often stylized as conforming either to a high-performance (commitment) model or to Taylorism and lean production. Both models represent a "regime," i.e., the pursuit of a range of managerial techniques and practices. High-performance management, when set against lean management, is stylized as being based on:

> methods designed to engage employees and mobilize greater discretionary effort, [which] will lead to advances in organizational performance. The assumption is that extensive employee participation in decisions governing work and organization may engender greater trust in management, greater commitment to organizational objectives and thus provide the foundation for improved performance.[40]

More pragmatic or skeptical employee relations researchers see imperfections in the claims made and the assumptions of each regime. However, based on the observed evidence that in the UK, while job complexity has risen, task discretion has declined for all occupational groups, and especially for professional workers, lean management – which is seen as indistinguishable from Taylorism – is often presented as being based on a loss of control over the work process, whether this results in either work intensification or task enlargement.

A study of UK and Italian sites in the aerospace and automotive final assembly sectors concluded that common to both high-performance or lean management approaches (and different employee segments or occupations might be subject to one or other of the approaches in the same organization):

> the experience of increased effort was not an inevitable outcome of the shifts in the composition of skills and tasks, but rather, a function of the workers' loss of any semblance of control over their work routines and range of responsibilities.[41]

Within the UK, two performance studies[42] using data from the Modern Management Practices Survey Series found that the Operations Management practices on their own were not sufficient to improve performance. These studies included four operations management practices:

- total quality management;
- JIT procedures;
- integrated computer-based technology; and
- supply-chain partnering.

They looked at the combined effect with three associated HRM practices:

- a learning culture through extensive training;
- empowerment; and
- teamwork.

None of the single Operations Management practices or the combination of all four was linked to performance. However, when seen *in combination with* the HRM practices, various links did become important:

- Teamwork interacted with most practices.
- These combined effects were positively linked to productivity.
- Supply-chain partnering enhanced the effect of all the other Operations Management practices.
- Adopting empowerment and extensive training was the key to productivity.

Another study in a sample of 448 UK firms subsequently examined the relationship between seven management practices associated with lean. It found significant relationships to productivity when executed as a total philosophy and concluded that:

> The implication for the practitioner is that there are no magical solutions or quick-fixes; the philosophy needs to be in place ... The challenge remains to fully embrace the philosophy, be it quality management, integrated manufacturing, just-in-time manufacturing or lean production.[43]

Employee engagement is of course a potential outcome from the pursuit of lean management flowing from appropriate and effective implementation. However, from a business and strategic perspective, there are still some important but little-understood questions that need to be answered:

- Is engagement a necessary *input* to the successful pursuit of a lean management strategy or just a product of it?
- Are there specific practices and values that employees must engage *with*?
- Is there is a need for employees to identify with both the end customer and the nature of the work process?
- Does a generic positive sense of engagement sustain and generalize – or not – into engagement with the broader strategic pursuits of lean management?

A study of practice in the UK aerospace sector found that employee engagement is created primarily through:[44]

- the information that employees can glean on the importance of workforce skills;
- judgments about the quality (or not) of knowledge held by managers, operators and technicians in enabling the work process to flow effectively;
- identification (or not) with end-customer value; and
  the general level of attention to and development of a lean mindset.

To summarize, the delivery of potential benefits from lean management is then only possible when the following lessons drawn from research are heeded.

THE DEPENDENCE OF LEAN MANAGEMENT ON PEOPLE AND ORGANIZATIONAL ISSUES

- The operations management and the HRM practices that together represent a lean philosophy have a synergistic effect on performance – i.e., both are needed before performance benefits may be sustained.[45]
- Successful implementation of lean management, even within the traditional areas of manufacturing and engineering, requires the creation of change in both technical and cultural aspects of the organization.[46]
- A series of conditions are crucial for the subsequent success of initiatives – they are enabling conditions. These include: clarity of strategy and alignment, leadership behavior, employee

engagement, the level of teamworking, levels of skill utilization, autonomy, the social climate and the participation climate.[47]

- The pursuit of lean management can on the one hand reduce or offset stress on employees through the elimination of rework and improved quality of processes, but on the other hand might increase stress through the intensification of the work process or the perceived loss of control that often results.[48]
- Parallel changes to job design are therefore essential for successful implementation.[49]
- The enhancement of the general employee problem-solving capability makes employees more valuable to themselves and to the organization to which they belong (both current and future).[50]

4.3 The implications of the pursuit of lean for HR functions

To summarize, by the 1990s, research was showing that lean systems cannot simply be placed into an organization without carefully attending to a number of HR issues.[51] Attention then shifted to "why" lean works (or does not work).[52] Most of this research still concentrated on the HRM practices that were needed to maintain lean practices over time.

Whilst people issues lie at the heart of lean strategy execution problems, and as strategies become stickier, complex and people-centric, an important issue is to think about the skills and roles that the HR function needs in order to have a more strategic impact on lean implementation. What is the interplay between lean management initiatives and the HR strategies and structures used to support them? We need to understand this in order to consider the potential role that HR functions might play in helping to ensure that lean initiatives are successful.

It is evident from practice that HR is not always involved, despite some of the connections we have made in the previous section. In this section we draw upon our own research across 13 organizations. Five of the case studies we have examined are firms that have traditionally done a lot of work on lean thinking in the manufacturing and engineering contexts (in automobile manufacturing, a service logistics company, a defence manufacturing and engineering organization, an aerospace, automation and control solutions company, and a nuclear decommissioning, reprocessing and waste management site).

Eight of the case studies are in firms that are now applying lean thinking in white-collar contexts (in the financial services, energy and petrochemicals, civil service directorate, national government, IT systems, services and products; postal services, and nutrition, health and wellness sectors).

In our previous book,[53] we found that many a Manufacturing Director in fact saw lean management as an employee engagement strategy. They argue that the reason why the oversight of lean implementation should be given to HR rather than any other function is that HR is the architect of organizational effectiveness:

> the power of the [lean management] tool is [that] it forces the line leader and the organization to engage with the employee and … forces the employee to become engaged in what the organization is trying to achieve … the Lean tool set is an employee engagement model first and a productivity model second.

The position held by senior line managers on the involvement of HR in lean management from our own research can be summarized by the following quote from one of them:

> HR needs to be an equal architect at the beginning … The reason I say an equal architect rather than one of the leaders is going back to my … model of people standing in front of a team board … if you want to improve safety, quality, cost, delivery and your organizational effectiveness you need all the constituent parts to be equally designing the jigsaw … And I think HR at the very least … needs to understand the principle so that they can support that, but [also] … actively championing it as well.

However, if HR is to respond to the above calls, there are a number of capabilities that an HR Director and their HR function need to have mastered. If they are to engage effectively with the line in order to add value during periods of business model change or contribute to the successful pursuit of lean as a strategic performance driver, they need to change what academics call the "HR architecture." This is the unique combination of the HR function's structure and delivery model, practices and system to create strategic employee behaviors and human capital[54] – to describe what becomes important.

BUILDING AN HR ARCHITECTURE FOR LEAN AROUND FOUR ELEMENTS

1. Employee role behaviors – role behaviors describe what is needed from employees who work with others in a social

environment given the specific strategy being pursued (in this case lean). Such behaviors might include: degree of repetition, degree of cooperation, concern for quality, quantity and process, leadership style, acceptance of responsibility, willingness to change, comfort with stability and breadth of skills used.

2. HR competencies – these include specific skills that HR is seen as needing, its fields of knowledge and the roles that must be undertaken to help sustain lean interventions.
3. Adjustments to HR practices – these include changes to or the importance of core HR functions and processes, such as recruitment, selection, training, development, coaching, leadership models, performance management, employee involvement and voice and so forth.
4. The intellectual capabilities needed by HR in terms of the structures and systems used to deliver HR support to lean initiatives and the location of this expertise within the structure.

From the chapter so far it is clear that there is an important role for HR to play in helping sustain lean management initiatives. However, this role also seems to have to have implications for all aspects of this HR architecture.

The HR delivery model within this architecture, at its heart, involves a set of HR professionals embedded within line businesses and working on processes and outcomes that are central to competitive success, supported by both efficient processes to handle the more transactional aspects of HR work and more strategically orientated expert HR knowledge handled by functional expertise or Center of Excellence structures.[55] If HR is to play a more pivotal role in creating the qualities for sustainable lean management, it needs to be seen to be working proactively with top management and earn their respect as a trusted business advisor. It has to play a role in developing, influencing and helping business leaders to build the foundations needed for sustainable business strategies, and it has to help manage the associated organizational changes that are needed to inculcate the values associated with lean.

If there is a role for HR in helping sustain lean management initiatives, can we establish what knowledge and skills are needed for HR to work with lean principles? A number of important questions need to be answered:

- If sustainability of performance gains is a business issue and a problem whose solution is highly dependent on people management issues, is HR responding to this opportunity in a tactical way or in a more strategic fashion?

- What specific skills and knowledge (i.e., HR capability) do HR Directors and their HR functions need to possess in terms of helping effective lean management?
- Are adjustments being made in the structure, role and skills of the function in the HR architecture?
- Who should own the "intellectual capital" surrounding lean thinking? Where are organizations locating such skills and strategic roles – i.e., within general line management directorates, within internal HR Centers of Expertise or within individuals placed in key line-to-HR interface roles, such as HR Business Partners?
- What does this mean for HR capability?

4.4 Conclusions

We have seen that the factors that aid the sustainability of lean are mainly *people-centric*. Regardless of whether the HR function is transactional or strategic in its relationship with the line, there is a need for a lead to be taken around a broad spectrum of people-related issues that have to be resolved in order to ensure the success of lean; these first became evident in the more traditional settings such as manufacturing and engineering:

- culture change;
- alterations in leadership and coaching behavior;
- changes in the underlying leadership model;
- technical performance improvement;
- teamworking;
- employee engagement; and
- communication.

Sadly, the role of HR in traditional lean settings seems to remain mainly transactional, even in "household" name organizations, with only three fundamental changes to underlying HR processes being made, and even these only being implemented sporadically:

- a shift in the selection and promotion criteria to only recruit people capable of working in the engaging lean environment;
- the need to link development to the performance management processes; and

- the provision of training on topics such as process design, change management, problem solving, coaching and leadership skills.

But in general terms there seems to be a "broad spectrum" of under-managed HR issues, with a realization that much more attention should be given to the following: visioning and policy deployment, facilitation, cultural change, leadership development, coaching and personal engagement, coaching conversations, listening, discipline, team building, conflict management and time management.

In short, HR is generally involved only reactively. However, the potential role of HR differs across the type of lean application and setting.

As lean is applied beyond its traditional areas into white-collar and knowledge work, adjustments need to be made to the way that lean is executed and as a result programs become more complex. There is a need to "translate" the learning and knowledge gleaned from previous manufacturing and production applications to deal with an additional set of issues that are now being raised.

This difference in the potential HR role between traditional lean organizations and white-collar organizations seems to be coming about for two reasons:

1. There is a need for "translation knowledge" when extending lean to service applications. A number of adaptations and translations have to be made in the execution process because the application of lean is more complex.
2. There is a temporal and institutional effect. As traditional applications of lean are now long-standing, more recent applications (which happen to be in white-collar settings) have benefited from the opportunity to learn from the difficulties experienced in early adoptions and hence have a different starting point.

All of the people issues triggered in traditional lean applications remain important, but a number of additional needs are triggered:

- insights into capability building and business acumen;
- the need for motivational and organizational skills, i.e., not just building generic employee engagement, but also creating a sense of engagement with the strategy;
- a strong human resource development focus;
- an HR-line relationship delivered through a consulting role;
- backed up by more centralized expert knowledge about lean implementation.

Given the complex nature of lean implementation, if HR is to add value and become more strategic, adjustments have to be made in the HR architecture, the portfolios of knowledge that HR needs and their location. Whether HR functions are able to deliver on such changes in their relationship with the line invokes questions about who needs to own the "intellectual capital" around lean management. There is a competition around who should own the most valuable and strategic knowledge about the performance driver of lean management once it is seen in its broader context as a tool for organizational effectiveness.

One way to think about this is to co-opt ideas about knowledge-based competition from the organizational learning literature. HR academics have used two dichotomies to help identify the sorts of expertise that are needed within HR:[56]

1. Knowledge about exploration (pursuit of knowledge that does not exist inside the organization to create value) and exploitation (refining and deepening existing knowledge).
2. Two different types of knowledge that have to be combined: component knowledge (knowledge of the parts rather than the whole, so deep enough operational knowledge of the line's lean management expertise to be able to assimilate, interpret, apply and recognize the value in it, but also to explore new possibilities); and architectural knowledge (the shared understanding of the interconnection of all components, or how things fit together, knowledge of the bigger strategic picture and the conflicts contained within any one strategy, and hence a greater ability to tweak and exploit the strategy being pursued).[57]

For HR to have component knowledge, it must have expertise around the specifics and mechanics of lean methodologies and the business problems to which such methodologies are being applied. For it to have architectural knowledge, it needs to have insight, expertise and learning that helps connect and apply the specifics of lean management into broader and over-arching HR issues, and the strategies to match.

In the majority of organizations at the moment, the HR function still lacks the component knowledge needed about lean management. They have some understanding of architectural knowledge, in that they generally understand the business strategy, but they have difficulty in understanding how the components can all work together.

We would argue that for HR to be more effective, it now needs what are called "knowledge integration and translation mechanisms" to support the effectiveness of the interventions that it is being called upon to make.

We will return to this issue in Chapter 8, where we lay out our model for HR in the future, the sorts of expertise that it needs and the implications for the broader HR architecture. But for now, using the case of insight into lean as one example, it should be clear that these integration mechanisms can include:

- the creation of Centers of Expertise and structural changes to the location of the intellectual capital associated with learning about the implementation of lean;
- the appointment of key boundary spanning individuals connected to important internal and external networks previously embedded in operations.

Where this knowledge is located is important. If HR is to add value and provide more strategic support, adjustments will have to be made to the HR architecture, the portfolios of knowledge that HR needs and the ownership of the "intellectual capital" surrounding lean thinking.

HR has to establish specific portfolios of knowledge about lean management that it then has to manage. There also needs to be a significant change to the HR architecture in order to assist the organization in the pursuit of lean. HR needs dedicated and specialized knowledge about the people management challenges that have to be addressed when implementing lean management.

THREE ADAPTATIONS BEING MADE TO HR EXPERTISE AROUND LEAN MANAGEMENT

- The development of a set of HR professionals, embedded within line businesses and working on processes and outcomes (with responsibilities for the relationship with line managers being picked up by those in HR business partner roles).
- More strategically orientated expert area of functional expertise acting as a Center of Excellence within the HR structure.
- Dedicated Centers of Expertise to provide HR insight sitting outside the HR function in a central change or transformation directorate.

The pursuit of each solution seems to be a product of the career positioning of the key individuals given responsibility for lean management and is based on the personal power and strategic relationships of these key actors. In some organizations, a positive decision has been made to locate all expertise (of which HR insight forms one part) within a central, but non-HR directorate. In other organizations, efforts are underway to incorporate expertise about lean management into HR Centers of Expertise or Academies.

It is currently an open question as to whether such specialized insight needs must lie within an HR function or within a broader structural grouping, and whether such specialization will in practice improve the effectiveness of interventions. We have seen a small (but growing) subset of organizations that have in one way or another been providing specialist HR support to the organization to help it execute lean management effectively. These have made changes to the internal HR architecture in response to lean activity. This is clearly an opportunity open to HR within non-traditional settings, but this opportunity is still largely being missed by HR functions.

chapter 5

Managing Beyond the Organization

5.1 Introduction

In our previous book *Leading HR*, we argued that HR is being repositioned as a function in part because of internal organization design pressures resulting from complex business models, but also:

> as a consequence of changes in the importance of external inter-dependence and partnership. The organizational "value web" is, in almost every case, extended across traditional organizational boundaries. This interdependence is a defining characteristic of business model change. Relationships with external bodies which were previously characterised as adversarial at best are suddenly having to be redesigned under a partnership model, as long term contracts are developed with other organizations in the same value web.

When HR functions find themselves operating in these more collaborative business contexts, they need what we termed "architectural design skills." Moreover, these skills have to be applied beyond the host organization. We concluded that this development is creating a new onus for HR functions:

> Rather like the new breed of industry regulators, they will find themselves overseeing all those parties and partners involved in people-related aspects of their own business model, regulating both internal and external HR systems, ensuring they perform in line with the overall goals of the organization. They will not just equate internal centres of expertise to existing HR processes, but will need to initiate external centres of excellence, think tanks and networks that can manage the proprietary HR expertise necessary for

long-term performance-driving processes – such as strategic competence, innovation, consumer insight, productivity, and partnership learning.[1]

In this chapter we build on more recent developments to argue that a fundamental shift in HR will be needed as a consequence of this. HR functions need to move from managing the employment relationship in the owned entities to which they belong, to managing the quality of people and organizational management across the whole network of parties being brought together.

It is important to remember, as we noted in Chapter 1, that the need for this more broadly defined role for HR is not new – it was first mooted in early work on strategic change and HRM under the original label of "network HRM" in the late 1990s.[2] It seems, however, that the world of work has finally changed to such an extent that the time for such a change in the design of HR functions is now inescapable. Organizations are becoming more specialized, decentralized and networked in their operations. Their structures are becoming more flexible and organic and we are seeing more organizations entering into strategic partnering arrangements.

We draw upon multi-disciplinary research mainly from the fields of operations management, strategic management, marketing and organizational behavior to demonstrate the growth of what are called "inter-organizational relationships."[3] Generally unbeknown to HR practitioners, there is a whole field of general management research, called *inter-organizational studies*, that has developed in order to understand the challenges involved in a series of business relationships and a variety of collaborative "organizational forms." What do these developments have in common?

CHARACTERISTICS OF INTER-ORGANIZATIONAL RELATIONSHIPS

Inter-organizational relationships exist when there are transactions between organizations that involve the flow of products, services, money, information or communications from one to another. They become important when there are:

- multiple stakeholders brought together by a mandate from funders;
- the parties have to engage in mutual problem solving;
- this in turn requires collaborative information sharing; and
- decisions over resource allocation.

The relationships may be formalized, based on written contracts or semi-formal, but require important choices and decisions about structure, process and governance, which in turn needs an understanding of:

- the best organizational form to adopt, dependent on the strategic behaviors and performance that are required;
- the structure and processes through which the business will be delivered;
- how best to identify and then disseminate the collective aims of the collaboration;
- how important intangible resources (such as people, skills and knowledge) will flow into and out of the collaborative venture, and how these flows will be regulated;
- how important duties, rights, functions and roles of the members of the collaboration will be identified and governed.

We shall provide insight into of the sorts of organizational behaviors and people management issues involved in the strategic management of these inter-organizational business relationships. Senior leaders, line managers and HR functions need to understand this work. We shall also draw upon emerging findings from a joint research project we are conducting with the UK's Chartered Institute of Personnel and Development.[4] This project has involved reviews of the business literature, and interviews with over 50 senior managers from six case study organizations in the private sector (Rolls-Royce, Shell and the Nuclear Decommissioning Authority) and in the public sector (East Cheshire NHS Trust, West Sussex County Council and Dorset Police).

With multiple stakeholders being brought together by a single mandate, key choices and decisions will have to be made about the desired organizational behaviors. Someone – and we argue this should include HR – needs to think about:

- the required level of integration between the partners;
- how best to support mutual problem solving between them;
- how to best educate and coach managers to promote the requisite and desirable management behaviors;
- promoting collaborative learning and knowledge sharing.

In this chapter we begin by explaining the nature of these more collaborative business relationships. We shall then look at three fundamental questions:

- How do we ensure governance of HRM in these important relationships that extend beyond the organization?
- How do we ensure appropriate risk management?
- How do we ensure the necessary mutual capability development across partnered business arrangements?

Throughout, we signal the implications of this for HR functions.

5.2 The situations in which HR needs to be delivered beyond the organization

Think about the range of situations in which senior business leaders now have to think about the organizational and people management challenges not just for their own organization, but across their partners as well.

5.2.1 Collaborative business models

We begin with collaborative business models. Initially under the drive of competitive pressure and need to differentiate services, then through the development of more complex financial offerings, organizations have begun to understand that they now operate increasingly as part of a highly integrated network economy:

> [As] we merge relationship thinking, service-dominant logic, and lean consumption with many-to-many, and thereby widen the circle to more stakeholders than suppliers and customers, [business] becomes co-creation of value [and we can] characterize our economy as a value creating network economy.[5]

In Chapter 4 we discussed some of the thinking on lean management and the idea of lean consumption. These ideas now play into another set of developments. For many years now, there has been a shift towards the innovation of more efficient service systems, and this often brings with it the need to develop business models that operate across, and much more closely integrate, separate organizations. Increasingly organizations see themselves, their products and services as part of a many-to-many set of relationships – a network not just of customers and suppliers, but also of competitors, intermediaries, governments and customer-to-customer networks.[6]

We witness the development of far more collaborative business models in which the rationale, or performance or design logic, requires a group of collaborating organizations to pursue a business opportunity. Business models are used to explain how an organization creates, delivers and captures economic, social or cultural value. In articulating how the performance logic works, managers have to explain the range of activities their own organization or business unit has to perform and how this contributes and adds value to the broader a product or service. They need to lay out how different components of the organization have to be structured and aligned, including their purpose, offerings, strategies, infrastructure, formal structure, management practices, and operational processes and policies. Finally, they also have to explain how financial and non-financial resources have to flow through different parts of the organization and how the value of these resources must be interpreted and acted upon at each stage.

This sounds complicated enough, but in many cases now this value chain – the chain of activities that exists in a specific industry through which products or services have to pass in order to gain in value – is becoming even more complex. A value chain may extend beyond a firm and be thought about across whole supply chains, distribution networks and even previously distinct industrial sectors. This broader context is called a *value system*. Strategists try to explore:

- how an organization can capture the value that is generated along the value chain by exploiting the upstream or downstream resources or information that flow along the chain, bypassing intermediaries; and
- creating new business models or ways of improving the value system.

In Chapters 2 and 3 we discussed the importance of innovation and customer centricity. We noted that in a service-dominant logic, a value proposition can broaden the view from thinking about the addition of services to manufactured products. This is the phenomenon of what is called "servitization" – whereby manufacturers start to add services to their offerings in order to develop more integrated solutions. This is also called service infusion, service differentiation or service business development.[7] An example is Volvo trucks, which in selling buses to India was known to have based its value proposition on a broader and more complete understanding of transportation needs, bus routes and timetables, consideration of the service level for passengers, environmental consequences, maintenance and replacement of bus types. The pricing of the buses and financial solutions offered was based around many component parts.[8]

Manufacturing companies such as Xerox, General Motors, Apple, Volkswagen, IBM, General Electric, Caterpillar, Johnson & Johnson and Rolls-Royce have all incorporated service strategies into their business model.[9] This move first into servitization and then into more collaborative manufacturing offerings is often highly dependent on the traits of the organizations and customers involved, and the development of a customer-focused culture and a more customer-centric organization design. These issues of implementation are considerable, complex and very people- and organization-centric.

We use the example of Rolls-Royce to illustrate this. The advent of more customer-centric through-life cost business models in the aerospace sector, as well as the growing importance of network resource management, now shapes and conditions the way in which all the functions within the organization need to serve each other and help enable the organization to perform. Similar developments now exist in the wider aviation industry, with Airbus' Total Support Package and Boeing's Goldcare offering to integrate airframe materials management. All these models illustrate the growing inter-dependency of HR across many organizations and sectors. HR increasingly now has to be designed to offer strategic support beyond the organization.

THE ROLLS-ROYCE COLLABORATIVE BUSINESS MODEL

Rolls-Royce Group plc is one of the UK's most successful manufacturers. In 2008, it produced revenues of £9.1 billion from its five divisions: Civil Aerospace, Defence Aerospace, Marine, Power Systems and Energy. Revenues are expected to double in the new few years, and by 2013 had reached $15.5 billion, with a £72 billion order book. In part, this is because of its revolutionary TotalCare® offering.[10] It developed an offering to combine its data, world-class technology and engineering know-how with a set of supply chain and cost management skills in such a way as to enable customers to be offered high engine availability and utilization, with minimal disruption costs. The TotalCare® lifetime care project involves a network of 70 international joint ventures. Rolls-Royce has 55,000 employees worldwide, with 45 percent of the workforce in the UK. Operations cover 85 facilities in 17 countries. A total of 33 joint venture facilities involve 25,000–30,000 employees and there are seven manufacturing technology partnerships and over 70 significant suppliers. The model is also being deployed into marine and nuclear businesses.

Why did this strategy, based on value co-creation, become important? A typical commercial jet engine contains 10,000 parts and has a life of around 20–25 years (some product and service life cycles can span 40–50 years). It has to be taken out of service approximately every five years for a full overhaul, costing several million dollars, often as high as the original purchase price. Before the advent of a through-life cost model, large airline operators had to develop huge support infrastructure, which created multiple duplications across the supply chain. As market pressures forced them to cut costs and focus on core business, this was not sustainable. Meanwhile, Rolls-Royce used to sell engines to customers at competitive prices, but only made margins 10 years later through sales in the spare parts business division. It also had to invest in technology programs that spanned more than 20 years into the future. This business model did not generate sufficient cashflows to justify the massive R&D investments and the industry needed a different concept to transform the risk structure of the business.

In the mid-1990s Rolls-Royce developed its business and service strategy and changed its business model. The model, in which Rolls-Royce gets paid by the hour that an aircraft engine operates, shifted its relationship with customers away from selling product and spare parts towards servicing long-term, multi-decade contracts to keep their planes flying. The majority of airlines now buy thrust through models where a flat cost per hour gives them the engine, all servicing, monitoring and spare parts with a guarantee for on-time performance. Around half of Rolls-Royce's revenues come from services today compared to 40 percent a decade ago – an annual compound growth in services of 10 percent – and more than 65 percent of its large in-service engines are covered by the business model. In civil aerospace it powers more than 30 types of commercial aircraft and over 12,500 engines in service with customers around the world. It is also the second largest provider of defence aero-engine products and services globally, with 18,000 engines in service and 160 customers in 103 countries.

For the model to work, however, there must be very close alignment across the support network, and data must be captured and used across this network in order to make support activity more intelligent and efficient. An aircraft engine contains a large number of essential components (pumps, probes, nozzles and cowling parts) provided by other manufacturers. Rolls-Royce manufactures approximately 30 percent of its gas turbine products by value, with the remainder of production provided by an external network of partners and suppliers. Extremely long lead-time products and high variability of demand raise the strategic importance of extending influence and control throughout an extended value chain that involves a highly complex and distributed global network of partners and suppliers. It therefore had to make a commitment to proactively co-ordinate key parts of this supply chain through a process called network resource management.

To support this business model, and manage risk, Rolls-Royce had to use its global base of suppliers differently and to share this supply base with its competition. In the past, relationships down the supply chains were based upon transactions driven by cost and efficiency. Now, if an aircraft engine project is successful, the project has considerable knock-on effects for the revenues and operational planning of suppliers of parts for the engines. It takes from three and five years to develop an engine, and every time an engine is ordered, it could be in service for up to 30 years, requiring future repair and overhaul to maintain the engine. Given the potential benefits for supplier manufacturers, a system of sharing some of the investment so that they could qualify for the rewards was needed. Rolls-Royce had to manage the risk, just as much as the revenue opportunity, in a mutually incentivizing way. It uses its primary suppliers, called Risk and Revenue Sharing Partners (RRSPs), to jointly finance and co-develop new products. Under the partnership, the suppliers invest capital in development of a new engine and provide product development engineers. This reduces both Rolls-Royce's investment in the project and the development time, but also gives suppliers more responsibility as business partners.

In the latest development of the model Rolls-Royce is enhancing its engine health monitoring with the intention of eradicating unscheduled repair or maintenance events. It has had to create additional data handling capability as 60 million Kb of engine health data is generated each year across over 40 customers. This data feeds back into improved engine design, but can also be used to predict engine problems before they happen, enabling preventative action to be taken, and to provide insight into the operational capability of airlines' pilots and other staff. Rolls-Royce is moving from a single-vendor to a multiple-vendor strategy.

As one of a number of IT initiatives, in 2012 Rolls-Royce signed a three-year outsourcing deal with Capgemini, which will perform the role of service integrator for Rolls-Royce, overseeing IT services provided by other outsourcers. Capgemini is tasked with working with Rolls-Royce to ensure that the different vendors and solutions are fully aligned, integrated and centrally controlled so that 40,000 Rolls-Royce IT users across 50 countries can benefit from a seamless service. Capgemini, selected partly on the strength of its security expertise and experience in working with police, aerospace, defence and security organizations around the globe, supports applications such as Rolls-Royce's SAP Enterprise Resource Planning (ERP) and supply chain software systems.

In summary, a business strategy based on value co-creation also shifts the points at which HR adds value. All of the long-term collaborative arrangements associated with engine-life deals combine the interests of the manufacturer, the supply chain and the customer, and encourage the integration of cultures and skills. But in addition to such cross-organization development, at what point and to what level does Rolls-Royce need to pool its human resources provision?

As customers become more reliant on Rolls-Royce for service delivery, customers provide Voice of the Customer team visits to ensure their environment is understood deep inside Rolls-Royce's organization in order to create mutual operational benefits. Similarly, as the way pilots fly aircraft and manage thrust affect efficiency and fuel costs, Rolls-Royce Flight Operations Advisors go to airlines and spend time with pilots advising them on more efficient and safe flying methods. It requires common learning and development models to support core engineering competence and commitment models across parties, and cost-effective but responsive customer interfaces between organizations.

When does the failure of one party's HR become a business issue for another? What kind of HR structure works best for the whole business model and the network of its contributors?

As the above example shows, manufacturers in complex and capital-intensive industries now often compete by integrating downstream activities. This is because of the size of the initial investments needed, the level of sunk costs and the depth of differentiating technical knowledge.[11] In practice, in the aerospace sector, this move towards product-service strategies evolved separately both across organizations and across major projects and business divisions within them. In part this was because in order to evolve a more seamless customer value offering, each part of the organization had to develop a stronger customer orientation, better knowledge and information management strategies, and engage employees.[12]

5.2.2 Open innovation and joint ventures

The second example is the rise of open innovation systems and of joint ventures. In Chapter 2 we discussed the need to manage innovation more effectively. One of the consequences of this is that many joint R&D, innovation and product developments are now managed under open innovation arrangements.[13] These arrangements must cover many situations. They must specify arrangements for the sharing of internal ideas, and internal and external paths to market, as the firms advance a technology. They involve the buying or licensing of processes or inventions, such as patents, from other companies. They must outline which internal inventions are not used in an organization's business and whether they may be taken outside the organization through licensing, joint ventures or spin-offs. HR needs to put in the systems, processes and practices that enable this to happen, and start making the investments in the sorts of talent systems, talent pipelines, career systems and skill structures that such open innovation implies.

Joint ventures are associations of two or more individuals or companies engaged in a solitary business enterprise for profit without actual partnership or incorporation.[14] Contractual arrangements join together the parties for the purpose of executing a particular business undertaking. All parties agree a share of the profits or losses of the undertaking. A new and distinct business unit may be set up to execute the business transactions involved. Strategic alliances are a strategic mode of integration that is achieved through a formalized collaboration, whereby two or more organizations co-operate on part(s) or all stages of a business venture, from the initial phase of research to marketing, production and distribution.

Joint venture arrangements are very people management-dependent. Twenty years ago it was argued that:

> In the context of strategic alliances that involve competitive collaboration, the competitive advantage of a firm can be protected only through its

> capability to accumulate invisible assets by a carefully planned and executed process of organizational learning. As this process is embedded in people, many of the necessary capabilities are closely linked to HRM strategies and practice.[15]

Similar issues to those seen in the aerospace sector, described earlier, are now faced in the energy sector. In our second example, Shell, these challenges of aligning HR across some of its partners became evident throughout 2011 and early 2012, when it reviewed what would be the best HR operating model to support the increasing number and scale of joint ventures in its business. In January 2013 it established a new role as part of this. In terms of new business in the upstream environment, and increasingly in the downstream environment too, working with a joint venture partner is now typically the way it works. This brings two risk issues to the fore for HR:

- non-technical risks;
- reputational risks.

Paul Kane, Vice President of HR Functional Excellence at Shell, explains why this starts to shape the sort of capabilities needed in HR:

> Shell determined over time that it is often the non-technical risk areas that are the most likely show-stoppers in moving ventures forward. Before you even get into doing the business directly with an outfit, it is dealing with the things that go in front of that. That is where HR, and all the other functions of the business, have a role to play in terms of working with the deal teams as a technical function … for us these are not something that can be solved personally, or just within HR. They run right across the whole game, and neither are they contained to just one partner. Within any project team or directorate the expectation is that you have people who understand and can advise on those risks.

DELIVERING COLLABORATIVE HR AT SHELL

Tor Arnesen, VP HR, Joint Ventures, Upstream International, Country Chair, Norway, Sweden and Finland and MD A/S Norske Shell

Our thinking in Shell led us to identify and review a range of different "archetypes," and to think about the different levels of Shell influence and control and support each might need. In our industry ventures can range from an arm's-length investor-type arrangement, to a need for heavier touch assurance with some senior level leadership development, to ventures that need to be developed and offered access to technical learning, through to collaborations that offer the opportunity not just for development but also leverage. Each archetype presents different challenges, reflects a different level of maturity in the collaboration and so comes with different risks, governance needs and a need for different bundles and packages of HR support. To address this, for us part of the solution was to create the role I operate in January 2013. The role provides central HR oversight across our joint ventures in the upstream part of the business. We have a range of upstream businesses. These cover assets we operate but in non-standardized businesses or countries, such as in China or South Africa and a few other countries. They include the Integrated Gas business, countries where we have joint ventures, and a specific line of business called Joint Ventures.

I have responsibilities for joint ventures in Brunei, Kazakhstan six countries in the Middle East, Italy and Denmark, working with Shell colleagues and the HR Directors of each joint venture. In doing this, I combine my current role with being a Managing Director and country chair for Shell in Norway. This double-hatting arrangement is important to doing a role like this.

For me, the initial task – which required considerable networking and face-to-face relationship-building – was to establish a small business team, the roles needed for HR and country management, and the way Shell wanted to work with the joint ventures. Each joint venture has its own governance, which in turn, depending on the stakeholders, brings together government representatives, other industrial organizations, senior managers from the venture in hand, and Shell. In HR terms, there may be questions about talent development for the venture itself, or indeed for broader issues of talent, culture and capability development in the country or labor market a venture operates in.

This means that HR has to be more thoughtful on the policy side. In many instances they are not in a position to be able to enforce Shell's policy position to another partner, so policy has to be clear.

For Shell the solution has been to build a cadre of HR Business Partners who are used to, and experience, the challenges of working outside of the Shell box. They believe that for many of its people, being able to work in joint ventures, will become just a normal part of their delivery of the HR agendas.

It also raises three needs that must be managed:

1. The first is about how to manage innovation (see Chapter 2). We carry out our own technology development and innovation in areas where we need to be the technology leader, and our intellectual property is an attraction to others. But we also see that most innovations today are open, carried out as joint industry projects. Joint venture companies are very interested in various models of how we can work innovation through collaborative industry projects and directly with governments. Using innovation, our technology and development is a way of creating mutual benefits and mutual wins in many parts of the world now. This requires more than just business development, but also social development and building of local capability. For me, this means establishing longer-term succession plans, often working on a 10-year journey, reviewing the status of where they are at the moment, which I map, but then also discussing with my colleagues and with HR people and HR Directors sitting in the joint ventures where they and we want to be in 10 years from now and how can we support you on that journey. On that basis I can have much more strategic discussions on where we as a partner should inject and support with HR capability, at this moment, or in five years from now.
2. The second is around questions of organizational effectiveness and organizational capability. It is related to overall organizational performance. I need people that are very good at looking at our contribution from a business performance point of view, and being capable of putting that in an organizational context. They need to support JVs with what is the right, not only before we make choices about structure, but also the right type of performance, management and culture for the development that joint venture needs to go through and focus on.

3. The third is how you build future talent over all the people, both in terms of leadership development but also in terms of technical and commercial development.

These questions inevitably impact back on the broader Shell HR environment. Traditionally, HR professionals come from a mindset where they like to operate, be in charge, have control, provide high levels of leadership and responsibility. However, from a commercial mindset, rather than being a primary operator, we may need to partner up with the right people, taking on those people that will make a difference and add value, but not necessarily making us the leader. In HR, as we continue to transition to an organizational effectiveness role, success revolves around having people that are client or customer orientated, listening and understanding the needs of others, rather than being marketers of Shell systems and processes.

Reflecting general research on joint venture success, the above example shows that a key contingency – or decision criterion – in deciding on the level of HR support is a judgment as to whether the alliance should be governed primarily on contractual or relational terms and, as the joint venture develops, and how to manage the effective transition from one form of governance to the other. There are, for example, six alternative ways of thinking about joint venture archetypes and deciding how to differentiate the level of HR support that they need. They might be categorized as follows:

1. On risk, by identifying the macro- and micro-level recurrent risks to performance.
2. On the level and nature of equity holding.
3. On the axes of long-term strategic intent versus the opportunities for capability and knowledge creation.
4. On the axes of exploitation or creation of knowledge and capabilities versus the degree for more immediate control versus arm's-length risk management.
5. On the identification of different behavioral, structural and control characteristics that might be triggered.
6. On the life cycle stage of maturity of the alliance (from young to mature).

JUDGMENTS TO BE MADE BY HR FUNCTIONS

We believe that in analyzing *each venture*, organizations need to consider a number of issues in terms of the level of HR support needed. These considerations can be applied to almost any form of partnered business arrangement:

- Which type of governance is in practice being applied or taking precedence in any particular joint venture, or in a family of ventures within their remit?
- How assured are they about the appropriate level of governance currently afforded by each potential governance mechanism (contractual or trust-based)?
- What level of risk to alliance performance is there, given historical or existing contractual arrangements?
- How strong an organization development oversight and task is that faced by the corporate HR function?

The "poorer" the contracts and trust-based governance mechanisms are upfront, the more "direct oversight governance" corporate HR functions need to exert, either through individuals assigned to the joint venture or through central units designed to make judgments about the level of organization development support that is needed.

5.2.3 Cross-sector social partnerships

A third organizational form that is creating the need to manage HR beyond the organization is that of cross-sector social partnerships, or multi-sector collaborations. Typically these are set up in complex social areas – such as economic development, healthcare, crime and poverty – where no one single entity or organization can perform alone, but has to work and collaborate with multiple organizations and stakeholders.[16] These partnering relationships between organizations are set to increase further, particularly as public sector organizations are entering into more partnerships with both the private and voluntary sectors as they move away from delivering services directly to more of a commissioning model. A 2013 PwC Global CEO Survey of public and private sector CEOs found that significantly more state-backed CEOs expect to initiate a new strategic alliance or joint venture (52 percent compared to 47 percent of private sector CEOs) and to outsource (40 percent compared to

30 percent). They exist in a range of settings, such as public administration,[17] public-private partnerships,[18] business-community partnerships,[19] business or government non-profit partnerships and the implementation of corporate social responsibility partnerships.[20] Beyond the achievement of contracted goals, their value is generally seen against a broader and long-term set of outcomes[21] – things that each partner in the collaboration could not achieve on their own.

What is the value created by the "whole network?" Why are they set up? They have typically been found to include important outcomes, such as the following:[22]

- Resolution of previous conflicted policy through the creation of a (sometimes subsequent to the initial start-up) shared understanding and goals.
- Creation of social capital, common identity and engineered changes in the structure of important networks.
- Development of new and emergent capacities for action.
- Shifts in the distribution of power.

However, this form of organization also presents very particular organization design and development challenges. Unfortunately, therefore, they are often found to:

- be designed in such a way as to exacerbate rather than solve the problems of collaboration;[23]
- be perceived to produce limited improvements to performance and not achieve the goals set for them;[24]
- bring together members who have contrasting goals and approaches;[25]
- run on norms that in seeking to build trust may end up creating a culture of non-confrontation and conflict avoidance;[26]
- be prone to gridlock and fragmentation of the people/communities involved.[27]

Ideally, one might assume that there is some kind of:

> single organizational entity that has the capacity to act, to exhibit agency, or to otherwise "make a difference" for the participants involved, their member organizations, and the broader communities and problem domains in which the cross-sector partnerships exist.[28]

In practice, partnerships do not always act as a single entity, yet much of the study of cross-sector partnerships still tends to focus on the issues that arise for each single firm rather than looking at the total entity.[29]

5.2.4 Underlying changes in the sorts of forms being used by organizations

Finally, attention is now being given to a number of other networked organizational forms, typically studied under a range of labels, including the following:

- Strategic networks, defined as sets of connections between organizations with the objective to establish a relationship between firms and partners (such as competitors, customers or suppliers).[30]
- Formal inter-firm networks, such as the *keiretsu* arrangement in Japan, which typically include large manufacturers, their suppliers of raw materials and components, and banks.[31] These are defined as groups of organizations that partner or co-operate with each other in order to provide expanded products and services. These networks might be alliances of related organizations that own a stake in each other in order to protect mutual interests, but must share knowledge and co-operate to control its sector of the business.
- Multi-employer networks, defined as situations where organizations collaborate across boundaries to jointly produce goods or provide services and where the employment experiences of workers are shaped by more than one employer.[32]
- Knowledge-based inter-organizational collaborations and knowledge-sharing networks. These are where organizations combine the competences needed for either minor incremental or radical innovations. The resources may be shared across customers, competitors, suppliers, sub-contractors and partners. The knowledge and resources must be shared in order to distribute risks.[33]

All of these more collaborative business models are in turn often driven by underlying series of business developments, such as:

- deep supply chain integration;
- the growth of inter-organizational information systems;
- collaborative manufacturing;
- the "projectification" of the firm; and
- more strategic use of outsourcing.

We see more strategic use of outsourcing, and cross-licensing, which involves a contracting-out arrangement in which one organization provides services for another that could also be (or usually have been) provided in-house. The arrangements can be applied to any task, operation, job or process that could be performed by employees within an organization, but is instead contracted to a third party for a significant period of time.

We also see the need for deep supply chain integration, where networks of organizations become linked through upstream (supply sources) or downstream (distribution channels) processes and activities, in complex ways that are necessary to produce value in the products and services for the ultimate consumers.[34]

Closely linked to this is the growth of collaborative manufacturing,[35] which reflects the phenomenon of companies competing as supply chains, not as individual entities, in response to the need for shorter lead times, customized products and better quality, whilst still competing on price. In collaborative manufacturing, designated individuals and organizations work together for mutual gain. These may be both internal to a manufacturing enterprise and may extend to its suppliers, customers and partners. To support this, information systems are integrated and information is aggregated and intelligently distributed for the manufacturing business both from and across suppliers, trading partners and customers. The possibilities emerge for partners in collaborative manufacturing environments to share employees (not just from support functions) at times when one entity has downtime and others need more employees, without disengaging them from the original entity. For example, the Toyota Motor Manufacturing Texas (TMMTX) plant houses 21 suppliers in the same premises with shared facilities. Similarly, the design, development and manufacture of modern aircraft are undertaken by a large globally distributed network of organizations. *The Economist* gives the example of Quirky in New York and Shapeways in the Netherlands. Quirky has a design studio in a converted warehouse and a small factory with 3D printers, a laser cutter, milling machines, a spray-painting booth and other bits of equipment. With the help of an online community, it designs two new consumer products a week, produces prototypes, which are then reviewed on line for developments to design, packaging and marketing, with manufacturers then sought, and products sold online or via retailers if demand is high.[36]

We also see the growing importance of (often international) project operations and what is called the "projectification" of the firm,[37] for example, in film or construction industry projects, or mission-based activities which bring together short-term and temporary collections of people, or in charities that need to bring together coalitions of professionals under a single identity. These all exemplify the increasingly fluid lines between organizations. Such projects create the demand for highly specialized skills, with project teams being drawn from multiple organizations, professions and countries, often with team members who are geographically dispersed.[38] Such projects have important common characteristics – they reduce risk and transfer much of it to other providers or vendors, who are expected to be able to better address these risks because of their presumed greater competence.[39] However, they create new challenges that become the problem of all:

- the need to mitigate the problems of co-ordination;
- to need to curb opportunistic behavior;
- to need to facilitate learning and knowledge transfer across what is a fragmented learning cycle (different people and organizations at different levels of understanding and development);
- the ceding of internal controls within a business function to the interests of the broader project – this in turn needs there to be high levels of trust in the other project stakeholders and their systems;
- the establishment of problem-solving and conflict-resolution arrangements;
- team composition frequently being of a fluid nature, with teams operating as a "partnership";
- team members being expected to have a high degree of autonomy, yet working alongside another "counterpart" team comprising employees from the partner;
- the need for co-operative work relationships rather than command-and-control;
- some team members staying for the entire duration of the project, with others performing specific tasks or functions that involve a shorter stay in the location.

These international projects are discontinuous, complex and difficult to manage from just within one partner. They produce challenges similar to joint ventures for the supplying firms, particularly around staff deployment, employing and supporting teams of workers in a temporary work organization with host counterparts, often in remote and sometimes dangerous locations, HR planning for project workers, career trajectory and job security, self-management of their own careers, including skills development, as a consequence of the intermittent and geographically dispersed features of international project work. A range of HR activities associated with the successful delivery of the project work become crucial: team maintenance, host country support, ensuring personnel safety, performance management and control, compensation and training.

5.3 Managing the issues of risk

Having laid out the some of the major changes in business relationships, we now show how the successful management of all of them centers increasingly around people- and organization-centric problems. All of these arrangements, whilst now becoming surprisingly prevalent, are known to be complicated and problematic to manage. The attention given to HR's role in their success becomes much more important.

Whilst we should better think about leadership for the "whole network," leadership beyond individual member organizations, the organizational behavior that drives these organizational forms, sadly still reflects a high degree of individuality and rationality rather than the pursuit of the supposed collective value. Yet much can be learned.

We use the insights from recent research to help answer three important questions:

1. How do we ensure governance of HRM in these important relationships that extend beyond the organization?
2. How do we ensure appropriate risk management?
3. How do we ensure the necessary mutual capability development across partnered business arrangements?

We begin by looking at the management of risk, outlining the challenges that have to be dealt with and the ways in which the risks can be managed. The management of HR across the different partnering arrangements outlined earlier is centrally concerned with the management of risk. Whilst the risks differ across each type of business relationship, a range of issues become shared across all the partners, even though they are not managed this way.

It is interesting to note that an understanding of the people- and organization-centric nature of risk tends to have come from research into outsourcing, joint ventures, supply chain and disaster management. This shows the following.

THE PROBLEM WITH RISK ...

- Changes are taking place in the "shape" of risk (i.e., its sources, nature, triggers, scale, rapidity and severity of consequences).
- Concerns about structures, systems, information sharing, interactions, personal exchanges and trust become important dimensions of the risk management process.
- There is an explicit link between risks and potential rewards.
- Key talent may themselves become a source of risk (see Chapter 7).
- When individual or collaborative groups of organizations propose tactical and strategic changes (with a view to enhancing

the performance of the parties involved), the actions taken to mitigate one risk often end up exacerbating another, and efforts to improve performance against one measure (such as cost or quality) inadvertently reduce performance or increase the risks associated with one or more other success criteria.[40]

- Even if the best skills can be found at the lowest cost beyond the organization, there are still challenges of co-ordination, communication and control, which are particularly tested by cultural divergences.

This has created the need for more diverse risk management tools and approaches, all of which are becoming important elements for HR to examine.

Research on the management of risk in outsourcing and offshoring – a type of business arrangement is considered to take the benefits and risks of outsourcing to its extremes – helps show this.[41] There are multiple regulatory regimes that can be adopted, but in practice outsourcing arrangements are based on two control mechanisms:[42]

- formal contractual relations in the form of bundles of obligations, incentives, rewards and penalties for when it is not clear that the chosen governance will mitigate all contractual hazards;
- a range of complementary social mechanisms such as trust, reputation and what has been termed "the shadow of the future," which together act to ensure self-regulation.

Greater complexity and density of these contracts is required for three reasons:

- to mitigate opportunistic behaviors by the vendor;
- to avoid over-dependence on the vendor; and
- to allow flexible responses to changes in the environment.

Building on the example of Shell earlier, the same themes emerge from research on joint ventures. Historically it has been assumed that firms could maintain their competitive position without substantially altering their internal organizational structure in response to these alliances,[43] but this assumption is increasingly questioned. Alliances might be driven by a motivation of scale. They have to produce significant economies of scale by reducing excess capacity in the areas where partners execute jointly. This most often has important impacts around research and development activities, manufacturing of common components and supply chain structures. Or they might be driven by the need for links[44] – where different resources or competencies and skills are combined to produce activities that previously did not exist.

But alliances are rarely concluded amongst equals.[45] They are often asymmetric[46] – for example, in terms of resource contributions, asset size, ownership, product markets, intensity of rivalry between partners, information and information resources. This asymmetry often creates a risk of opportunistic behavior. Partners may vary in scale, grandeur, number of employees, revenues or capital. The nature of their strategic rivalry might be imbalanced – A may view B as a bigger threat than B views A.

Reflecting the importance of social mechanisms as a form of risk management, research on alliance success or failure shows that there are four social and behavioral risks associated with the management of joint ventures:[47]

1. *Co-ordination* – necessary to reduce uncertainty and manage dependency. This depends on the balance in the level of autonomy of each partner within the relationship. Inter-dependency is defined as the degree of replaceability and dependency of each company on its partner both in terms of investment and resources.
2. *Commitment* – reflects both the economic costs of maintaining the partnership as well as the emotional ties to the relationship; the implicit pledge of relational continuity between the exchange partners.
3. *Inter-dependence* – mutual dependency means that the relational governance of the partnership becomes crucial. This is governed by levels of trust.
4. *Trust* – determined principally by two things: the symmetry of the relationship (the extent to which partners value one another's resources); and communication behavior, which in turn depends on three aspects of the quality of information, the extent of information sharing, and participation in planning and goal setting.

Finally, we can draw some lessons from supply chain researchers. They were some of the earliest to understand that an increasing percentage of the value creation for lean and agile organizations takes place outside the boundaries of the individual firm.[48] Even by the mid-2000s, it was evident that major supply chain disruptions reduced the stock market value of a company by 10 percent[49] and also were the source of conflict between various parties in a collaboration.[50]

Supply chain researchers therefore recognize the importance of a customer orientation (we focused on the importance of customer centricity in Chapter 3), but argue that this cannot be managed be single partners. It brings with it the need to integratee the performance systems across the upstream, downstream and internal organizations – what they call the "behavioral backbone" of inter-organizational management.[51]

Table 5.1 shows the questions – each associated with identifiable risks – that can be seen to be important.[52] They are all very people- and organization-centric.

We end our discussion of the people- and organization-centric nature of risk management and the need for a broader role of HR in collaborative business contexts (see Figure 5.1).

We look at research in two contexts: supply chain and disaster management.

TABLE 5.1 Issues and risks identified with supply chain management

Major issues	Questions to focus on	Risks
Contracts and incentives	What is the most efficient contract? How best to align the incentives for all parties? What is the most efficient division of labor?	Asymmetric information; goal conflicts
Governance structure	What exchanges and transactions must be captured? What assets need to be specified? How will the arrangements handle market failures?	Opportunism Parties driven by bottom-line safeguards against specific investments
Competence development	Which competences does each party need and contribute? How will access to complimentary resources be enabled? What new capabilities are created by combining and re-using the existing capabilities of the partners?	Calculated trust Information sharing Mutual adaptation to data, systems and knowledge
Relationships	How will inter-firm relationships be handled? What should be the roles, positions and responsibilities of the participants to the partnership? How will adversarial relations be avoided?	Access to collective/shared resources
Performance measurement	How will the behavioral and outcome-based contracts be aligned? How will the true activity based inputs into the collaboration be captured?	Goal conflicts
Joint learning and transfer of knowledge	How will joint learning take place? What new competencies get created? What knowledge will be important to share? How can this create a win-win situation?	Information sharing Communications and interactions Personal trust

FIG 5.1 **Identifying risks in your partnership arrangements**

THINKING ABOUT COLLABORATIVE RISK IN SUPPLY CHAINS

Supply chain researchers have investigated the type of support that is becoming important.[53] In a cross-organizational context, there are three dimensions to risk: its magnitude, its likelihood and the breadth of exposure.[54] Risk is defined as "the extent to which there is uncertainty about whether potentially significant and/or disappointing outcomes of decisions will be realised."[55] Some risks dissipate as they travel across the organizations in the network, while others get amplified. For example, when Rover ceased car manufacturing in the UK, the impact on the downstream car distribution channels and agents was much greater than the impact on upstream suppliers.

But risk and uncertainty are not the same. Risk is measurable in the sense that estimates can be made of the probabilities of the outcomes. It is therefore manageable in the sense that its impacts may be identified, analyzed (estimated and evaluated) and controlled. This management has to be a continuous and developing process that runs throughout an organization's strategy and its execution, and is embedded in the mindsets of senior managers involved in the collaboration. Uncertainty, by definition, is not quantifiable and the probabilities of the possible outcomes cannot be known.

The source of risks may be internal (resulting from the situation itself) or external (resulting from those outside factors which impinge on the situation). There are typically four families of risk: those that stem from infrastructure, business controls, business values and relationships. Four major factors impacting supply chain risk are: lack of trust, withholding of information, dependence on outsourcing and standardized contracts.[56]

However, the understanding of risk in supply chains has moved away from looking at risk in the more physical and tangible connections towards the importance of information and financial flows and the more behavioral aspects of relationship development across these networks. There are three sorts of risks that can be designed for:[57]

- systematic (i.e. unavoidable) risk, at least in the short to medium term (e.g. it may be difficult to reconfigure the supply chain);
- partner-specific risks (e.g. financial solvency, quality standards and inadequate information systems). Such risks are usually a form of unsystematic risk, which may be avoided by the organization through appropriate strategies;
- node-specific risks emanating from the organization's ability to respond to demands of others in the supply chain (e.g. ill-equipped or poorly trained staff, inadequate management control and ineffective communications). In a review of the management literature conducted in conjunction with the Chartered Institute of Personnel and Development (CIPD), we have suggested that wherever the risks are considered to be, they are likely to relate to the 6Cs of risk, i.e. issues of co-ordination, communication, control, culture, capability or conflict.[58]

We can also learn from research into both disaster management and military operations. This adopts a network-centric approach to identify the importance of building situation-awareness,[59] which in turn focuses on the importance of communication links, processes and information hand-offs between important actors in the network. Not surprisingly, in these situations, organizations fall back upon the co-ordination of the commitments made within the collaboration within a small number of important individual relationships.

LEARNING FROM DISASTER MANAGEMENT: BUILDING SITUATION AWARENESS

When a disaster strikes, previously autonomous teams have to combine into inter-dependent decision-making teams, collecting and exchanging relevant information from multiple sources, verified for accuracy and distributed to the vital sources, all in a short timeframe. During the collaboration, shifts occur in terms of the urgency, scope, impact, type of appropriate responder and the needs of responders for information and communication. The state and the configuration of those who need to be part of the network shift. Research continues to show the high chance of failure in these situations,[60] but also the importance of organization design to deal with the limited capacity and resources and problems caused by the division of tasks and labor across a collaboration. When attention is given to disaster management and a risk management lens is adopted, it shows that problems of conflict and debates around resource allocation, at every stage of the collaboration, are lessened when attention is given to plans for mitigation, preparedness, response and recovery, which in turn heightens the importance of prevention, early signal detection, intervention, after-crisis care and evaluation. The need is to have an organization design that in crisis enables rapid situation awareness and sustainability, and delivers speed of command. Those cross-organization processes that foster joint development, pooled resources, co-ordination of efforts and interpretation of information help avoid the collaboration fragmenting into "isolated islands" of effective operation.

5.4 The governance challenge

The second major business issue associated with more collaborative business arrangements is that of governance. We now look at how collaborating organizations must ensure that the necessary structures and control mechanisms are in place to minimize risks to the business and its activities. There is of course some overlap between the themes of risk and governance and we cross-reference between these two issues where appropriate. Governance mechanisms are important for two reasons:[61]

1. To control against the risk of opportunistic and self-interested behaviors, where the investments of one party to the partnership lose value because of the way others redeploy that investment (typically studied by economists using a transaction cost economics perspective).
2. To gain other benefits within the relationship, based on the way in which organizations in the chain share potentially unique assets, knowledge, resources or capabilities by combining, exchanging or investing in these (typically studied by strategists using a resource-based view of the firm).

The overall purpose of governance arrangements is to create expectations about the exchanges that must take place between partners. They shape a series of important behaviors that are needed to help the partnership evolve and perform over time:

- co-ordination;
- collaboration;
- vigilance; and
- safeguarding.

TYPICAL GOVERNANCE MECHANISMS

- Legal contracts requiring behaviors such as joint problem solving, joint planning, collaborative communication and symmetrical access to information.
- Incentive structures that reinforce long-term gains over short-term opportunistic behaviors.
- Governance forums (e.g. steering groups or advisory committees) and monitoring systems to enforce goals, supervision and progress on the basis of input controls, behavior controls or output controls.
- Social enforcement, based on personal trust as a control mechanism and the potential for reputation loss as a risk reduction mechanism.

Two streams of research have evolved around problems of governance. Each is driven by different assumptions about the motives and behaviors of partners in the business arrangements, and therefore each argues for the importance of different mechanisms to govern any partnered business relationship:

1. Research that focuses on the structural design of transactions, i.e. the required contractual arrangements as an effective governance mechanism. This is rooted in assumptions from transaction economics.[62]
2. Research that has studied the relational (trust-building) processes necessary to govern inter-firm relationships, i.e. the role of key individuals (or units) in safeguarding and co-ordinating the business relationship.[63] This is rooted in assumptions from social exchange theory.[64]

In this section we look at research on governance as it specifically relates to two different types of partnership: supply chain management and joint ventures. Again, we will show how the theme of governance is surprisingly people- and organization-centric. It is in essence about the appropriate balance needed between formal control and relational mechanisms.

The first major stream of research has been that on the contractual design – also called structural design – that must be used to govern inter-organizational working.[65] This work rests on the assumption that contractual partners will be naturally opportunistic, either where one partner has more specific or asymmetric assets (for example, HR capability) *or* where there is just general high uncertainty. Taking a structural approach has been criticized for ignoring the social context, previous history and role of time in shaping behavior in the business relationship.

THE LESSONS FROM STRUCTURAL GOVERNANCE RESEARCH

In thinking about the regulatory focus, the need for productive relationships and avoidance of any violation of expectations, the following lessons emerge:

- the initial structural design of transactions is the most important factor in explaining subsequent performance;[66]
- therefore, a key issue is how formalized and complex the content of contracts need to be as a safeguarding mechanism;
- the mitigation of the risk of opportunistic behavior requires the inclusion of penalties for violating behaviors;
- technical detail around strategy and governance is needed for co-ordination and legal enforcement is needed for risk management, but the former clauses are more conducive to constructive exchanges;[67]

- the contractual interface between parties – particularly around monitoring performance and behavior, task division and flows of information – can be designed to be broad or narrow;
- narrow contract interfaces concentrate on defining milestones, target dates and performance standards. Broad interfaces also define contractually the behaviors that are needed both outside the alliance and as affecting the execution of the alliance;
- broader interfaces are better and are associated with improved quality of joint sense-making (in the problem definition and solution space of the venture) when partners face unanticipated problems. Overlapping task divisions also assist sense-making;
- denser contracts exist when there are high switching costs, higher strategic centrality of the partnered activity and higher uncertainty about future needs,[68] but are associated with higher monitoring and enforcement costs;
- where one partner has a strong bargaining position, they tend to ignore the need for broad contracts;
- in addition to a safeguarding role, contracts also serve a co-ordination role. They need to provide precise divisions of labor and provide for procedures that integrate dispersed activities. They need to simplify decision making;
- contractual clauses can be couched in more productive terminology that does not lead to subsequent violation of expectations,[69] with clauses added that play a positive and technical co-ordination role without provoking levels of distrust;[70]
- in order to align expectations, partnership contracts clauses that provide a co-written and rich task description and provide detail on the processes to be involved[71] are shown more effective than enforcement clauses.

There are important messages for HR and what they need to influence. It is possible to promote superior levels of collaboration and vigilance by couching clauses in terms of either prevention (loss to the partnership) or promotion (gain to the partnership). Perceptions about partnership behavior can be coloured in a more positive light. The way in which contracts are framed has been shown to determine the subsequent emotional reaction to any ambiguous behaviors from parties to the contract. The design of contractual arrangements is therefore important for two reasons:

- formal contracts serve to foster distrust and bring about the very actions they are designed to prevent;[72] and
- contract design needs to not only sufficiently define the exchange (in terms of roles, responsibilities, contingencies and proper economic safeguards), but also be framed appropriately so that they induce the emotions and behaviors that ensure the reaching of the relationship's goals.[73]

The second stream of research is on relational (trust)-based forms of governance. A trust-based approach rests on the assumption that given the importance of the partnership, all other things being equal, partners will behave in a trustworthy manner, especially where there is a history of previous transactions.[74] This type of research concentrates on two key trust-inducing behaviors needed in partnerships:[75]

- interpersonal (fairness, honesty and reciprocity); and
- joint sense-making (problem definition, problem solution and adjustment to alliance performance).

Trust can be defined as the intention to accept vulnerability based upon positive expectations of the intentions or behavior of another. Trust only exists between and among individuals; it does not exist between organizations. However, inter-organization trust is considered to be a psychological state[76] that can be built up in order to manage risk.[77] It is created *at both the operational and the managerial level* when key players in the partnership are prepared to accept vulnerability because they have positive expectations about the intentions or behavior of the other partner.

TRUST BEYOND THE ORGANIZATION[78]

- Organizations cannot really trust each other. However, organizations can build and pass on to new individuals a series of important conditions that underlie their mutual competitive and risk-taking behavior.
- Risk conditions, and risk management mechanisms, can be channeled into important institutions within and between the organizations.
- There are different types of trust that have to be developed: process-based trust and relationship-based trust.
- Trust can be an outcome of business relations, it can be a predictor or antecedent of performance or it can act to moderate other factors.

As shown in Figure 5.2, there are three areas in which both forms of trust need to be developed: around predictability, reliability and competence.

Relational research[79] focuses on the informal (non-contractual) governance arrangements and mechanisms that enable trust to become an effective mechanism. It examines the way that inter-firm relations evolve over time and over transactions, and how partners move towards the less rigid application of contractual terms. In thinking about knowledge and information exchange, levels of reciprocity, problem definition, problem solution and the necessary adjustments to collaborative performance:

- Trust-based governance is not an alternative to contractual approaches, but determines the extent to which contractual terms may be adhered to inflexibly, or the negative cycles of behavior that may be entered into.
- Trust-based governance provides an assurance that knowledge and information will be used for the greater good and that opportunistic hazards will be minimal, reducing the need for costly and inflexible safeguarding mechanisms.[80]
- Members of different partner organizations will engage in more extensive communication and information exchange when it is informal, and adjustments to uncertainties are therefore mutual and conducted in parallel, increasing effectiveness.[81]

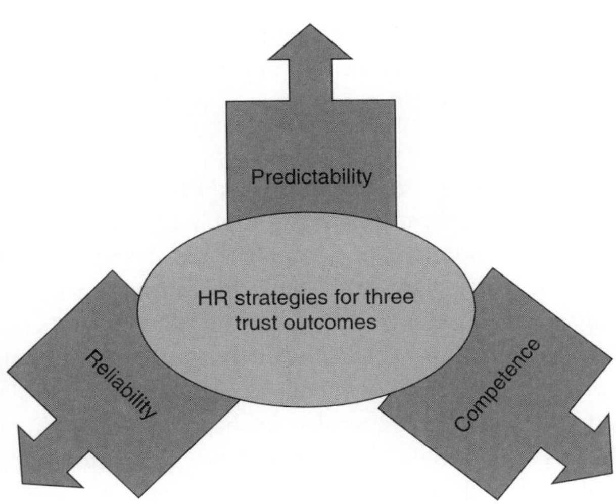

FIG 5.2 HR strategies for promoting trust across the partnering arrangement need to focus on three outcomes

- The quality of joint sense-making at the operational level influences the level of goodwill trust at the managerial level.[82]

Summarizing research on governance, it seems to us that there are important lessons about the new HR roles that are needed. Applying an HR lens to the governance process has the potential to increase the effectiveness of partnering arrangements. HR has a role to play in both the structural and trust-based approaches to governance, as the way in which formal contracts are framed affects the expectations and behavior of partners. It can provide its insight into the way in which contract clauses engineer subsequent organizational behaviors to inform decisions about the appropriate balance required between structural and relational governance mechanisms. However, it is not invited to do this, nor do most procurement functions have the capability to think beyond their immediate and narrow world.

5.5 Building capability for the whole network

The third and final theme that HR needs to focus on in order to support their organization's collaborations and partnering arrangements is the need to build the capability for learning and knowledge sharing across all partners, not just within their host organization. We discussed this issue and provided examples in Chapter 2 when we covered the challenges of open innovation. But in the context of this chapter, we need to reinforce the point that as well as being responsible for ensuring internal learning and knowledge-sharing capabilities within their own organization, someone now has to support development of these capabilities across the partnering arrangement as a whole. But which organization – and whose HR team – bears the responsibility and cost of doing this?

For example, within the textiles and apparel industry, as we have noted, competition is in practice between competing supply chains, and so distributors are keen to help their suppliers and manufacturers develop important capabilities in areas such as logistic and supply chain management by providing training programs and sharing knowledge on the topic. Translating the knowledge acquired from clients backward throughout the supply chain to the textile manufacturers and the fiber producers increases the value of the whole industry, and so distributors and retailers are happy to educate partners both about operations within the whole supply chain, and customers' needs and preferences. Each individual organization is now becoming heavily dependent on the management of these issues across the whole network.

COMPETENCE MANAGEMENT ACROSS EXTENDED SUPPLY CHAINS

There are many situations now – especially in the more dynamic, innovation-driven and customer satisfaction-dependent sectors – where the development of specialized management and technical competences is central to strategic success. But the technical capability is now distributed across many actors within an extended supply chain. An example is the manufacture of complex products, such as aircraft or motor vehicles. We saw in the Rolls-Royce example that to better manage costs, risks and complexity, aerospace products are composed of many parts, the production process is shared among several companies, and only a few large companies manage the agreement with the final customer (such as an airline company or national government). Assembly of the whole product may be distributed and several organizations work along the different supply chain levels in order to produce components and sub-components.[83] They have to manage sophisticated technologies, innovative materials, knowledge-intensive processes, and the exchange of large and accurate data across all parties.

But the issues of capability require subtle judgments. For example, Alenia Aeronautica, a leading Italian company that as part of the Finmeccanica Group was involved in the design and manufacture of aircraft components on several programs (such as the C27J, ATR, F35 JSF, Eurofighter Typhoon, Boeing 787 Dreamliner and unmanned aerial vehicles), found that in managing the competencies considered to be highly strategic, and in developing plans and actions for the continuous monitoring, scouting and development of these competencies, even apparently similar competencies were subject to differences.[84] These included differences in terms of organizational shape, culture, availability of resources and the depth of organization development surrounding each competency.

However, lessons such as this learned from traditional manufacturing sectors have now become relevant for new settings, such as healthcare management.[85] Even here, we see the application of operations research techniques to understand how to optimize inventory levels of drugs and ordering process of care-related products and pharmaceuticals. Even patient logistics require planning

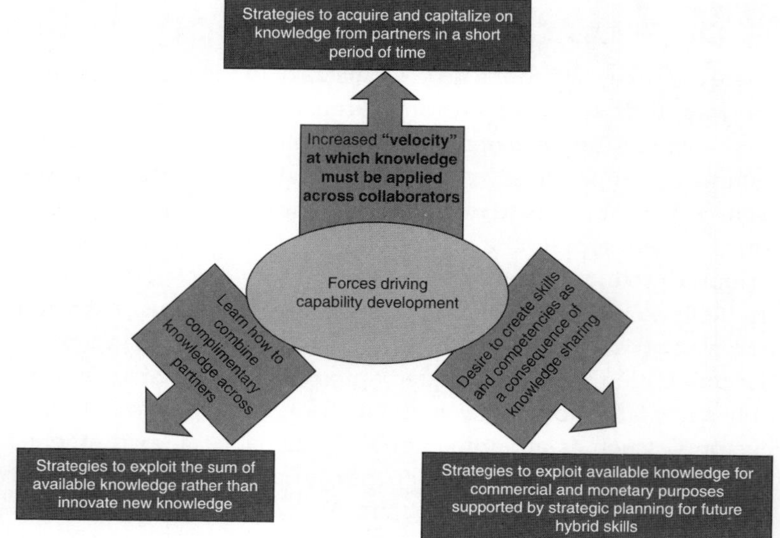

FIG 5.3 Three forces driving capability development across collaborative arrangements

and control decisions aimed at matching supply and demand throughout the entire healthcare supply chain, from the production of medical products, drugs and services through clinicians involved in end patient care.

To summarize, sharing knowledge and learning across organizations in the chain is neither free of costs (time and resources have to be invested in the knowledge sharing) nor free of risks (those firms that supply much of the knowledge or capability development become more vulnerable as they get locked into relationships). They have invested resources in other partners and there are risks around how others will use that knowledge. Organizations need to simultaneously reconcile the tension between the amount of time, resources and capability development devoted to knowledge exploration and the amount devoted to knowledge exploitation activities. In the management literature, those that are able to effectively balance this tension are referred to as "ambidextrous organizations."[86]

5.6 Conclusions

In conclusion, managing beyond the organization involves a significant shift in the way we are working. In this chapter we have focused in turn on each of the three main themes that past studies in the area have shown to affect the success of arrangements: risk, governance and capability development. We have seen that there are now many opportunities being presented to organizations through partnering and collaborating. We have also shown that there are risks that accompany these opportunities. These require careful governance, both to set expectations and responsibilities for the arrangement and also to mitigate potential crises. Again, it seems clear that HR needs to support the development of learning about these issues. It needs to develop the knowledge-sharing capabilities required both within an organization and across the whole network of partners. In short, we need HR functions that can ask the more important questions.

THE MORE STRATEGIC QUESTIONS TO ASK TO DETERMINE THE LEVEL OF HR SUPPORT AND INTEGRATION ACROSS THE NETWORK

Does the long-term strategic intent of the collaborators remain *competitive*, is it *co-operative*, or is it now *complementary*?

What is the importance of the collaboration to your organization relative to other strategic activities in the *overall business portfolio*?

What is the degree of desired control over your organization's *strategic resources*?

What is the strategic purpose of the collaboration: is it a consolidation arrangement (where the value comes from a deep combination of existing businesses), skills-transfer (where the value comes from the transfer of some critical skills across partners), a co-ordination arrangement (where the value comes from leveraging the complementary capabilities of both partners) or a new business arrangement (where the value comes from combining existing capabilities, not businesses, to create new growth)?

Is there a need for immediate and *tight control* of joint operations or can they be controlled through an "arm's length" strategy of *risk management*?

To what extent does the partnering arrangement require the *exploitation of current resources* (e.g. cost reduction, short-term HR expertise or resourcing needs) versus the need for the function to build new collaborative capabilities?

Does either the initial collaboration or a *future evolution* of it involve the *creation of new knowledge and capabilities* (and the desire to leverage these capabilities) where the management of learning and network capability will be more important?

What is the *strategic permanence* of the business arrangement? Is the arrangement based on an ongoing business concept, requiring permanent provision of support and resources, renegotiated co-operative agreements over time and jointly owned assets and liabilities? Or is it a looser project-based cooperative network?

Historically it has been assumed that when working beyond the organization, individual organizations could maintain their competitive position without substantially altering their internal structures and service delivery mechanisms. This assumption has also been applied to HR. We hope we have shown that this assumption should increasingly be questioned. The importance and level of external inter-dependencies of organizations is increasing the pressure to adapt the internal organization design. HR not only has a role in advising on the people and organizational issues that must be served in these collaborative arrangements, but also to best support the chosen organization forms. It also has to adapt its HR delivery model – a topic we will return to in Chapter 8. This will create a number of practical challenges:

- having to drive through another set of business-led changes in HR;
- taking up the opportunity to redesign internal systems more strategically; and
- making HR central to discussions about the new business relationships.

HR will need to build the internal capability of its own function to deal with the common challenges involved, while constantly learning from direct experience of managing partnering arrangements. In responding to these challenges, there are seven overarching issues for HR. It now needs to:

- evaluate the suitability of its existing structures and delivery mechanisms to meet these new needs;
- develop a blueprint to manage partnering arrangements;
- be flexible enough to differentiate the level of strategic HR support between arrangements and across partners;

- inform its choice of HR philosophy, services and practices by understanding the way in which the whole partnering network operates;
- develop leadership for the network;
- equalize the "felt" HR across all parties and deal with the issue of dual identity;
- design HR not just to deal with the assumed way in which the partnership will operate, but also with how the partnership operates in crisis situations.

Without attending to the issues that we have laid out in this chapter, crisis situations there will be!

chapter 6

The HR Imperatives of Engagement, Organizational Well-Being and Fairness

6.1 Introduction: the need for HR to start looking out again

The previous four chapters have focused on a series of important strategic performance drivers: innovation, customer centricity, lean management and the need to deliver HRM beyond the organization's boundaries. We have been looking into the strategy of the organization – one of the major roles of HRM. These are all very important challenges that must shape the design, focus and attention of much of the HR architecture. They all help to show that HR is indeed needed. They all require that any HR function of value is highly networked and interconnected with both internal expertise and the external developments that shape each performance driver. But, of course, the HR function, as the intermediary between the organization and its people resources, has to cope with those external developments that are beyond the organization's immediate control, but will serve as powerful drivers of employee behavior nonetheless. The focus on customer centricity outlined in Chapter 2 brings the outside into organizations under the guise of strategy and markets. But this outside world also impacts the internal labour market via the attitudes, mindset and culture of the workforce. And this in turn impacts engagement, which as we saw in Chapters 2 and 4 respectively, plays a crucial role in innovation and in lean management.

Independent of the recent context of austerity in much of the developed West, important questions are now shaping the employment relationship, introducing more varied societal conversations. These conversations are about risk and responsibility, justice, engagement, well-being and fairness.

Over the past seven years, we have been going through extremely turbulent economic times, which have adversely affected families, businesses, public sector workers and, indeed, the fabric of nation states, and their ability to survive and grow in the future (see, for example, Greece, Italy, Spain, Portugal and Ireland). As recently suggested:

> threats to jobs, incomes, homes and education, and uncertainties over our ability to meet daily needs have been unleashed on a scale not seen since the Great Depression of the 1930s following the collapse of the stock market in the Wall Street crash of the 29 October 1929.[1]

Indeed, as President Franklin Delano Roosevelt said during the Depression:

> True individual freedom cannot exist without economic security and independence. People who are hungry and out of a job are the stuff of which dictatorships are made. The hopes of the Republic cannot forever tolerate either undeserved poverty or self-serving wealth.

Within organizations we see conversations about how the current stagnating and shrinking cake should be distributed, and the role of employers in addressing unemployment, low pay, falling standards of living, the legacy to future generations and the sustainability of a future based on continuous economic growth. In essence, we need to work together to resolve these issues. There are many positives to this challenge[2] (the need for determination, bounce-backability, perspective and resilience), but also of course many negatives, which we are seeing much of in many countries (greed, blame, anger and disgust).

In this chapter we look at three debates about engagement, organizational well-being and fairness. They are highly inter-related, underwritten by trust and are also pivotal to the question as to whether we need HR. They also all have implications for performance.

6.2 Employee engagement

There has been much debate in recent years about the nature of employee engagement and, depending on the definition of engagement, discussion of the implications of engagement (or the lack of it) for organizational performance. Engagement (defined in its broadest sense) may explain three different levels of performance, as noted below.

THREE DIFFERENT AND INCREASINGLY MORE COMPLEX PERFORMANCE OUTCOMES[3]

1. Proximal performance outcomes, e.g., an employee's immediate task performance, what is called their contextual performance (otherwise known as organization citizenship behaviors or going the extra mile), their commitment, satisfaction and turnover intentions.
2. Intermediate performance outcomes that capture the delivery of a strategy, e.g., customer service or the brand value proposition, innovative behavior, the efficiency and effectiveness associated with an understanding of the organization's broader business model and performance context.
3. Distal or organizational performance outcomes associated with the organization's financial performance, e.g., the typical business unit dashboard measures of quality or financial performance that form part of the organization's service-profit chain.

However, what are the important antecedents that bring engagement about and therefore what is the most appropriate fulcrum around which organizational performance interventions must pivot and should be designed? Although organizations need to focus employee engagement around what it is they are trying to achieve, this engagement naturally exists outside of the world of strategy. Of course, performance-led HR also has to focus on employees and the external factors that drive their performance.

One of the ways in which engagement is understood is as the positive end of a continuum, with job burnout on the negative end, based around exhaustion, cynicism and inefficiency, and engagement on the positive end, based around energy, involvement and efficiency.[4] As such, engagement is seen as a persistent emotional (called affective) and mental (called cognitive) state. Much applied research treats engagement as:

> a positive attitude held by the employee toward the organization and its values. An engaged employee is aware of business context, and works with colleagues to improve performance within the job for the benefit of the organization. The organization must work to develop and nurture engagement, which requires a two-way relationship between employer and employee.[5]

THE DRIVERS OF POSITIVE ENGAGEMENT AND WELL-BEING

The antecedents of engagement include the job and personal resources afforded to an individual. It has proximal performance consequences (outlined above) that result from positive emotions, better health and the application by the individual of their job and personal resources.[6] This is called job demands-resources theory.

Feelings of loyalty, commitment and discretionary effort act as forms of social reciprocation by employees to a good employer. Engagement is expressed in two bonds – job engagement and organizational engagement – which are in turn based on a series of antecedent HR practices.[7] These HR practices create different levels of engagement through their impact on the characteristics of jobs, the level of organizational support that employees perceive they have, the quality of the employee–supervisor relationship, the nature of rewards and recognition, and the level of fairness in processes. Job and organizational engagement each predict different proximal performance outcomes. These may be employee-level proximal outcomes (such as job satisfaction, motivation, discretionary effort and commitment) or collective or group-level intermediate variables (such as morale, organization citizenship behaviors and contextual performance). This is called social exchange theory.

Individuals choose how much to invest in terms of different levels of cognitive involvement (their cognitive resources and mental energies), emotional involvement (satisfaction) and physical energies and efforts at persistence (motivation).[8] As work is a "performance" in its own right, at which we may be more or less convincing as an individual, the more people draw on their selves to perform their roles, the more stirring are their performances. Two assumptions are made about the link to performance:

- there is a hierarchy of engagement, beginning with physical, then cognitive and finally emotional attachment; and
- an important antecedent to engagement is person-job (P-J) fit or person-organization (P-O) fit.

There are, however, competing views about how engagement feeds into organizational performance:

- The *job attitudes cause performance perspective*, influenced by the human relations movement and more recent marketing literature, argues that attitudes facilitate and guide behavior, and serve to energize positive feelings, which in turn strengthen identification with the job, unit or organization, heightening motivation, which serves as either a component or a consequence of commitment.[9]
- The *performance causes job attitudes view*, influenced by expectancy theories of motivation but also some marketing research, argues that performance comes first, and this creates internal and external rewards which in turn create positive attitudes. An engaging environment stimulates discretionary employee actions, which cause improvements in intermediary outcomes (such as employee turnover or the customer perceptions of service quality discussed in Chapter 3), and these accumulate and result in improved financial performance.[10]
- The *reciprocal relationship view* argues that engagement and performance influence each other through bidirectional connections. Satisfaction and financial performance mutually reinforce each other. Within business units with more satisfied employees, employees engage in discretionary activities that benefit the organization, but financial success reinforces satisfaction, thereby leading to better pay, benefits and job security. However, the causal path that goes from employee perceptions to performance outcomes is stronger than the reverse, particularly in regard to things like employee retention and customer loyalty.[11] This reciprocal relationship requires there to be global satisfaction with one's organization.

6.3 Organizational well-being

6.3.1 The economic consequences of well-being

MATT STRIPE, GROUP HR DIRECTOR, NESTLÉ

For me the future HR issues fall into two critical areas:

- the future world of work; and
- organizational wellness.

The challenge for HR in the next five years is to break out from our functional constraints and really become the architects of the workplace of the future, which means changing our lens on the workplace and adopting a more holistic value stream approach. This starts with:

- What talent and capabilities does the organization need in the future?
- How do those people want to work, be led and connect to be engaged and effective?
- What technology is required to allow that to happen?
- Where in the world is that talent and where do we need it to be?
- Finally, if we need physical space, how does that support this culture?

This is a fundamental change of mindset as most organizations lead the development of these different components to their current functional owners: HR for people, IT or finance for technology and facilities for office design.

The second critical issue is employee wellness. Wearable technology will become the norm and therefore wellness and well-being will be critical components of the employee proposition. In the very near future, employees will be able to understand how the way they are being led is affecting their state. Imagine an employee bringing a grievance to a line manager using wearable technology to demonstrate his line manager is causing him stress in the workplace. Future leadership will be more transparent in this new reality and those who cannot adapt to this new world of work will be obsolete. The next generation of talent management will allow a measurement of the whole person with the use of analytics to include wellness and engagement dimensions alongside 360 data and climate surveys. From a manufacturing perspective, the new insights gained will force the reassessment of existing shift patterns and current ways of working. Finally, as organizational transparency becomes an increasing requirement to attract future talent, this data will be available to all.

We are beginning to see the consequences of the changing economic landscape throughout society and they are having an impact on organizational well-being and the way that organizations are beginning to think about this.

For example, in a recent national survey of UK families, the Centre for the Modern Family[12] found that as a consequence of the recession, 78 percent of the sample population felt that family life is tougher now than it was before the recession, with 20 percent reporting that they were struggling to cope financially and another 39 percent who were "just getting by." Indeed, only seven percent of the UK sample population was finding family life comfortable at present. In addition, three times as many families were saying that their financial problems were a more significant cause of stress compared to the percentage who saw the pressures of bringing up children as being the major cause of stress. What is encouraging in this national survey is the importance of the family network in providing financial and emotional support during times of hardship, with one in five reported as being able to borrow money from relatives, and 76 percent of young people claiming that during these difficult times, the family had been an enormous source of emotional support.

In terms of the workplace, the European Agency for Safely and Health at Work recently published its second European-wide opinion poll on Occupational Safety and Health,[13] which surveyed over 35,000 workers in 36 European countries. As a result of the continuing recession and downturn, 77 percent of respondents said they thought job-related stress would increase over the next five years, with only seven percent saying they thought that it was likely to decrease. This is not surprising, however, given the tough conditions currently being experienced throughout Europe and the increasing challenge of having "to do more with less human and other resources," with high levels of job insecurity, with the increasing demands on people working longer and longer hours and with a more robust management style prevalent as the excessive pressure from top management is increasingly being delegated downward throughout organizations. This stark statistic illustrates the work that still needs to be carried out to persuade senior management that improving the health and well-being of employees is a strategy for growth and not just for improving employee health. If we can convince employers that enhancing the engagement, well-being and resilience of employees, improving their work-life balance and reducing their excess pressure levels will positively impact productivity, and down the line bottom-line growth, then we might be going some way towards reducing the effects of job-related stress on both the workplace and individuals.

This link between well-being and growth is on the global agenda. As Jane-Llopis and colleagues recently highlighted:[14]

> In 2004, the Organisation for Economic Co-operation and Development (OECD) began its program to redefine progress to develop broader

understanding on what drives well-being of people and nations and what needs to be done to achieve greater progress. The European Union followed with its program on Beyond GDP. In 2008, Nicolas Sarkozy, President of France, launched the work of the Stiglitz Commission[15] and in 2010, David Cameron, Prime Minister of the United Kingdom, was the first national leader (outside Bhutan) to define well-being as his goal and to commission the United Kingdom's statistical service to measure population well-being as a national statistic. Under the leadership of Bhutan, the UN General Assembly passed a resolution in 2011 calling on governments to do more to promote the happiness of their people and mandating a UN conference that was held in April 2012 to further explore its implications.

6.3.2 The costs of a lack of mental well-being

Impaired mental health accounts for tremendous costs to society and businesses.[16] The economic cost to society is substantial: depression alone is estimated as absorbing one percent of Europe's gross domestic product; globally, mental ill health is estimated to account for a cumulative US$16 trillion global output loss in the next 20 years.[17] For individual companies, mental health is now often the most common cause of sickness absence in richer countries, accounting for 30–50 percent of all new disability benefit claims in OECD countries,[18] for up to 40 percent of time lost[19] and with presenteeism (lost productivity while at work) adding at least 1.5 times to the cost of absenteeism.

There have been major reports by the Health and Safety Executive (*The Management Standards on Work-related Stress*), the National Institute for Clinical Excellence (*Guidance on Stress Management Interventions*), the Government Office for Science Foresight Project on Mental Capital and Well-being and the Dame Carol Black's Work and Well-being overview in the Department of Work and Pensions. They all come up with roughly the same conclusions, based on the large amount of data available on the links between various aspects of the workplace and their stress or well-being outcomes (see Figure 6.1).

The science reviews from the Mental Capital and Well-Being report[20] found a number of workplace issues that lead to ill health and lack of well-being, based on a large number of science reviews. These are highlighted in Figure 6.1 above and all of these are also found in the other reports mentioned above. First, there is the issue of management style. There is a huge volume of work, which suggests that a bullying or abusive manager can damage

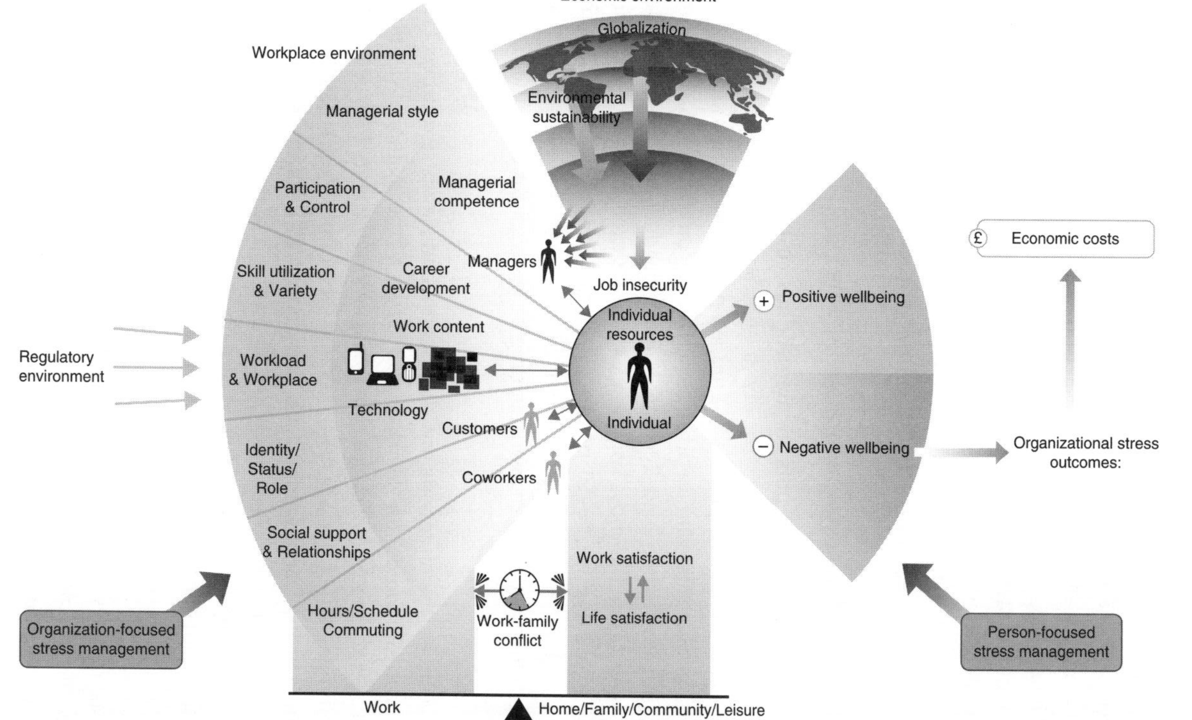

FIG 6.1 Well-being at work
Source: Foresight Mental Capital and Well-Being Project (2008)

people's health[21] (see the insert from Nestlé above). Managers who manage by praise and reward and not by constant fault-finding are likely to get the most out of their subordinates and will be less damaging impact on their health. Second, the issue of control and engagement is another source of well-being or stress. The more people have autonomy and control over their job, the healthier they are likely to be. Third, using people's potential and skill base, and the provision of job variety, are important for enhance well-being and lower stress levels. Related to this is their workload. The more an individual has an unmanageable or excessive workload, the higher the risk of ill health and lower productivity. Fourth, it is important for individuals to have a clear understanding of the nature of their role and status within the workplace. People who have ambiguous or conflicting roles are more vulnerable to stress, and their ill-health manifestations. Fifth is the issue of relationships. The worse an individual's relationship with colleagues, and particularly their boss, the more their well-being will be undermined and their health compromised. And finally, with the UK leading Europe in the longest working hours, the evidence is conclusive that consistently working long hours will damage your health, personal life and productivity in the long run.[22] Striking a better balance between work and life is fundamental to individual health and well-being.

6.3.3 Strategic stress management and enhancing well-being at work

The business case for well-being interventions is overwhelming. In 2008, PricewaterhouseCoopers assessed 55 wellness program interventions throughout industry, finding an average 45 percent reduction in sickness absence, 18 percent reduction in staff turnover, 16 percent reduction in accidents/injuries, an increase in employee job satisfaction of 14 percent, an eight percent increase in productivity and a drop of seven percent in health and employer liability insurance claims.[23]

So what should organizations do to manage the downsides of stress and enhance well-being? A three-pronged strategy for stress management in organizations has been suggested.[24] For the prevention and management of stress at work, the following three approaches represent a comprehensive strategic framework:

- primary prevention (e.g., stress reduction);
- secondary prevention (e.g., stress management); and
- tertiary prevention (e.g., employee assistance programs/workplace counselling).

STRATEGIES TO REDUCE WORKPLACE STRESS FACTORS

- Redesigning the task.
- Redesigning the working environment.
- Establishing flexible work schedules.
- Encouraging participative management.
- Including the employee in career development.
- Analyzing work roles and establishing goals.
- Providing social support and response.
- Building cohesive teams.
- Establishing fair employment policies.
- Sharing rewards.

Primary prevention is concerned with taking action to modify or eliminate sources of stress inherent in the work environment, thus reducing their negative impact on the individual. The focus of primary interventions is in adapting the environment to "fit" the individual. They are often a vehicle for culture change. The type of action required by an organization will vary according to the kind of stress factors operating. Therefore, any intervention needs to be guided by prior diagnosis or a stress audit, or risk assessment, to identify the specific factors responsible for employee stress.[25]

Secondary prevention is concerned with the prompt detection and management of experienced stress. This can be done by increasing awareness and improving the stress management skills of the individual through training and educative activities. Individual factors can alter or modify the way in which employees, exposed to workplace stress, perceive and react to their environment. Each individual has his or her own personal stress threshold, which is why some people thrive in a certain setting and others suffer. Awareness activities and skills training programs, designed to improve relations techniques, cognitive coping skills and work/lifestyle modification skills (e.g., time management courses or assertiveness training), have an important part to play in extending the individual's physical and psychological resources. The role of secondary prevention is, however, one of damage limitation. Often the consequences (rather than the sources) of stress, which may be inherent in the organization's structure or culture, are being dealt with. They are concerned with improving the "adaptability" of the individual to the environment. Consequently, this type of intervention is often described as "the band aid" approach. The implicit assumption is that the organization will not change,

but will continue to be stressful; therefore, the individual has to develop and strengthen his or her resistance to that stress.

Tertiary prevention is concerned with the treatment, rehabilitation and recovery process of individuals who have suffered, or are suffering, from serious ill health as a result of stress.[26]

Intervention at the tertiary level typically involves the provision of counselling services for employee problems in the work or personal domain. Such services are provided either by in-house counsellors or outside agencies, which provide counselling information and/or referral to appropriate treatment and support services. There is evidence to suggest that counselling is effective in improving the psychological well-being of employees and has considerable cost benefits.

Counselling can be particularly effective in helping employees deal with workplace stress that cannot be changed. It can also help non-work-related stress (bereavement, marital breakdown, etc.), which tends to spill over into work life.

6.3.4 Questions to ask about the well-being agenda

The following indicators represent some of the characteristics of a healthy workplace. It targets large and medium-sized organizations employing over 250 employees. It is not an exhaustive list, but represents the key activities that one would expect to see in an organization committed to the health and well-being of its employees. These are not simple "box-ticking" exercises. Some of them will require a process of continued monitoring and established procedures for dealing with any issues highlighted.

INDICATORS OF A HEALTHY WORKPLACE

Does your organization:

- Carry out an annual or bi-annual stress/well-being audit using a standardized psychometric instrument (for example, the ASSET an organizational stress screening tool or HSE's Management Standards) and are the results acted upon in an appropriate and timely fashion?
- Have an in-house counselling service or Employee Assistance Program provider, and do you use the data compiled from these services to identify problem areas within the organization and take action to resolve them?

- Provide resilience training for employees, across different levels of employee, with processes that encourage them to attend and that provide data on the level of attendance?
- Provide social skills or interpersonal training for line managers?
- Encourage flexible working arrangements, particularly notifying employees that they have the right to request flexible working? And do you monitor how many and who (e.g., gender or grade) takes it up and from which part of the organization?
- Have a bullying policy and a safe reporting procedure?
- Keep data on the working hours of your employees and attempt to ensure that they do not work excessive hours?
- Publish, as Key Performance Indicators (KPIs), data on job satisfaction, sickness absence rates and other potential indicators of well-being in your Annual Report?
- Have these same KPIs for line managers throughout the organization?
- Carry out an employee survey which is less comprehensive than a stress or well-being audit, but still have a rigorous procedure for ensuring that stress, bullying, poor work-life balance, etc. are dealt with appropriate and in a timely manner?
- Keep systematic records or details of the "causes" of sickness absence and make an effort at monitoring presenteeism in the organization?

6.4 The changing contours of fairness

The example provided at the beginning of the chapter from Nestlé, with the hidden consequences of people having wearable technology, reminds us that what is considered fair or not is changing, and there will be a cost to this. Should HR go where angels fear to tread and enter the perilous territory of fairness? Well, we believe they really have no choice.

HR functions have invested significant resources in employee engagement or insight units. However, if their broader set of HR policies triggers significant inequality of outcomes, perceived problems of justice, a lack of burden sharing and no sense of proportionality, will engagement only be skin deep? Without a broader strategy on fairness, will organizations be able to:

- sustain and deepen employee engagement?;
- develop organizational advocacy?;

- build an employer brand?;
- develop trust in the organization's customer centricity?
- take responsibility for individual well-being?;
- be seen to have authenticity (or not) in the values and competencies that its leadership models or talent systems promulgate?

6.4.1 The rising cost of fairness

It seems evident that a lack of fairness comes at a cost. In the US in 2007 the Level Playing Field Institute (LPFI) and the Center for Survey Research (CSR) estimated the number of Fortune 500 staff who left their employer because of unfair treatment study, based on a review of studies on discrimination, harassment and bullying, and then the cost of replacing them.[27] It also built in an estimate of disengagement and the fall in productivity of those who choose to ignore the unfair treatment or to deal with it themselves. On this calculation, unfairness in the workplace was estimated to cost US employers $64 billion each year – a new take on the $64 billion question! The situation in the UK seems little better.

IS FAIRNESS BECOMING AN ISSUE?

Data from the 2013 CIPD *Employee Outlook* survey showed that 41 percent of employees had encountered particularly unfair workplace behaviors in the past 12 months, 59 percent believed that the rules and agreed procedures were not applied consistently by decision makers, 49 percent believed that rewards were not distributed fairly and 64 percent felt that there was a lack of consultation among those who were affected by the implementation of decisions.[28] The most prevalent unfairnesses were around pay (freeze, long hours, senior management pay/bonuses, differences in pay), distribution of workload, bullying, victimization or harassment, or favoritism.

The Centre for Learning and Life Chances in Knowledge Economies and Societies (LLAKES) at the Institute of Education, London has run a Skills and Employment survey every five or six years since 1986, showing employment trends over time, funded by the Economic and Social Research Council.[29] Over 3,000 workers aged between 20 and 60 were interviewed in 2012, with the findings showing that British workers were at an all-time low for job satisfaction and security, and were feeling more pressurized at work than at any time in the past 20 years. A total of 52 percent of workers were concerned about the loss of job status, with the biggest concerns relating to pay reductions and loss of say over their job, and 31 percent were afraid of unfair treatment at work.

According to the 2014 CIPD/Halogen Employee Outlook survey,[30] 41 percent of employees reported excessive pressure at work every day or at least twice a week. Perceptions of pressure were statistically associated with lower satisfaction. A total of 30 percent of UK employees felt that their organization's performance management process was unfair. To be fair, 40 percent were happy with this process and did consider it to be fair, but nonetheless nearly a third of employees are clearly disengaged from a core HR process. Although levels of job satisfaction in the UK, with a 42 percent net satisfied score, had improved marginally by two percent from 2013 to 2014, job-seeking intentions were still high at 24 percent of employees, and trust in leaders was at a two-year low. Some 35 percent of UK employees felt engaged, and whilst only four percent would claim to be actively disengaged, 61 percent of employees were totally neutral about their employer. A total of 32 percent of employees felt that progression within their organization was unachievable and 20 percent felt that their managers did not effectively communicate objectives and expectations.

6.4.2 Whose problem is it?

Organizations and employees face significant challenges and one of the problems this is creating is that what is meant by "fair" in today's world is becoming a more complex judgment. People may disagree about whether something is fair or not – they may *see it differently* – but that is not necessarily the same as the situation actually *being* fair or unfair.

Although fairness refers to the idea that an action or decision is morally right, and these morals stem from philosophy, ethics, religion and law, in practice people make judgments about fairness not just as employees – they also make these judgments as consumers, parents and citizens. In addition, there is increasing transparency around what happens inside organizations and more vociferous social judgment. In any situation there are many allocations that could be considered as fair or not.

Fairness invokes questions about: the contextual equality of society, the expected division between society and organizations in supplying individuals with benefits; about opportunity; and about outcome. However, as we noted in Chapter 1, we are living through a period where substantial transfers of risk, responsibility and accountability are taking place, and these transfers are between markets, states, organizations and individuals – and indeed also amongst different generations. As we consider the future of work, therefore, and expectations of the employment deal, questions of fairness are becoming more complex.

Organizations are no longer happy to have standard 9-to-5 arrangements and expect employees to engage with the organization, and have a more effective and collaborative relationship, to deliver value over and above that which is definable in a job description and to encourage greater co-creation of value with employees. They recognize that there are different employee segments in their workforce and treat each segment as a separate internal market, each with its particular needs. They see the need to engage the whole person – to engage their employees as parents, as consumers, as citizens. Yet many issues hit the headlines daily and invoke deep questions about what is fair or not, including the following:

- pension provision;
- questions about the adequacy or excessiveness of rewards;
- use of zero-hours contracts;
- the quality of careers across age groups;
- the global sourcing of work; and
- social mobility.

Fairness has now become an issue at all levels of the organization:[31]

- At a strategic level, chief executive officers, boards, the senior leadership talent, investors and other stakeholders ask questions about the sustainability of an organization's values, the viability of its business models over the long term, the credibility and trust to be placed in its leadership, and its fairness to its suppliers, customers, shareholders and investors.
- Functions such as HR, marketing and logistics deal with fairness at a more tactical level, having to think about how fairness impacts the organization and its employer brand, corporate reputation, and the authenticity of its value proposition or employee voice.
- At an operational level, line managers, operations managers and those involved with quality assurance, health and safety have to cope with the

impact that "fairness" has on employee engagement, the delivery of service, the impact on quality, standards, health and safety, and strikes, and any breaks in service delivery.

- Finally, line managers are also instrumental in creating a workplace climate and positive (or otherwise) perceptions of fairness. Again, this has consequences. A recent study of over 2,000 UK employees showed the important role that leaders play in influencing the relationship between perception of unfairness and a series of important employee outcomes. Both employees' trust in their senior leadership and the quality of the relationship they have with their immediate supervisor mediated the relationship between perceptions of organizational unfairness and any negative consequences for their subsequent job satisfaction, advocacy and turnover intention respectively.[32]

We use everyday words to mean the same as fairness – equitable, impartial, unprejudiced, unbiased, objective and dispassionate. There is also a distinction between what seems equitable (or just) and what might in a more philosophical sense be seen as fair. For example, HR might have to find ways of rationing out flexible work hours. Whatever solution is arrived at may be perceived to be fair to some but unfair to others, so we fall back on what is the most "reasonable" solution, which is to have some kind of equitable (impartial and just) decision process – fair to all parties in that it is dictated by reason, conscience and conformity to legitimate rules or standards.

6.5 Five perspectives on fairness

We need to think about the implications for HRM of these challenges from a cross-disciplinary perspective. In order to signal the broader sets of expertise that are now needed inside HR, we lay out five different perspectives, or "lenses," on fairness. Each lens can be used to shed light on a range of issues and contexts faced in modern people management. In thinking about each lens, the important questions to ask are as follows:

- What seems to be the most appropriate lens for each scenario that the organization is faced with? (We believe of course that you need to apply all five to each issue, however...)
- Do some problems lend themselves to a dominant way of thinking? Different functions and professions within the organization tend to come from the different lenses. What assumptions might their disciplinary

background lead them to make and will these assumptions colour their core judgments and lead to blind spots?

- What does each lens in practice suggest about how employees or other relevant people might react to and deal with the issue?
- Can the broader set of lenses help clarify the organization's position?
- Can they help organizations ask the more intelligent questions and predict the judgments that employees are really making, and the actions and stances they will take?
- Do the different lenses help us to understand the different employee segments that exist?

Finally, and most importantly, we need to consider these questions. Are these issues best left to the other professionals who currently deal with them (as we shall see, the economists, the political and social policy experts, etc.)? Does and should HR play a role in these debates? If so, is it equipped to do so?

6.5.1 Organizational justice

The first lens on fairness and the one that is most familiar to HR professionals and line managers – hence our starting with it – is called organizational justice. We see this lens used around the design of management policies such as employee voice and employee engagement, or to help formulate key practices such as appraisal and performance management systems. It is used to think about the provision of access to important organizational resources, such as career systems, or information. It is important because an employee's perceptions of decisions as fair or unfair will influence many of their subsequent job attitudes and behaviors at work. It also draws attention to the possible behavioral reactions to unfairness – people may reduce inputs, increase outcomes, elect new referents or decide to leave or exit the situation.

SHOULD HR ENSURE THAT POLICIES ARE JUST?

The dominant paradigm in HR research on fairness is that of organizational justice. This gives attention to three judgments:

1. Distributive justice[33] concerns the fairness of allocated outcomes – the *problem* of how things should be distributed. Employees make judgments about the equity and inequity of a situation based on comparisons between themselves and others – an input-output ratio – comparing what a person perceives as having contributed with what they perceive they get

out of the exchange relationship. Whether it is "fair" depends on their point of comparison (their referents). This may be internal (one's self at an earlier time) or external (other individuals, groups, organizations and sectors). Outcomes are only equitable when they are awarded in proportion to their inputs (such as how hard they work or how productive they are).

2. Procedural justice[34] concerns the fairness of the process used in making outcome allocation decisions – *the best approach* to take. Employees are naturally attentive to the justice of events and situations in their everyday lives, such as issues related to perceptions of fair pay, equal opportunities for promotion and personnel selection procedure. Employees judge fairness based on four rules: a fair process requires all parties involved to be treated with respect (dignity); must treat (and be seen to treat) all individuals the same, applying consistent and transparent rules (equality); must take full account of all available information, exhaustively establishing the facts of each particular case (accuracy); and must be trusted by all parties as truly seeking a fair outcome for all (legitimacy).
3. Interactional justice[35] is about the quality of the interpersonal treatment that people receive when procedures are implemented. Employees judge fairness based on perceptions of their interpersonal treatment during the implementation of policies at work. They make two separate judgments: about how employees are treated (i.e., perceptions of respect and propriety by authorities, managers and their third parties); and about the accuracy and quality of explanations about procedures (i.e., the adequacy of the explanation, its timeliness, specificity, and truthfulness and authenticity).

6.5.2 Thinking about fairness in the executive pay debate

One of the criticisms leveled against HR has been its apparent inability to influence the design of legitimate executive bonuses and rewards incentives. In a recent initiative with the CIPD we used the example of the executive bonuses debate.[36] This debate draws upon the second fairness "lens," which concerns what is called the "socially just distribution of goods." The models that are used to justify "fairness" this way come from the field of economics and philosophy. This perspective seems to matter most in discussions of executive pay (fair pay), bonuses and rewards. It also has implications for industrial relations and is involved in consideration of social policy, such as welfare. Why is this important? Because it can be used to identify the typical rules or strategems that "players in the game" will likely first wish to follow and the fall-back positions taken. It can be used to predict the behaviors that are seen as breaking the rules, and the rational and emotional responses that are likely to follow.

Is the problem that HR risk operating out of their depth? The systems are designed by people who think like economists – their models assume we are at heart rational and calculating, and reactions can be predicted by weighting an individual's expected outcomes against the probability they think of this occurring. To one school of economists, rational means maximizing the individual chooser's expected utility. We play to rules depending on how we think the game works, and as long as the rules can be applied, we will accept the outcomes as long as it has some subjective benefit to our welfare:

- What is fair pay in today's corporate world?
- How might you better debate reward with an economist?
- What is socially just reward and what creates imbalanced, dysfunctional or socially harmful incentives?

The answer depends on how you believe people operate.

USING A GAME THEORY LENS: IS EXECUTIVE PAY BEING HANDLED FAIRLY?

Fairness is a matter of ensuring that the protocols adopted maximize the benefit to all the players in a game. Executive pay becomes unfair if the rules of the game are not working as they should. Seeing executive pay through a game theory[37] lens might trigger the following questions:

- Do people think that high levels of executive pay might be bearable in a non-zero-sum game (a game where the value of the pie can get bigger, and therefore increases in the size of the pie brought about by one person lead to more pie for everyone, so they can have a particularly large slice of pie)?
- However, in a zero-sum game, the pie is just divided up differently, so one person's bigger slice means a smaller slice for another. Is the problem that executive pay is sold to people on the grounds that everyone's pie will get larger, but people believe that it is really a zero-sum game (there are winners

and losers, and they are the losers)? We can also think about widening pay dispersion between the top and the bottom.

- Is the issue that you feel that executive pay is not actually driven by the rules of economics – i.e., the rules of the game can too easily be manipulated? So is the problem the fact that the form of payment that makes up the total cash compensation – for example, cash or shares – can be artificially manipulated? Or that executive pay is still rising despite declining business performance? Or that an insistence on belt-tightening among the general population who cannot manipulate rules is unfair when asked for by those who can?
- Or is the issue that those who govern the pay awards – the compensation committees – are themselves financially linked to the organization or the value of the currency (for example, shares) it uses as part of the reward for executives?
- Is the problem that the "relative" others against whom the level of rewards are being justified are part of a closed shop, a perceived cartel, inflating the mutual value of their rewards?

These are all complex questions, but are questions that would be asked about executive pay if you used a rational choice way of thinking about "fairness." However, are we in practice not so rational? Do we, should we, behave in more reciprocal ways?

Another school of economists attempts to describe what is seen as an ideal – normative – standard of justice (this is based on what is called the theory of justice).[38] Justice is whatever the best procedure results in. In an uncertain world, "fairness" is only what can be *justified*, not independently calculated. If you are tasked with designing a fair disciplinary procedure at work, is the fairest way to ask yourself "how would I design this if I knew I was going to be in the worst position my design creates?" and "how would I want this procedure to be set up if I were wrongly accused of a firing offence?" If you have the products of social co-operation – wealth, opportunities, rights, powers, freedoms and status – to divide between citizens, is the best solution to ask one of them to split these products into bundles any way they choose, but tell them that they will get the worst bundle that they make? The just distribution of social goods ends up being a more equal distribution, unless we can show that an unequal distribution improves the absolute position of the worst off

(perhaps by incentivizing the talented to do things such as becoming doctors or researching new forms of energy generation).

A RECIPROCAL VIEW ON EXECUTIVE PAY

- Is it the judgment of fairness based on what you believe is the true cause or source of organizational performance, and might this be perceived to be the efforts of others (the collective of the organization) rather than just the actions of some individuals?
- Does it make a difference what the timescale is to be used for the assessment of performance, or the restrictions on when the reward can be vested – if the reward is based on a short-term (for example, one-year) horizon, is this a true measure of performance or not?
- Is it that the social desirability of the non-salary perks (retirement plans, health insurance, properties and forms of travel) seem to require little return contribution to society in the form of taxation (so that it is a free good that is not fair)?
- Is the problem the level of risk-taking behavior that the system creates – the unintended consequences or perverse incentives?
- Is it because the organization providing the reward might have received money from other sources (for example, the government/taxpayer) and the perceived use of the reward is not seen to reflect the interests or aspirations of those providers?

6.5.3 The fair pay debate

We noted in Chapter 1 that pay in the UK is becoming more unevenly distributed, and the gap between the top one percent and the rest of the population has been widening steadily over the last decade. Such pay inequality poses a serious challenge to society and government, and also to HR functions. Various reviews such as the Hutton Review of Fair Pay have taken place. But what is this fair pay debate based on? The third lens on fairness then is based on what are called principles of outcome, again mainly driven by economists.[39] It is also used in discussions of executive pay, fair pay, pay distribution, corporate social responsibility, employment law and tribunal mediation, and in issues such as apprenticeships and access to social mobility opportunities.

On the one hand, arguments are set against what is called tournament theory – a model that is often used to justify the star-based talent systems (discussed in the next chapter) and high levels of differential reward. It argues that prizes should be fixed in advance and not based on absolute performance – just that relative to others in the same position. Rewards at higher levels of an organization serve to motivate and incentivize those at lower levels, who will strive to get promoted, either under a meritocratic model (where people should get what they deserve for their talent and hard work) or a market model (where people should get what the market will pay for their services). As long as the high performance of individuals striving for the next "prize" boosts the overall performance of the firm (i.e., increases the size of the cake for all), they are entitled to a greater distribution.

On the other hand, we see principles of outcome, such as norms of proportionality and ideas about luck and due desserts. Here pay is determined by two factors – the demands of a post as determined by the labour market and the contribution and performance of the post-holder. In making decisions on pay, managers believe that fairness cannot be understood as simply about equality of outcomes. Pay triggers judgments about an individual's "just deserts," which varies according to their differing contributions and choices and the extent to which the influence of chance and external circumstances is minimized. Both the processes and outcomes must be fair, and fair pay must therefore be proportional to an individual's contribution and set by fair pay determination processes. The value of an individual's contributions reflects both the weight of their particular posts and their actions and efforts within them. Some form of proportionality of treatment – whether in respect of need, merit or a mixture of both – implies limits on pay dispersion. The argument is then made that a maximum pay multiple is a mechanism for maintaining such limits, which as well as being morally desirable would bring instrumental benefits to organizations by supporting greater employee engagement and morale, as well as to society as a whole by helping to avoid inequality traps and assisting social mobility and incentives to productive work.

6.5.4 The women on boards debate

The fourth lens that we need to use on fairness has its roots in social policy research. It is called capability theory[40] and is used in the discussion of HR and social policies to deal with issues such as:

- diversity (for example, equal opportunities);
- discrimination (for example, age, gender, sexual orientation, disability, race discrimination);
- positive discrimination (for example, women on boards);
- corporate social responsibility issues (for example, child labour, wage exploitation, fair trade and supply chain standards);
- social mobility (for example, access to training or education).

The capability approach defines people's real freedom to act by realistically establishing what resources are available feasibly to achieve their desired outcomes. Although resources and income have a profound effect on what we can or cannot do, the capability approach recognizes that these are not the only things to be considered when establishing "fairness." It switches the focus from a means to a good life, to the freedom to achieve actual valued improvements in one's life.

People are able to focus on whether they have real freedoms (or not), i.e., are they able to value or access important resources (such as income, commodities and assets)? Every individual has innate potential which can be realized only through access to these valued resources, but there are individual differences in their ability to transform these resources into actions. Access to resources is important because this determines their real level of "functionings" (the choices people can realistically make to better their lives), i.e., what they are capable of (able to do), want to be capable of and should be capable of. But there is a distribution of opportunity within society. Therefore, people need the resources (the internal powers) to realize their desired functionings – but also the capabilities. They are not equally placed to realize their human capabilities, due to barriers arising from structural inequalities (such as class, race, disability, gender and sexual "oppression"). Policy therefore has to intervene to provide the additional assistance that some people may require to develop their capabilities and to transform them into functionings ("conversion factors"). In order to be "fair," policies have to make opportunities "real" and feasible in two ways:

1. They have to ensure access to valued resources in order to give people the substantive freedoms to transform their potential capability into desired functionings.
2. They have to help make this "conversion" easier. It is not just a case of putting people into the positions (for example, positive discrimination); you have to ensure they have the holistic opportunity to cope with all the other factors that enable success. There must be no hidden systemic barriers.

THE QUESTION OF WOMEN ON BOARDS

The debate acknowledges that based on women's merit alone, there should be many more represented at board level. It is not just the outcome (for example, the percentage of board members who are women) that can be used as a measure of fairness; it is also access to, and treatment by, a range of HR processes (selection, potential assessment, promotion and development). Many organizations rely too much on the "representation" measure and too little on the "process" measure. Despite the multi-faceted nature of the issue, the emancipation of women from systemic injustices justifies the application of a human rights approach to intervening robustly. The capabilities approach argues that we must look at all the factors that thwart women's progression and serve to intervene through policy to ensure fairer access to such resources and enhance their ability to translate this access and opportunities into desired outcomes.

6.5.5 Fairness and the pensions problem

The fifth and last lens on fairness that we introduce is that of temporal perspectives.[41] This lens is not a way of thinking about justice, as the previous four are, but it raises questions about a particular *problem of justice*. What do we owe to people who don't yet exist, or to the future existence of those who are now born? These ideas force us to ask questions about fairness from one generation to another – how fairly do we pass the baton over time? The lens draws upon theories of intergenerational equity and burden sharing. They have come from either:

- a legal perspective – are you sure you are not irretrievably compromising the subtle rights and obligations that are embedded in constitutions or other legal instruments?; or
- an environmental management perspective – are you allowing people the same resources, and access to these resources, that will give them the same freedoms of choice and action as you have or are you borrowing against someone else's future?

It features in discussions about pension funds, corporate social responsibility, corporate governance and the long-term viability of the organization, sustainable business models, human rights, the use of sovereign funds and how to deal with levels of debt (national, corporate and personal). What issues might this "lens" evoke? How does this help us "frame" the questions?

The first line of argument is that "fairness" is judged on how the baton is passed from one generation to another, and at any one moment in time the present generation may present this baton to the next generation in such a way that it irretrievably compromises key principles, such as constitutional rights, access to resources and the chance to benefit from those resources. Indeed, most national

constitutions actually convey a set of legal rights and obligations that create important conditions or constraints. For example, they dictate principles about access to power and authority, and access to a social pact. These principles are enshrined and apply across time – fundamental entitlements that must not knowingly be compromised. In other words, one party cannot "land grab" or "resource grab" across time in such a way that the next generation would find it impossible to implement the values within the constitution.

There is an implicit commitment of successive generations – a long-term perspective – concerned with the interests and rights of future generations as well as of people today to respect and maintain fundamental balances (inviolable rights), and this requires the commitment of those past and present to keep (at least) a minimum level of actual conditions so that the basic principles and values are feasible.

The second line of argument comes from what is called burden sharing. There are competing factions: each owning part of the nation's stock of exhaustible natural resources. To avoid this, all factions have to move on to burden-sharing views of fairness. This view is based on ideas of sustainable development, in turn defined as development that meets the needs of the present without compromising the ability of future generations to meet their own needs. It is driven by the efficiency principle, i.e., the argument that the current generation owe to the next generations – and must ensure that their current actions still leave – a set of conditions that ensure the same availability of important resources (for example, financial wealth, lack of debt and quality of the environment) necessary to maintain a certain standard of living and production capacity. To meet this obligation, the next generation must have the option or the capacity to be as well off as we are, for example, use of equity funds to maintain a sufficient level of money to ensure that the fund can always be a "guardian of the future against the claims of the present."

THE PENSIONS ISSUE THROUGH THE LENS OF INTERGENERATIONAL FAIRNESS

Asking whether the Baby Boom generation should pay more for their pensions raises problems of inter-generational fairness. The fundamental issue is one of the distribution of the burdens of population aging, lower fertility rates, rising life expectancy and how we face up to the financial consequences of these. It is not just whether we can redistribute the costs more equitably, but how we do this and whether we can look at which generation bears the cost of one part of the problem (for example, aging and pensions) without looking at another (for example, fertility rates). If the costs of pension promises made to sets of individuals historically, and at the time on a basis to be considered legitimate, are to be met in full, what are the adjustments that need to be made? Given that it is important that pensions are sustainable and affordable over the long term, an inter-generational "lens" on "fairness" triggers the following sorts of questions that need resolving:

- Societally, how can we be reassured that shared costs and contributions are being contained, and that the revenues taken from current and future contributors used to fund a pay-as-you-go pension benefit match the pension benefits of no-longer contributors?
- Is the degree and balance of fairness between the employee and the taxpayer based on sustainable principles over time?
- Are we paying fairly for the benefits that are being offered, and if we withdraw these benefits, are we being fairer to the next generation or denying them rights that their predecessors fought for?
- Are the costs of any reform process or those of the related consequences, such as welfare support for those with inadequate pensions or means-tested welfare payments, being borne fairly across different employee segments?
- Do the cross-subsidies still work in the same ways now, and into the future, or do we change the funding exchanges? Should those who are paid the least subsidize the pensions of those who earn the most in a defined benefit scheme or do you adjust benefits to career earnings?
- Is this best achieved by changes in the age at which pensions can be drawn to match the expected increases in longevity, cutting the value of pension benefits or increasing contributions?
- But then are the assumptions we make about longevity (that we will all be healthy for longer) simply based on extrapolations of statistics or based on a social reality – will all people have the resources to trade income for life expectancy? Will the current middle-aged sector of the population be as healthy in older years as a generation starved in youth through world wars? Are you modeling and joining up the correct data fairly?

- Is there a way to reform the system without a race to the bottom – without further eroding the value of these pensions – and for the majority, are these arrangements really gold-plated?

6.6 Conclusions

To conclude, as we move away from domestic markets into global markets, into more and more mergers and acquisitions, and in a world where the emerging economies will replace the aged economies of Europe and North America, individuals and their organizations will have less control over external events, but can control their own culture. It is safe to say that the three issues raised in this chapter – (dis)engagement, stress and well-being, and fairness – are here to stay and cannot be dismissed as simply a bygone remnant of the pre-recession decades prior to 2008. The challenge for HRM in the future is to understand that developing and maintaining a "feel good" factor at work and in our economy generally should be about enhancing the quality of working life and well-being of our employees, from top floor to shop floor. As the social commentator Studs Terkel once wrote:

> Work is about a search for daily meaning as well as daily bread, for recognition as well as cash, for astonishment rather than torpor, for a sort of life rather than a Monday through Friday sort of dying.[42]

HR has the capability of beginning to action its frequently heard rhetoric "the most valuable resource we have is our human resource." This will not only help our growth agenda and GDP per capita, but will also create the quality of life aspects of what all our societal institutions – business, government and NGOs – should be supporting. It was in 1968 that Bobby Kennedy summed this up nicely as he was campaigning for the nomination as the Democratic candidate for the presidency of the USA:

> Too much and for too long, we seemed to have surrendered personal excellence and community values in the mere accumulation of material things ... Yet the Gross National Product (GNP) does not allow for the health of our children, the quality of their education or the joy of their play. It does not include the beauty of our poetry or the strength of our marriages, the intelligence of our public debate or the integrity of our public

> officials. It measures neither our wit nor our courage, neither our wisdom nor our learning, neither our compassion nor our devotion to our country. It measures everything in short, except that which makes life worthwhile.[43]

We believe that employee engagement, organizational well-being and fairness are worthy design criteria for the sorts of HR functions that will still be needed in the future.

chapter 7

Strategic Talent Management

7.1 Introduction

In Chapters 2, 3, 4 and 5 we laid out a series of strategic performance drivers that organizations continue to grapple with. One of the ways that organizations are responding to these challenges is to become much more analytical – they are bringing skills around big data and HR analytics to the fore, a discipline that itself draws upon some of the ideas about human capital (or workforce) analytics or accounting (HCA) and later also on strategic workforce planning (SWP). What ties all of these developments together is the question of talent – and our changing understanding about what makes people talented in today's business environment. We have clearly entered an environment of unprecedented business risk – nations are pitched against capital markets, markets could disappear overnight along with the ability to finance business models, and consumer behavior may take years to revert to normality, or indeed may start to create a new normality. As organizations continue to navigate their way through turbulent waters, even as business confidence is returning, the demands placed upon those deemed to be leading talent are extreme.

In this chapter we shall make it clear that talent management has to about marshaling thoughtful strategy. The recent crisis has laid bare in many instances the (limited) depth of talent that many organizations really have. We need to put the strategy back in talent.

Two questions have been asked of the undoubtedly sophisticated pre-financial crisis talent management systems and continue to dog our current systems and capabilities:

1. Did the financial crisis show that the wrong people were in some key roles, i.e., should the talent management system give more attention to risk management?
2. Given that the reality now is the need to manage in a very unstable environment, do organizations need to evidence different competencies?

We consider the answer to both questions to be yes. This signals a number of challenges that organizations now need to address:

1. As evidenced in the previous chapters, the new realities raise deep questions about the sorts of skill sets needed by top talent. In our previous book *Leading HR* we noted that by 2010, 59 percent of HR Directors reported that the organizational capabilities featured in their planning processes were new to the strategy. A total of 40 percent reported that there had been a shift in the jobs, roles or skill groups that were consequently seen as critical to performance.
2. Given the natural limitations of strategic leaders who now operate in a hypercompetitive business system – strategic leadership in a world turned upside down – can we risk top teams having illusions of control or escalating their commitment to what might be a defunct strategy? We have to both sharpen up and also de-risk our talent systems.
3. There is also a gap between the *intentions* asserted by many organizations (their assertions that everyone has talents) *and the existing processes* that they have put in place (the central systems that may only focus on a handful of high talent). To deal with this tension, many organizations have been decentralizing their talent management operations, handing over responsibility to line managers for the conduct of wider review processes.
4. At the same time, competitive forces are requiring organizations to take control of the skills supply chain through the use of more forward planning activity, such as strategic workforce planning. Many organizations are also having to globalize their talent systems.

So how should we make the necessary changes to our people management? To answer this, we first need to take us through the complex and contested topic of talent management, laying out the practical and the academic issues and challenges that this aspect of HRM lays bare.

7.2 How did HR capture the talent management agenda?

The intellectual roots of talent management were in the human resource planning movement of the 1980s and early 1990s. This movement focused on forecasting of staffing needs to meet business needs and the need for activities, such as planning and managing staffing needs, succession planning and short-term management development moves. Around the same time, organizations began to integrate previously separate resourcing and career development traditions into a life-cycle perspective. Talent management began to be seen as involving cradle-to-grave processes to recruit, develop and retain employees within an organization[1] or as an integrated set of processes and procedures used to attract, onboard, retain, develop, move and exit talent in order to achieve strategic objectives.[2] This life-cycle management thinking was applied in the first instance just to a small group of high-value managers.

By the late 1990s and early 2000s, talent management was being used as a label in its own right, with debate focusing on how organizations could develop, sustain and manage talent pools, engrain a talent mindset in the culture of an organization, align various HR programs and processes to the needs of talent, and understand how to pursue talent strategies that balanced recruitment versus the development of talent. It was argued that organizations should see talent as a strategic resource and source of competitive advantage.[3]

In parallel with this was the emergence of the argument that the HR function should be seen as a strategic business partner.

Structurally, a role emerged in some larger organizations that focused upon the general stewardship of a cadre of senior managers and directors, typically the top 500 employees. It was often the Head of Resourcing role that was the one that was developing into that of Talent Director. Their responsibilities included the systematic attraction, identification, development, engagement/retention and deployment of the senior cadre, which meant role rotation, development, identifying those members of the cadre with the highest potential for board level roles and, where necessary, the exits of low-performing members.

These emerging Talent Directors became important players in the HR hierarchy, because CEOs, and the boards they led, became increasingly aware of the need to possess talented employees in terms of competitive advantage. The portfolio of responsibilities for many Talent Directors included high potential identification, succession planning, critical role analysis, external search and recruitment, executive strength benchmarking and in some organizations performance management and strategic workforce planning. A key output for many Talent Directors was the periodic production of Talent Review reports for the board to assess the overall level of competitive advantage. Still a sub-function of HRM, talent management began to emerge and develop its own identity as the internal talent teams inside organizations looked for frameworks that would aid the categorization of all their managerial employees, in particular, frameworks that would identify and highlight so-called high potentials.

7.3 Talent management in theory and in practice

However, talent management still meant many things in practice. It could refer to the specific competencies, capabilities and talents that very effective people have, to the individuals who have such talents, groups and pools of such people, or be used collectively to refer to the entire employee population. It could refer to specific HR processes or component practices involved in the management of the above. It might be seen as an outcome of such processes or as a goal of the HR strategy. These outcomes or goals in turn might be expressed as a set of metrics, standards or achievements that the rest of the organization holds the HR function to account for. In earlier work,[4] we have noted that the talent strategy of any one organization varies across what we called "4 Ps": Philosophy, Providers, Practices and Principles.

We shall lay out the four different philosophies noted in Figure 7.1 later in the chapter, but at this point we wish to signal that each of these philosophies makes some very different assumptions about how talent systems should work and how they create value for the organization. However, at this stage it is important to note that in addition to the different philosophies, the systems that HR has pursued *also* differ depending on whether the providers of some of the key tools and activities have been occupational psychologists, HR development specialists or executive search consultants. This is important because the models of performance and potential – what is under the bonnet – differ across these providers. The range and scope of practices that get bundled together under the label of talent management also vary across organizations, so some might tie talent assessments tightly into performance management and rewards, while others might focus on the internal workforce, and others put energy and effort into building secure pipelines of external talent, shaping the employer brand. Systems might be more or less globally integrated or local market and business unit-driven. Finally, at least after the global financial

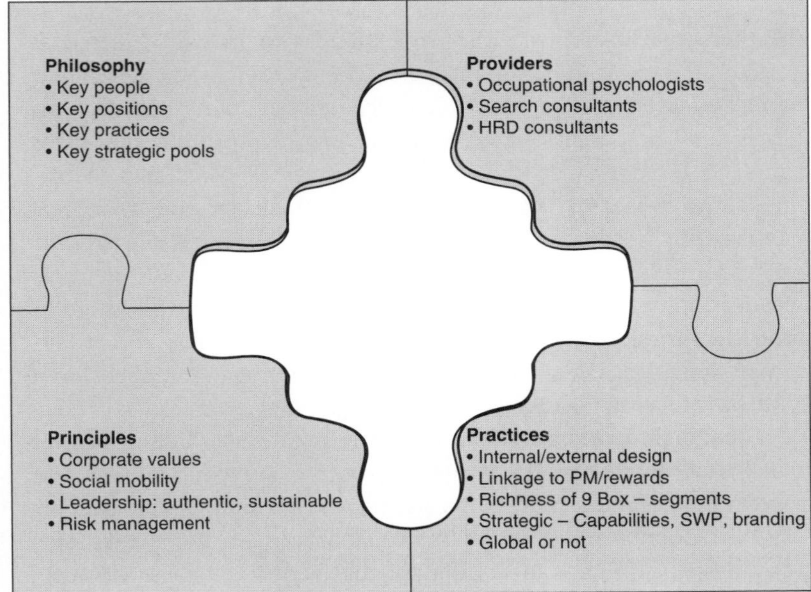

FIG 7.1 The 4Ps of talent strategy
© CPHR 2011

services crisis, organizations might try and force certain principles or values into the way talent is managed, drawing attention to models of leadership that are based on sustainability or authentic behavior, or requiring more risk-based assessments around who is talent and who is not. In short, you do not have to dig very deep into an organization's talent system to understand how unique, idiosyncratic and difficult to benchmark it really is.

However, that said, for the majority of organizations, as shown below, talent management has come to operate around a few core technologies and tools – notably systems that categorize people as talented based on evaluations of their performance and potential.

TYPICAL TALENT MANAGEMENT SYSTEMS AT THE BEGINNING OF THE 2010S

Most large organizations had defined their talent processes by the turn of this decade, since which time processes have been periodically refreshed, but the core architecture has remained the same.

For an organization like IBM, the talent system was directed at building their leadership pipeline. The Leadership Acceleration and Development System (LEADS) brought pipeline data into an integrated database, enabling Talent Insight reporting on issues such as gender diversity and global resources. Managers identified employees for the talent pool (the Business and Technical Leadership Resources) through a Pipeline Identification Process that identified employee potential for both business and technical leadership, whilst Business and Technical Leadership Partners in the HR function managed the cycle of talent reviews and placement activities. There were three talent segments: employees on a pathway to senior leadership; senior employees on a path to executive leadership; and the pool of existing executives. Talent reviews facilitated the placement of talent across the lines of business, and individual development plans, managed through a CareerSmart system, documented the actions to close gaps in the capabilities, competencies and skills required to build leaders critical to the business. For technical leadership, attributes such as providing industry insight, managing major projects, selling, consulting, defining system architectures and enabling IT solutions were tracked.

In contrast, within the UK civil service, the system had to be seen as fair and open, and when filling senior vacancies, diversity of talent was seen as critical to future success. It was driven by the philosophy that everyone has talent, with a 70/30 focus on growing internal talent. Mainstream development programs were mandatory, universal and linked to standards. Tiers of different processes open up as one advances up the hierarchy. At lower levels – the 88 percent or so of frontline staff or managers – two populations were managed: a fast stream group and "Reach" programs to target under-represented groups. The top 12 percent of the hierarchy were tracked by People Development Forums, which identified three elements: critical roles and the characteristics of those roles, emergency cover and succession for these roles, and development opportunities; the strengths and development needs of people, their next moves and risks of attrition; and contextual organization data such as demographic data, attrition levels and engagement scores. Middle management levels – about 10 percent of employees – were seen as early talent. Less than two percent of employees at senior management levels were emerging talent and only around 0.3 percent of staff as senior civil service directors were part of an executive talent pool. Talent management processes were kept simple and created two talent pools: fit for future individuals identified with potential for future senior roles; and fit for now individuals capable of addressing current business goals and plans.

At BAE Systems, there were five mandated core business management processes to support the delivery of corporate strategy and foster high performance. Talent management was seen within a business performance context. An annual Integrated Business Planning process was used by individual businesses to establish and plan for the delivery of objectives in line with corporate strategy, supported by quarterly business reviews, customer reviews and data from employee surveys. Project performance was assessed by Contract Reviews. Performance was reviewed throughout the year through the Performance Management Process. A Performance Centered Leadership framework was used to integrate management, resourcing and people development, focusing on the traditional outcomes of performance (financial, project and behavioral), reward and development. There was behavioral performance feedback and a performance-potential rating (called Spectrum). Line leaders and functional directors ensured the framework was implemented. HR's role was one of assisting in development interventions and providing some oversight and governance of the processes.

At Nestlé, international experience was highly valued. At any one time, the international assignment program covered around 4,000 employees. The organization had both an informal network and *also* a hierarchical leadership culture. Talent management was driven by the need to move people globally and manage replacement. Managers took pride in "knowing their people" but were also "process-oriented." Talent management was defined as the development of a supply of right skills for the business and was embedded in the strategic business planning cycle. At the market (country) level, a series of overlapping processes shaped the talent process. Local HR, in each market, ran an aligned career development cycle, identifying market-critical positions, leading management development initiatives and validating the corporate talent calibrations. Senior leaders ran Talent days in which they reviewed data for the top 50 managers in each market. Factory heads identified issues such as retaining technical knowledge or recruitment shortages. A common global approach was then identified, and attention shifted from the management of a cadre of high potentials towards a system where all managers had to grow their business and grow their "people" – a view that everyone had potential. Transparency and validity became important, which meant the talent management process had to be understood by all. Calibration was on a 9 Box performance-potential matrix, with data globally integrated, and the leadership framework and curriculum was driven by values and behaviors. Individuals received development plans, 360-degree feedback and online tools were developed. HR's role was to be a facilitator and "broker" of the system, with HR expertise for talent management residing across Centres, covering resourcing, talent and people development and organization development, and a network of HR Business Partners.

By 2010, talent management had received a remarkable degree of practitioner interest, but, intriguingly, academic interest specifically in talent management, only really began after 2010, as evidenced by a number of special issues published on the topic in the last four years.[5] This work has started to delineate the topical research issues and build a community of academics. Given the potted evolution noted above, academic articles on talent management continue to demonstrate:

1. there is no precise definition of what is meant by talent management, a problem which is slowing down the development of the field;[6]
2. there is no consensus around the intellectual boundaries that will help us understand the topic and design the best systems;[7]
3. until recently, discussions around the practice of talent management have been dominated by study of Anglo-Saxon organizations and by the analysis of US academics;[8]
4. the effectiveness of and types of talent management activities have yet to be fully understood in different national contexts and in different types

of organizations,[9] and in the context of the different strategic capabilities firms might be pursuing;[10]

5. there has also been a lack of theoretical development in the area.[11]

The field of talent management is then maturing, but is being impeded both by the scale of debates taking place and the fact that many of these debates bring about different values, assumptions, allegiances and philosophies. Yet, despite such debate, the field of talent management makes a series of implicit value claims, some of which are taken for granted, while others are more tentative. Even within the general management literature, let alone that on talent management, there is still disagreement about what value creation actually is.[12]

The same observation could be applied to the talent management literature. We argue that in order to understand which elements of talent management are the most valuable for organizational performance (or effectiveness), we need to ask the deeper question, which is how does a talent management architecture generate value? For HR practitioners, this question is one of being able to articulate and argue what the return on investment is on the organization's approach to talent management. For academic researchers, the issue is one of clarifying the link between talent management and value creation, and using this to direct future research efforts. In the next chapter we do this by incorporating understanding from a range of other literatures, notably: the resource-based view of the firm; the organizational and dynamic capability perspective; global knowledge management; and concepts of value creation, capture, leverage and protection.

However, we first need to demonstrate the existing tacit or explicit assumptions about the value of talent management. Talent management philosophies are underwritten by beliefs about how organizations work and values as to how they should work. For some, these philosophies differ on two dimensions:[13]

- assumptions about whether talent is exclusive or developable in all; and
- whether it is a stable and enduring trait or a temporary potential.

Another way of laying out different philosophies is to consider the focus of attention that each philosophy engenders. Four of these have been outlined:[14]

1. People approach: talent management as a categorization of people.
2. Practices approach: talent management as the presence of key HRM practices.
3. Position approach: talent management as the identification of pivotal positions.

4. Strategic pools approach: talent management as internal talent pools and succession planning.

However, one of the challenges the field faces is that the various philosophies tend to be presented as competing approaches to and alternative conceptualizations and definitions of talent management, and better or worse ways of doing it. We use this categorization to discuss the nature of strategic talent management, outlining the assumptions about human capital that are implicit in each, the resultant practices and strategies that are signaled, the implicit dilemmas and their subsequent critiques.

7.4 Categorizing people

This philosophy focuses on the people (not the practices) aspects of talent management and the differential management of a small elite of employees with unique skill sets – their skills (in the broadest sense) are assumed to be rare, hard to find, difficult to replace, and to add a disproportionate amount of value to the organization compared to other employees.[15] Such individuals are therefore much sought-after by competing organizations. The philosophy advocates differentiating the management of these people using practices designed to attract, retain and develop high-performance and high-potential employees.

PEOPLE AS A STRATEGIC PORTFOLIO

George Odiorne[16] recommended utilizing the Boston Consulting Group strategic portfolio matrix as the basis for constructing what he termed a "Human Resources Portfolio." By the early 1990s, many HR functions were basing their high-potential identification and succession management practices around frameworks that were derivatives of Odiorne's Human Resource Portfolio and this portfolio approach provided an influential framework for early Talent System architecture. Odiorne felt that potential was best seen as the likelihood of the job holder making a future contribution to the organization, and this was felt to be based on six factors:

1. past performance
2. intelligence and aptitude
3. future availability to the organization
4. interests and desires

5. supply and demand factors
6. and biographical information.

Talent management practitioners converted the original strategic product market portfolios of business units (that could be categorized as stars, cash cows, problem children and dogs), through to a human resources portfolio of high-low potential and high-low performance (which categorized people as stars, work horses, problem children and deadwood), to the now ubiquitous 9-Box model which uses a 3x3 differentiation. The message was clear: HR was the function that categorized people, and people represented a strategic portfolio.

Although the categorization and differentiation philosophy was famously captured in the *War for Talent* dialogue of the late 1990s, it is actually underpinned by three enabling concepts, each with long prior histories.[17] Even those who ended up disliking the War for Talent mentality (and it still has plenty of supporters) might be prepared to accept the following three insights that led up to it.

THREE IDEAS THAT ENABLED THE WAR FOR TALENT DEBATE

As noted above, an implicit strategic portfolios approach that differentiates investments in people (in the same way as businesses were placed in a portfolio) on a two-dimensional matrix of performance versus potential.[18]

There was a belief that businesses were at a moment of dramatic change – an inflexion point – that required a significant shift in policy, because "informated" workplaces (designed for the circulation of information) and their more fluid, social, distributed and less hierarchical work arrangements were changing the value of talent by upgrading the need for people with intellective skills, i.e. those defined as having the power to understand business and the social opportunities that now existed.[19]

The individualization of organizations and understanding of management competencies, shifting organizations and their selection systems from a pay-for-the-job approach (which assumed that jobs could be designed, evaluated and differentiated depending on their size and complexity, and employees fitted to the job) to a pay-for-the-person approach (which argued that jobs were too flexible, uncertain and unpredictable to be "sized," so HR systems must enable highly skilled people with job-crafting capabilities to design their jobs in the most appropriate ways).[20]

The key people philosophy implicitly stresses two competitions: one between individual talent (an inter-personal talent management focus) and one within the individual so that they could "be of their best" (an intra-personal talent perspective). The inter-personal competition was couched in terms of a series of competitive HR and marketing strategies and a cultural *mindset*, designed to land and "upskill" employees in a cut-throat free-agent employment market, to position talent management as a leadership imperative and to require attention to be paid to underperformance through explicit categorization and segmentation of employees into A, B and C players, with the elite recruited, retained and lavishly rewarded, and the tail slowly removed from the system.[21] This required an underpinning of internal (employee value propositions) and external (employer brand and market mapping) marketing to drive attraction and retention behavior and convey statements of explicit obligations that the organization would commit to for talent.

Two forms of competition become important:

- competition between people (inter-personal); and
- competition within oneself to be of one's best (intra-personal).

This inter-personal versus intra-personal distinction is best seen as part of the giftedness or excellence literature,[22] which stresses that high-level performances are not feasible for everyone, hence the justification for differential investments, with the caveat that an intra-personal perspective also lends credence to a more egalitarian and positive psychology view that everyone has talents and can improve their effectiveness. The notion of an intra-personal competition, concerned with the need to maintain peak personal performance and avoid career derailment, is couched in the language of sports psychology and coaching.

Interestingly, academic insight into the dysfunctional consequences of over-relying on a star-based talent system pre-dated by about eight years the subsequent post-financial crisis acceptance that perhaps organizations (and their HR functions) had designed inappropriate talent systems. It was in around

2000 that the warnings first started to appear – only a couple of years after the consultants at McKinsey had pushed the War for Talent agenda. The categorization of people philosophy has attracted three different but unco-ordinated criticisms, some pre-dating the excesses that led to the global financial services crisis, others coming after the fact.

The first criticism concerns where the real *locus of organizational effectiveness* lies. This argument, based on studies of productive systems or CEO failure,[23] objects to the proposition that human capital, rather than systems, is the primary source of competitive advantage.[24]

PROBLEM 1: IS FIGHTING THE WAR FOR TALENT HAZARDOUS FOR YOUR HEALTH?

Jeffrey Pfeffer famously considered that fighting the war for talent, which emphasized a fight for sourcing talented individuals, was hazardous to an organization's health:

> The consultants at McKinsey were preaching at Enron what they believed about themselves. They were there looking for people who had the talent to think outside the box. It never occurred to them that, if everyone had to think out of the box, may be it was the box that needed fixing.

His key objections were as follows:

1. The star approach to talent shifts the emphasis on individual performance at the expense of teamwork and gives rise to a system that can create disharmony between employees who otherwise need to work collaboratively. The HR practices that go along with such an approach, for example, individual-based performance-related pay, can make it hard to share knowledge, ideas and best practices.
2. The celebration of individual brilliance can lead to an elitist attitude marked by arrogance and a poor learning attitude, where those dubbed as "Stars" have their way over an otherwise perfectly good idea coming from a "B" or "C" player.
3. The very fact that most companies that adopt the "A" player approach to talent management rely heavily on monetary incentives to attract and retain these key individuals makes this approach non-strategic as it is easily imitable. If money is the

major motive behind the functioning of these star performers, other companies can offer more money and lure away these stars. Retention of stars tied to a company only through monetary incentives is big problem.

4. Probably one of the biggest issues is how to treat employees labeled as "C" players. Labeling by itself can have damaging effect on the performance of these employees, leading to a negative self-fulfilling prophecy. Lower expectations leads to less resources being available to these employees and can lead to demoralization and thus poor performance; exactly the opposite becomes true for the "A" players.
5. The "star" perspective on talent also seems to suggest individual ability as a fixed invariant trait, which is again a dangerous assumption that is not supported by research. There is ample evidence that performance appraisals, the bedrock of the "star" approach to talent management, are susceptible to the horn and halo effect, i.e., a tendency to allow one's judgment of another person to be unduly influenced by an unfavorable (horns) or favorable (halo) first impression. Past performances can bias a supervisor's judgment of current performance and future potential.

As outlined above, this argues that a focus on elite human capital (i.e., people, or stars) is the wrong fulcrum for improving effectiveness, detracting attention from the right fulcrum (which is systems), and some of the practices that the philosophy creates (e.g., the level of reward given to those differentiated by the system) create a set of side-effects in terms of behavior and performance that nullify any returns on human capital.

COUNTERPOINT: THE FORCED RANKING DEBATE

Is it right to be critical of a full-blown forced ranking and an extreme differentiation approach within talent management? Certainly, forced ranking has not been well received by history and the cultural backlash is palpable. Another business crisis would destroy any remaining pragmatic support for the practice. However, what constitutes "forced ranking" (less flatteringly known as the "rank and yank" system, but also variously called Topgrading, the Vitality Curve, Forced Distribution or Differentiation) of performance management is still open to debate and practices are often not clear in terms of how differentiation happens in practice. The operation of Talent Systems has suffered, in terms of their effectiveness, from issues of manager patronage, leading to an inability to really differentiate high potentials from what could be termed "solid citizen" managers. As a consequence, some organizations introduced forced ranking/forced distribution of their management population in an attempt to create a performance management culture. Talent Directors are divided about its benefits and in practice, even if they do use it, may adopt a softer version that can be called guided or shaped distribution (i.e., an emphasis on teasing out differences but with less differentiation of reward and softer management of underperformance based on these data). Advocates point to the following advantages: it can jolt managers out of complacency, combat artificially inflated performance ratings, and reduce favouritism, nepotism and promotions that may be based on factors other than performance. It might raise significant variations in the talent data provided by the performance appraisal system and the data provided by the forced ranking process. However, there are also pragmatic doubts that the data used to rank performance may be robust enough – or perceived to be discrimination-free enough – to withstand potential legal issues. Transparency also remains a challenge. Sadly, the forced ranking debate will run on and on, but whilst the practice remains, there is a risk that in taking a forced ranking approach, organizations will continue to be tempted to narrow their definition of what they mean by potential.

The second criticism of an over-reliance on a star-based talent system also dates back to 2000. This has been called the *cognitive limits* problem.[25] Derived from work on management cognition and the psychology of strategic management, researchers asked "how could organizations with high-profile and historically successful track records fall prey to catastrophic chains of events that led to their demise?" Drawing attention to limitations in the mental models of strategic leaders operating in a hypercompetitive business system, it suggested two bellwether judgments be made about the knowledge possessed by talent:

- is the individual capable of high-quality strategic thought?; and
- does the "capital" that they possess enable them to make a potential contribution to value creation?

These researchers argued that organizations needed to build their "strategic competence." This strategic competence was defined as the ability of organizations (or more precisely their members) to acquire, store, recall, interpret and act upon information of relevance to the longer-term survival and well-being of the organization. Being able to effectively capture value from talent was therefore a very risky venture. It also meant that organizations needed their talent management system to be embedded in a broader knowledge management and organization cognition framework.

Talent (in an organizational context as opposed to the many other human endeavors) therefore must be defined in the broadest sense to include:[26]

- human capital;
- social capital;
- reputational/political capital; and
- business model (intellectual) capital.

The third criticism concerns the level of balance between a categorization approach and other parts of a talent system (or the attention given to other employee segments). There are two strands to this argument. It reflects either:

1. an organization effectiveness and design perspective – this perspective argues that whilst star talent management is necessary, it is not sufficient. Organizations must therefore seek a balance between sourcing great individual talent and building such talent into a more collective organizational capability by ensuring that the knowledge of star talent is turned into the actual delivery of performance by the whole organization;[27] or
2. a critique based on cultural discomfort with a differentiated approach to talent and argument that a more egalitarian, universal and inclusive focus that looks at talent management practices as it relates to the majority of all employees is needed.[28]

From the preceding review and analysis, it can be seen that a series of claims is made about value generation through a talent management approach.

DO WE NEED A CATEGORIZATION OF PEOPLE APPROACH TO TALENT MANAGEMENT?

The categorization of people perspective makes the following arguments about value generation:

- the "informating" of work has changed the potential value of talent and has increased the level of power, business and social opportunity open to those with intellective skills;
- consequently, those elite managers (or expert talent) that possess such intellective skills can generate value (create value) for an organization in a disproportionate manner. Therefore, organizations should prioritize and invest their limited investment resources on their elite managers first;
- however, this raises the need to understand the true locus of organizational effectiveness and how elite human capital interfaces with more systemic sources of organizational performance (for example, systems or broader organizational capabilities);
- in turn, this draws attention to the cognitive limitations of strategic actors and therefore the need to leverage whatever insights human capital as a collective has through knowledge transfer, thereby understanding how individual elite talent is embedded in a broader capability system, i.e., seeing talent management as one (and only one) mechanism for building and distributing broader capability around the organization.

7.5 Key practices needed for talent management

The second talent management philosophy is the Practices approach. Whilst the People approach outlined above argues that the differentiator for high-performing firms is *not* sophisticated HRM processes, but rather a fundamental belief held by leaders throughout the organization about the importance of individual talent and the creation of internal "talent markets," the Practices approach acknowledges that there is a need for a dedicated set of advanced and sophisticated practices.

This reflects arguments aired in the HR bundles debate,[29] with talent management being seen as a collection of key activities, components or practices, all of which need to be connected and integrated. These component practices have to be more than just a string of HR programs, practices and processes, and have to form part of a broader system and core business process, matched to the business strategy.[30] This philosophy therefore adopts much of the thinking implicit in the HR architectures literature.[31]

We explained the notion of HR architectures in Chapter 4 when we discussed the challenges of implementing lean management. To recap, an HR architecture is reflected in a combination of the systems, practices, competencies (skills) and employee role behaviors needed to develop and manage the firm's strategic human capital.

In terms of delivering competitive advantage, it should also be evident from the previous chapters that different strategies (we have discussed innovation, customer centricity, lean management and collaborative business models) each emphasize different internal business processes.[32] Indeed, we made it very clear in Chapter 2 that the leadership models and social capital needed to manage innovation are quite distinct.

Therefore, when thinking about the sorts of talent that are needed and which talent will prove to be successful, it seems evident that the skill sets that will end up being critical for the creation of value are different across the various performance outcomes we have discussed in previous chapters. The business processes involved in innovation, customer centricity, lean management and collaborative arrangements place different demands on talent. They also need the HR architecture to be different, as these systems will depend upon the sort of strategic outcomes that the organization is trying to achieve.

There are different prescriptions of what the bundle of talent management practices should be, and the descriptions are usually case study-based. For example, one leading team of talent specialists has identified three important sets of practices:[33]

1. to establish clear strategic priorities and shape the way high-potential leaders must be groomed and aligned with corporate strategy programs;
2. to ensure careful selection of candidates and communication of who is in the pool to the rest of the organization through a combination of nominations and objective assessments; and
3. to enable active management of a talent pool to ensure development, reward and retention by rotation through matched jobs.

This last need – the active management of a talent pool – in turn requires a further three core elements:[34]

1. a sophisticated performance development review process;
2. assessment of both an individual's contribution to *organizational-level* capabilities coupled with more traditional individual leadership competencies;
3. an embedded system or surrounding package of HR practices (including deployment decision forums, high-potential review processes, external resourcing strategies, reward and recognition policies driven by data from employee motivation surveys, talent benchmarking system based on 360-degree feedback and personal development plans, and a partnership approach with managers driven by personal coaching).

More recently, without invoking the HR architecture literature, the definition of practices has been broadened to mean "activities and processes," especially those associated with the identification of key positions, development of diverse talent pools and delivery of employee commitment.[35] Typically, these key activities, or components, revolve around seven necessary components.[36]

SEVEN KEY ACTIVITIES OR COMPONENTS OF TALENT MANAGEMENT

1. Identifying and recruiting talent (analysis of labor pools, benchmarking competitor strategies, decentralizing or centralizing recruitment strategies, co-ordinating preferred suppliers, and establishing brand and reputation amongst key employee segments).
2. Attracting talent to the organization (creation of employee value propositions, management of an employer brand).
3. Minimizing attrition through engagement and retention (effective onboarding, aligning rewards and recognition structures, improving line management skills and engagement with talent, retention initiatives).
4. Identifying key internal talent (systematic and effective approaches to affirm individuals with the status of talent, high potential identification systems, identify the roles that are most talent-dependent, and the use of assessment instruments and frameworks).

5. Managing talent flows (developing effective succession systems, creating flexibility in internal mobility, career management and planning systems, succession management).
6. Developing employees (coaching and mentoring, flexible portfolios of development activities, learning opportunities and options for employees, team learning processes, strategic and operational leadership development programs, coaching).
7. Delivering performance (organization talent review processes, linking data on organizational performance to the selection of talent, stretching the performance of talented individuals, managing underperformance).

Importantly, the potential for value creation increases when the scope of practices is extended beyond traditional HRM concerns, as for example seen in:

- the extension into communication and marketing concerns of branding, value propositions and advocacy;
- the extension of interventions down the supply chain and skill formation process (called talent pipeline); and
- the crossover between interpersonal and intrapersonal competition activities.

Many of these practices bring new ways of adding value. A series of high-performance work practices, including the collection of branding, marketing, communications and HR concepts that together form employer branding, act as an external and internal organizational signal. They create impressions of both quality and prominence – two key elements in managing employer reputations.[37]

The ability of such brands to create identification and engagement of employees has a leveraging effect upon (i.e., it amplifies) the value already inherent in the organization's strategic positioning. Branding leverages value by shaping how the organization and individuals manage diverse career orientations and personal reputations, thereby linking talent to the organization's need to be simultaneously *different* from competitors whilst securing general recognition, approval and esteem by remaining *socially legitimate*.

From the preceding review and analysis, it can be seen that a series of claims are made about value generation through a key practices approach to talent management.

DO WE NEED A KEY PRACTICES APPROACH TO TALENT MANAGEMENT?

The key practices perspective makes the following arguments about value generation:

- Talent management is only effective if it is managed as part of a broad architecture (a set of systems, practices, competencies and employee role behaviors designed to engineer human capital in a set way).
- However, this whole architecture must then be aligned towards important strategic outcomes (such as competition in terms of innovation, quality, efficiency and effectiveness) if the talent management system is to be a contributor to the direct creation of strategic value.
- The set of practices in the talent system can also serve to improve or amplify the efficiency of the existing strategic positioning (for example, by optimizing an individual's existing talent or by aligning it more effectively to the strategic positioning).

7.6 Talent management as the management of key positions

The third talent management philosophy, through its attention to the management of key positions rather than key people, picks up on the critique of the People perspective outlined earlier and the debate about where the locus of organization effectiveness (and implicitly value creation) really lies. Whilst some HR professionals have ethical objections to classifying people as "A, B, or C," there is less emotional reactivity to classifying positions – or segmenting jobs – within the organization.[38] "A positions" have two major characteristics: a disproportionate role in a organization's ability in executing some part of its strategy, but wide variability in the quality of work displayed by among the employees in that position. "B positions" may still be strategic for the company, but the skills required to perform them are common and there may be little variability in the performance of employees in these positions. "C positions" serve functions, but may be deemed non-core or outsourced.

Supporters of this philosophy advocate a matched strategy combining this approach with some elements of a people categorization philosophy through the systematic identification of key positions which differentially contribute to the organization's sustainable competitive advantage accompanied by the development of a talent pool of high-potential and high-performance incumbents to fill these roles.[39]

Two observations have been made about the key positions philosophy:[40]

1. Whilst it is invariably always used as a matched strategy, it becomes of particular importance when there is a high level of strategic uncertainty, and a new business model is in operation, for in such contexts the relative contribution of important roles to the success of organization change may become crucially dependent on the job design of a small number of mission-critical jobs.
2. The assessment of how "valuable" a role is is itself complex and needs a range of important processes inside the organization. The strategic value of key positions varies and must be judged across two dimensions: the extent of business model change and its potential for added value.

In our early work in the Centre for Performance-led HR, we argued that the added value of HR should be seen in three ways:[41]

1. Value creation (operationalized as: the ability to build, capture and develop talent in line with the dictates of the business model; to develop a value proposition that aligns such talent to the organizational capabilities inherent in the business model; and to develop performance outcomes of innovation, service, efficiency and effectiveness).
2. Value leverage (operationalized as enhancing a business model (and talent) through learning how to best execute a strategy in hand, transfer of knowledge and learning, and manage through structural channels to ensure engagement of the broader organization with the business model).
3. Value protection, i.e., ensuring that value once created and captured is not lost (operationalized through the design and maintenance of effective governance processes of talent). These processes have to ensure the constructive surfacing of risks in business models, the discussion and creation of risk mitigation strategies, and the impact of the risks associated with the choice of talent on the reputation of the organization and across its stakeholders. They also have to ensure the ability of the organization to retain its best capabilities. However, understanding the risks associated with any particular view or specification of talent is not that easy. Often it is only the accident that shows the true value (or lack of value) associated with a role, a job or of people who were assumed to have talent.

From the preceding review and analysis, it can be seen that a series of claims are made about value generation through a key positions approach to talent management.

DO WE NEED A KEY POSITION APPROACH TO TALENT MANAGEMENT?

The key positions perspective makes the following arguments about value generation:

- the systematic identification of such positions (and how they differentially contribute to the organization's sustainable competitive advantage) becomes a key contributor to the efficiency (through aligned organization design, control and co-ordination) of strategic execution, and indirectly the speed of execution;
- such an approach capitalizes on whatever value resides in existing talent (especially when the level of business change is high and therefore clarity over the requisite component and architectural capabilities is low) by creating, leveraging and protecting/preserving value.

7.7 Strategic pools and human capital management

Finally, in a refinement of the Positions perspective, the fourth philosophy is one of human capital management, drawing upon some of the ideas about HCA and later also on SWP,[42] as discussed later in this chapter.

Two capabilities are needed to convert any human capital planning cycle into a talent management system:

1. measuring the impact that human capital (human capital in this context might refer to either an individual elite set of talent or may be seen as a collective set of talent such as a particular skill group or otherwise segmented population). The impact of human capital in turn might be measured in different ways. The impact might be on the ability of the organization to execute important business processes or it might be seen in terms of impact on operational outcomes; and
2. the forward-looking skills of trending, forecasting and predicting (which has been described as a necessary yet dangerous art!).

THREE CORE BELIEFS THAT UNDERPIN A STRATEGIC POOLS PHILOSOPHY

A strategic pools philosophy is embedded in human capital management traditions, which in turn are underwritten by three arguments:

1. the costs associated with the development and retention of talent should be viewed as investments on behalf of the firm (human capital theory);
2. people can make choices about the investments they choose to make in themselves and will make more investment if there are signals that they are in an area of especial importance to the organization (expectancy theory);
3. strategic assets (for which we can read talent) have associated risks and assets, on which organizations might take an option.[43] Where the business model is fluid and the successful winning technologies are as yet still to be demonstrated, organizations manage risk by explicitly taking different "talent options" out against the various projected developments of their business model. They attempt to "future-proof" their organization by attracting pools of talent associated with several alternative ways in which the organization might need to develop (real options theory).

Those coming from a human resource accounting traditions long ago argued that the debate about talent management either ignores, avoids or throws gratuitous or simplistic platitudes at the question of human value in business environments.[44] A number of key writers have addressed this problem.

A dominant view on talent management is that it is best defined as the process through which employers anticipate and meet their needs for human capital.[45] This approach to talent management draws upon supply chain management theory in order to embrace planning in environments characterized by uncertainty in supply and demand and an inability to forecast away uncertainty and plan years into the future.[46] The ability to capture the full benefit of talent-sourcing strategies is greatest when supported by a complementary set of organization capabilities. It is these capabilities – to do with knowledge sharing, HR analytics and information management systems – that the talent management function must master.

Another set of talent experts, in asking the question "how do you create value from your human capital," bring with them the notion of "pivotal talent pools." These are groupings and clusters of talent (viewed either as people or positions) where human capital investments will most improve organizational capabilities and have the biggest impact on strategic success and competitiveness.[47] This is a refinement of the strategic portfolios notion, arguing instead that if investments have to be rationed, they are best differentiated for maximum return, and differs from the strategic positions philosophy through its advocacy of both the use of *metrics*, and a more open form of strategic thinking needed, to identify pivotal pools.

In our own work we have drawn attention to the tasks that face HR in helping the organization future-proof its talent. In Chapter 2 we picked up some of these issues under our discussion of the need to understand and put in place the skill-formation strategies that in turn build long-term organizational capability.

WHAT DOES GETTING INVOLVED IN "FUTURE-PROOFING" TALENT MEAN?

HR functions need to work with the business to do three things:

1. take technological options or bets on expert talent, and develop targeted searches to map the market for such specialist talent;
2. develop skills strategies to help create and develop new hybrid skills or insights. These skills strategies can only be achieved as follows: by HR understanding the nature of what may be a totally new and previously non-existent hybrid skill that is emerging from, or required for, the future strategy; by HR being involved in a deep dialogue with operations in order that both functions understand the possibilities, relevance and consequence that exist in bringing together different, but already existing, component skills that the organization already knows how to manage; or finally by HR working with the business during the discussions of future potential strategies in order to capture new insights into the nature of future skills through analysis of the business dialogues that helped to articulate the strategy;
3. develop strategies to transform or evolve the existing skill or knowledge base into the new mindsets that "glue" together the business model.

You can see from this that in future, organizations might start to believe that the function of talent management, once seen as more than just categorizing managers in terms of potential and performance, is an activity that better sits within an Operations function. HR might just need to own the job analysts who can help the line better articulate the nature of a future skill, but only the line has the insight into the nature of this skill.

For a third set of talent experts, the question of value and human capital can only be addressed by using a risk optimization, management and mitigation framework to look at human resource strategy and SWP.[48] Cautioning against the illusion of predictability, they call for increased precision in predictions about future supply and demand for skills, and the application of quality-control tools to talent management processes to achieve the same "low-defect" rigour seen in engineering and operations processes. Risk-aligned talent strategies balance the risks in talent planning, with investments in talent for several future scenarios, according to their relative likelihood and risk. They argue that human capital strategies have to be built on the reduction of uncertainty, elimination of bad outcomes and insurance against bad outcomes. They use four phenomena to show that senior leaders are concerned about, but do not really focus on, human capital risk:

1. the risk-return trade-off;
2. behavioral causes of risk-seeking and risk-aversion;
3. the consequences of loss-aversion; and
4. the consequences of risk-seeking.

We should note that the above views about talent management, driven by a human capital management philosophy, have been criticized. But these criticisms are mainly only on pragmatic grounds. However, we need to be aware of them:

1. decisions in practice are not based on such frameworks, but are still driven by the informed preferences, or intuitive instincts, that senior managers have of the visible talent within their organization;[49]
2. even when informed by data provided by HR functions, organizations and their managers often lack a synthesis, and any metrics and analysis provided rarely come with important nuances explained;[50]
3. decisions are bounded by the cognitive limits of managers who have neither the time, the capability nor the inclination to access data and an inclination

to select those who are "good enough," i.e., managers are driven by their previous experiences and beliefs about what talent should look like.[51]

What is the value of a strategic pools and SWP approach?

DO WE NEED A STRATEGIC POOLS AND SWP APPROACH TO TALENT MANAGEMENT?

The strategic pools and SWP perspective makes the following arguments about value generation:

1. Measurement of the impact that human capital (talent as either an individual elite or seen as a collective of particular skill groups or otherwise segmented population) has on operational outcomes creates value through the diagnosis of, and translation into, the true needed capabilities, feasibility assessment of make or buy options, and assessment against strategic considerations.
2. Value is created through the identification and translation of the organizational capabilities articulated in the strategy into specifications for talent; the creation of insight into the relative value of specific talent to the execution of strategy; the assessment of the consequences or feasibility for build or buy talent strategies; and the use of frameworks to segment the existing or target talent population in different ways against strategic considerations (either on the basis of the centrality of the roles to the strategy or through the application of marketing and consumer thinking and treating talent segments on the basis of their expectations of the organization).
3. This then broadens out the assessment of value by bringing in broader concerns around the protection and preservation of value, and the associated prior investments in talent that such protection necessitates. This broadened assessment is best achieved both through the use of risk management, optimization and mitigation disciplines, and also by the techniques used to ensure supply chain management under conditions of uncertainty.
4. Value is protected through the making of necessary investments and taking of actions needed to avoid any loss of value, and value is leveraged through the ability to understand the potential of any scaling of necessary HRM responses.

We believe there are three ways in which HR now needs to de-risk the organization's talent systems:

1. Change the competencies: shift the focus of the underlying leadership model to one based not just on ideas of authentic leadership, but also on the skills and competencies needed to ensure organizational competence in the context of hypercompetition and strategic uncertainty. It lays out what research on strategic management shows these competencies to be.
2. Broaden the data capture: augment the talent system data with much better qualitative data around the depth of strategic insight and capability that individuals have. The report argues that this data needs to pull out what is called the business model, social and political capital of individuals, and suggests ways of doing this.
3. We need to design talent management systems that can manage the collective wisdom of talent. They need to focus less on just identifying talent and more on getting effective brokerage out of the talent data, i.e., by getting talent to talk to each other. HR needs to proactively manage the talent data and design talent systems as "distributed capability systems" rather than just basing them on critical people.

7.8 Placing talent management in an HR analytics context

We also believe that an area where HR needs to build its capability, and rapidly, is in the area of HR analytics. Analytics of course can be applied to the whole range of HR activity. However, as noted in Chapter 6, many organizations learned the tools of their trade by looking at employee engagement and its link to performance. Why has discussion about the nature and importance of HR analytics become so widespread?

A decade ago, there was a famous strategic planning meeting at Tesco, at which each function presented to the CEO its contribution to the analysis. The marketing function took everyone through their analysis of the customers, their buying behavior and needs, and how this opened up some interesting and profitable business opportunities. HR came along and took everyone through some rather mundane analysis of the workforce, standard metrics and demographics. The CEO was not impressed and famously said "we seem to know more about our customers than we do our workforce."

If HR wished to do anything with its seat at the table, it needed to be able to link its knowledge and insight into the workforce to some useful organizational outcomes. It needed some data that could predict something, not just describe things. The response is now history. Tesco set up an employee insight unit, applied marketing thinking to its research, identified a range of different employee segments – for Tesco, these were called the want it alls, the live to works, the work to lives, the pleasure-seekers, and the work-life balancers! It showed how each segment could be engaged through appropriate employee value propositions. It adopted a core retail model – the service-profit chain – which we outlined in Chapter 2. It used its data on employee engagement to show that gains in engagement were linked to (were correlated with, but were not necessarily causal of) important business unit outcomes around store profitability and customer service. HR had gained a way of being able to show the rest of the business that if some business initiatives, or leadership behavior, ignored engagement, there could be a price to pay.

Subsequently, some of that insight team moved on, one of them to McDonald's. We have captured this work under the label of performance recipes.

BUILDING EMPLOYEE INSIGHT AT MCDONALD'S UK

The work that was done at McDonald's shows how expanding the scope of analytics work becomes important. McDonald's too adopted service-profit chain thinking and identified how this model could be applied to the more transactional service environment of fast food. Every organization needs to "decode" how its particular chain works, which means understanding the links between internal service quality, customer expectations, organizational image, brand proposition, customer orientation of its staff, external service value, customer satisfaction, customer loyalty and customer advocacy. For McDonald's, the chain worked as follows – committed leaders created more competent and confident staff (it has a young demographic and a record of building social mobility). Once engaged, the staff created a simple, easy, enjoyable restaurant experience (measured through metrics of food quality, service and cleanliness). These metrics in turn were predictive of customer visits, and these customer loyalty business metrics were predictive of business growth measures of sales and profits. They began by simply "linking" the metrics – and there was good news. Where staff were engaged, customer visits were 66 percent higher and sales 28 were percent higher. But correlations are not causal. McDonald's was aware of this and used our Centre to bring more advanced statistical know how to its data analysis. The data helped HR learn about what we called the performance recipe. How exactly did aspects of people management really create business success and how did the business metrics really link to each other? The Operations Director saw what was going on and the data got more visibility and usage in the organization. HR was helping the rest of the organization learn about some of its measurement and control systems.

What did the analytics show McDonald's? It dispelled a number of myths that existed. First, it was clear that staff could be dissatisfied, but could actually still display a strong customer orientation. It also became clear that whilst store leadership was a very important predictor of engagement, just having managers who were seen as strong leaders was not enough. Although leadership correlated with engagement, there was a missing ingredient. We noted in Chapter 6 the importance of job resources in order for employees to be engaged. The data at McDonald's supported this. Leadership behaviors only actually caused engagement to go up if the leaders also made employees believe that they had the resources to do their job, so HR spotted the need to build the provision of important resources for employees if the engagement–customer service link was going to work. Finally, when the employee attitude data was linked to the business unit performance metrics, it could be seen that the customer orientation of staff did indeed lift food quality, service and cleanliness, and subsequently profitability. When employees knew that they had the resources to do the job, this had important impacts on productivity and food costs.

Building an analytics team enabled HR to unravel how store profitability and service perceptions were very staff-dependent. The HR function at McDonald's deciphered how they had to manage the subtle ingredients that led to a chain of performance. But their analysis got better. Once they had a culture and a system of analytics in place, they were able to extend their insight. There was a niggling question. Although the engagement data could be seen to be useful and predictive, there seemed to be a link between some of the demographic qualities of their store staff profiles and performance. Age seemed to play a part, but how and with what result? They ran some controlled tests on the data, being able to compare the performance data of 178 company-owned McDonald's restaurants where one or more members of staff aged over 50 is employed with the performance data of 239 company-owned McDonald's restaurants where nobody over the age of 50 is employed. To their surprise, the stores that had one or more 50 year olds in the teams had a 22 percent higher level of customer service. They were already able to show the financial utility of that kind of performance improvement – massive. Moreover, the customer service uplift could be created in both poor-performing and already high-performing stores. The data were telling them not that older employers were better, but that the demographic mix of their teams did change the store dynamics and ultimately the customer experience. As the *Financial Times* summed it up, "the kids are alright but they need help."

The above example shows that in relation to building an HR analytics capability, McDonald's had gone through a journey. Many organizations are now on this journey. The journey is not easy, nor does it automatically suggest that you have to build a dedicated analytics resource in your organization.

For McDonald's, these measurement capabilities need to be linked to the field and operations management structures of the business. It had to learn how to reject the overly simple "employee engagement = business success" proposition and instead figure out what is a more complex performance recipe. Linking back to the discussion of engagement and the link to performance in Chapter 6, the analytics work helps lead us to a number of generalizable conclusions:

- It shows that sometimes being in a good-performing unit makes you engaged and not the other way round – the issue of reverse causation that we mentioned.
- Sometimes performance effects only begin to become important at extreme levels of engagement.
- Sometimes engagement works through intermediate outcomes (such as job resources or design).
- Sometimes engagement only works when it creates a collective capability – a bunch of individually engaged staff does not create the performance.

- There are different employee segments – different types of employee respond differently to the same conditions.
- Engagement levels co-vary with lots of other things: relatively new to the organization, young, gender, hours of work and pay patterns, country they work in, work for a core or a more peripheral organizational unit and treatment on pensions. How good are your HR analytics skills?

The above example shows that there is often a good story to tell when it comes to the strategic importance of HR. Once we "decode" various contributions to the organization, then HR is one of the under-exploited business functions – it can help improve performance to the benefit of all.

7.9 Conclusions: meeting the growing discontent amongst practitioners with a more strategic HR understanding

Looking across the different talent management philosophies outlined above, it is fair to conclude that organizations and their HR functions have learned how to engineer and hone sophisticated talent management processes. But it is also evident that three problems remain:

1. It is line managers, and not HR, who operate the processes, and to many, talent management is a dark art that lacks transparency, is subject to bias and is capable of simply reinforcing all that is narrow about an organization and its culture.
2. Even the best processes can still have little impact at board level.
3. Good processes for the few can lead to denuded resources for the many and, depending on whether the organizational problem is one of customer centricity, innovation, efficiency and effectiveness or globalization, allowing resources to be denuded in the wrong areas would be a fundamental failing by HR.

From some of the criticisms about talent management that we have raised, it seems as if that at the very time that talent management was peaking in practitioner attention and HR functions were giving separate attention to the problem of talent – in around 2007 – questions and discontent amongst fellow practitioners also began to surface (remember that academic concerns were first raised in around 2000).

For example, in a series of studies from 2007 to 2011, drawing on interviews with executives from 70 organizations, a team of researchers noted that whilst firms such as GE, Unilever, PepsiCo and Shell had developed a reputation for effective practices in the area, such practices were not the norm.[52] They found that only 15 percent of major organizations in North America and Asia, and 30 percent in Europe, believed they had enough qualified successors for qualified positions. Programs were aimed at identifying and managing a pipeline of high potentials, but were typical "battle strategies," i.e., they were not easy to execute, nor were they transparent. On transparency and high potential, they noted:

> We are surprised to discover how many companies launch high-potential programs without first clearly establishing what they mean by "potential" ... The only real reason to keep [who is on the list] quiet is that you suspect the process is overly subjective and unfair.[53]

Realizing that they would be hard-pressed to make sustainable judgments about performance versus potential, other practitioners started to ask more questions in relation to their achievements:[54]

> as practitioners in this area we have both bought into this notion and worked for many years to make it happen. We have worked with CEOs, undertaking extensive talent reviews. We have worked with psychologists assessing people's capability. We have worked with technology specialists to introduce databases to capture skills across the workforce. We have worked with "the talent" as coaches. We have worked with recruiters to scour the market for more talent. And yet when we reflected on the difference this activity was really making we felt that it was still not enough ... the struggle was systemic ... in truth, we had metaphorically put sticking plasters over the obvious issues without really getting to the root cause of the problem ... it felt to us that organizations were operating in a talent "doom loop."

Their critique of their own practice was as follows:

- Talent management needs to be about knowledge, innovation and relationships today rather than executive potential tomorrow.
- The vital many were as important as the special few.
- The inter-dependence between people within and across organizations is critical.
- Individuals control when and who they share their potential with, so the idea that organizations can manage talent is an outdated conceit.
- The social dimension matters more than the capability and resources of individuals.

- We need to manage how talent works – the whole ecology of an organization and its ability to create social capital.

Clearly, HR functions continue to struggle with their practice. From our original analysis of leading talent management practice, we concluded it was "time to question the tablets of stone."[55] Our work with Talent Directors identified the following points.

FIVE MAJOR AND ONGOING CHALLENGES FOR TALENT MANAGEMENT

- The quality of conversations around strategy, organizational design and development.
- Achieving and enabling the full potential of talent management and a return on investment.
- Managing the 3Gs of diversity: gender, geography and generation.
- The need for better relationship management between those who design the talent systems (HR functions) and those who have to deliver that system (line managers).
- Operational integration.

The first issue concerns the sorts of conversations needed to link talent management to strategy, organizational design and development. This is about:

- getting top teams to have talent conversations;
- building the SWP and data-handling capacities of the function and the top team;
- enabling talent functions to bring to the talent conversation issues of long-term development and the challenges of changing business models and changing critical roles; and
- ensuring governance to align business risk and talent.

We use some example quotes from Talent Directors to help articulate these:

> "How to move to more to more value add with the Board? It needs a return on investment conversation ... and what we call sustained conversations."
> "Understanding our business model is changing ... and so is the internal landscape in the organization."
> "We need to identify critical gaps roles, build success profiles around these role gaps, understand the pipeline and look for issues and specific actions to facilitate movement in the pipeline."

"[Doing more with what] we know are the mission critical roles in the organization are. We do a capability analysis – and focus on the areas where we need a better skill set."

"We need to look more at critical roles – then the competencies piece – but understanding the strategic piece for the next 5–10 years, not in the next couple of years."

The second set of challenges has related to how to achieve and enable the full potential of the talent function. This is about:

- articulating the link between talent and such talent providing sustainable contributions and performance;
- managing the volatility in the talent population; and
- learning how to combine quantitative and qualitative data insights.

Again, some typical comments from Talent Directors are as follows:

"Data is improving on every employee – but it is not fantastic – a big issue is joining up the data – lining up the quantitative and the qualitative. Making us more profitable is about understanding this two-dimensional aspect to talent data. We need qualitative data on things like sales acumen, business intuition."

"How can HR challenge the quality of talent data and the issues they have to deal with ... There are two dimensions to it. One is the data and the second is the presentation of this data – what should be on the talent dashboard."

The third set of challenges relate to some of the things that the board should discuss but does not always do – with the subsequent challenge for talent functions that in the context of very business-focused talent discussions, they also need to move their organizations into more sustainable models of talent. Individuals from what are called the 3Gs of diversity are increasingly pressing their claims to be seen as part of the talent population. However, how does HR build a business case for the 3Gs at the board level? And how does it look more strategically at its resource planning for the under-represented Gs?

The business case for diversity, how we motivate senior leaders to take the diversity agenda into the board ... understanding the various glass ceilings and doing something about it, and in terms of resource planning there is a fear that we will struggle to attract [talented] people from more diverse backgrounds.

The fourth set of challenges concern issues of relationship management. Creating a talent mindset is not just about the willingness of the line to discuss the capabilities of talent, it is also about how HR engages them with this issue and how well HR equips line managers to have these discussions and to carry them out well. In order for line managers to accept HR's role in so equipping them, they have to see the value in the line owning the talent process, but being required to operate this process effectively and being held to account for its operation. All these challenges are fundamentally about the design of the relationships that have to exist within the talent system. In short, a new skill set is needed by Talent Directors to work with the line in this way. Organizations also have to prepare line managers to have the right conversations and shape what these conversations should be about. For this to happen, there needs to be clarification about the roles needed in the talent process, enabling objective and subjective conversations to help managers accept the talent proposition:

> Clarification of roles within the talent process – being clear about these depending on the way you have structured your talent processes, the organizations' contribution, the line managers, and the people running talent ... It is the execution and the way you design the talent system that will make it work or not.

Finally, the fifth set of challenges picks up operational issues of how organizations align and integrate the talent processes with other parts of HR. This is about having the confidence that the talent system allow you to get the right people, at the right time and in the right place. It about being able to manage the totality of talent data and aligning the systems on a global basis:

> It is still about joining up HR – to what extent we are aligned with design and reward – so it is not about jargon but about how that linkage works, how the metrics we use drive policy.

As this chapter has made clear, HR functions need to reposition their talent management function. They need to think more strategically about the nature of talent, not only by building their HR analytics capability, but also by designing their function in ways that maps much more clearly onto the question of strategic value.

Too much management practice, and indeed research, simply assumes that strategic assets are valuable, and then too quickly asks how firms avoid others imitating these assets without first asking the more important question. This question is what makes particular assets and resources valuable in the first place? In order to answer this question, it has been argued that we need to design our management around a theory of value.[56] In the next chapter, we look to the field of strategic management and use some of the thinking within it to lay out how we should think about the value of HR and some of its key technologies, such as talent management.

chapter 8

Creating Value in HR: The Example of Talent Management

8.1 Introduction

In the previous chapter we showed that organizations and their HR functions have learned how to engineer and hone sophisticated talent management processes. However, many are also looking at their talent Centers of Expertise and both broadening their remit and linking them much more flexibly to related areas of expertise such as Learning and Development, Resourcing and Engagement, and to broad change programmes. This is allowing us the option to think more strategically about the role, remit and value of talent management.

In this final chapter in the book we bring what we know about strategic management and strategic value creation to bear on the talent management debate. We ask the following questions:

- Is a professional service model – with its language of centers of expertise and competence – the right one for HR to be following? Is there a more valuable strategic test that can be applied to the choice of specialized know-how? We differentiate Centers of Excellence from Centers of Expertise as a way of thinking about this.
- What are the critical tests that should guide the design of our talent systems? Can we use these to lay out a series of design principles that should be used to guide and evaluate the value of a talent management system?
- Does this help us to articulate and argue what the *return on investment* is on the organization's approach to talent management?

The discussion in this chapter is intended to inform debates about HR analytics and HR metrics, and also for making choices about how best to integrate and combine currently very siloed Centers of Expertise. It also has implications for related activities, such as Organizational Effectiveness, Organization Design and Learning and Development. Specifically, in this chapter we shall:

- draw upon a number of non-HR literatures from the field of *strategic management* on value creation, strategic resources and dynamic capabilities, and global knowledge management, in order to help HR practitioners think about the nature of strategic "value";
- use this to inform the choices about the design of a talent management system or architecture;
- develop a framework based on four separate value-generating processes that a talent system needs to include (we call these value creation, value capture, value leverage and value protection).

Strategic management academics have long since argued that we need a "theory of value."[1] Only then does it become clearer which elements of HR management are the most valuable for organizational effectiveness. Once we see how strategists address the question of "value," it might move both senior HR and line managers out of their comfort zone. But we believe that in asking more searching questions about their practice, they will see a clear path through to their future activities.

Although we apply this theory of value in this chapter to the practice of talent management, we believe of course that the framework of the four value-generating processes of value creation, value creation, value leverage and value protection could equally well be applied to HR functions across all of their activity base.

8.2 The battle lines of the future for HR

8.2.1 From centers of expertise to centers of excellence

In this final chapter we ask – as we have implicitly asked throughout the book – how should HR think about its added value? We hinted in the opening chapter that building its own expertise on very functional and process-driven lines does not bring this value to the fore. One problem is that HR seems to have adopted the concept of Competency Center or Center of Expertise that historically was developed and used by IT specialists and that is embedded in Professional Service Model thinking, but that this specification is not the way that strategists would use the label of "Center of Excellence" or would expect HR to use it.

Professional service firms have bodies of knowledge, and this knowledge has to be turned into outcomes that impact the productivity of their client. Centers of Expertise are then in effect equal to knowledge centers (also called Centers of Competence in some other literature). Drawing upon discussion from IT and business process specialists is informative and shows us why in many existing centers in HR we might have ended up with faltering demand. From the perspective of a professional service model, which is what HR functions have adopted, a Center of Expertise or Competence may be considered to be:

> a highly effective way to implement and sustain specialist capabilities where a consistent, expert and cost effective service is required across organizational boundaries and where a comprehensive view is required to ensure synergies are identified and exploited.

But using this sort of definition, it is not surprising that the solution nearly every HR organization seems to have taken is to hive off the existing "peak" of its core functions and processes – high-level process expertise – and simply relabel this expertise as a "Center," simultaneously claiming that this somehow therefore has a transformational and strategic mandate.

Under this definition, Centers are seen through the lens of a Professional Service Model, which means that:

- Centers represent teams of expertise that can link their knowledge to productivity. The related activity of embedded HR (HR business partners) is to then transfer that knowledge into the client;
- the range or portfolio of Centers is supposed to clarify what these organizational capabilities are and to help the HR function craft its necessary investments and policies so that it can maintain a specialist and critical core of knowledge that influences strategy;
- Professional Service Models are seen to be at heart concerned with time and cost savings, achieved through rationalization and re-use of processes and services. They introduce greater predictability into service delivery through more consistent process and management controls, and through operational efficiency and excellence that is in turn achieved through the use of best practice tools across the organization.

Professional Service Model thinking suits an IT environment, where there are high levels of technical knowledge and where services have to be designed for customers who have varying levels of internal capability. And of course

HR shares some of these problems (although, unlike IT, everyone thinks they are a people expert). But is this sort of model really right for HR? Under Professional Service Model thinking, the challenge for a service provider is to optimize costs, evaluate risks and ensure predictable delivery. In the world of IT, it is assumed that standard methods and approaches produce faster learning curves, that consistent processes reduce the risk of rework and that the role of a Center is to ensure that processes and methods are implemented to an appropriate quality standard.

The key characteristics are a focus on a particular domain of expertise, providing shared and consistent services, introducing end-to-end life cycle responsibility and operational support, market awareness of best practice, communication of that knowledge, and delivering this knowledge through strong governance of processes and defined expertise around a set of expert skills. Such Centers are about commoditizing knowledge.

So as a commodity, it is not surprising, as we noted in the opening chapter, that almost every HR function that you look at has the same old Centers. Some call them centers of expertise, some centers of excellence, yet, as we shall see, these labels are supposed to mean different things.

The question that strategists ask is that if every organization has this expertise and everyone chooses to group their expertise in similar ways, how does this provide competitive advantage? According to strategic management theory – and note they use the term "Center of Excellence" and purposefully differentiate that from a (lower status) Center of Competence – Centers of Excellence should only be allowed to exist where it is accepted by all in the organization in the context of the business model, and this means not just seen as important by the function to which they belong (in our case HR).

A Center of Excellence, according to the strategists, is defined somewhat differently from the way Professional Service Models think about it. It is supposed to be:

> "An organizational unit that embodies a set of capabilities that has been explicitly recognised by the firm as an important source of value creation, with the intention that these capabilities be leveraged by or disseminated to other parts of the firm."[2]

> "Small groups of individuals recognised for their leading-edge strategically valuable knowledge, and mandated to leverage and/or make that knowledge available throughout the ... firm."[3]

Looking at the above definitions, Centers of Excellence should only be established inside organizations:

- As a part of deliberate (cross-functional) organization design, where managers decide to grant autonomy to units that have been given a specific strategic mandate by the Board.
- Where they have already been seen as high-value units that have a strategic role due to the possession of products, services or functions they offer – and capabilities that cross organizational boundaries and markets.

The organizational capabilities they leverage do not equate simply to expert functional knowledge. However, if there is line of sight to the business model and a business case to be made that the organization must leverage or disseminate the capabilities that the unit embodies to other parts of the firm in order for the organization to deliver its competitive advantage strategy, then there is a case for a Center of Excellence.[4]

To conclude, for a unit to be truly deemed a Center of Excellence, there must be an accepted intention to derive value from the unit's capabilities for the broader organization, and an explicit recognition and declaration that, through its role, the unit can truly add value.

THE 4P'S TEST FOR A TRUE CENTER OF EXCELLENCE

In the context of your organization's current or desired business model, do your Centers pass the 4Ps test?:

- Proposition.
- Purpose.
- Performance.
- Prosper (and Survive).

Proposition: What is it?

- What is the argument to build the capability in a Center of Excellence yourself rather than just have a good "scanning unit" that can pick up and transmit intelligence back to the HR Director?
- What capability-building investments (such as the granting of additional finance, release of resources, transfer of skills, knowledge and expertise) are required to build it and then run it? Must these investments be mandated by corporate HQ or elsewhere?
- What is the required decision-making autonomy of the unit? How will it be given the ability to identify and pursue market

opportunities without permission? How will it attract and hire new managers?

- What is its connectivity to other sources of competence – how can it continue to create new knowledge and not just exploit it?

Purpose: how does the Center of Excellence really add value?

- Is it a focal point for a superior set of capabilities that creates value – either through its tangible resources (policies, practices or processes) and/or through its intangible resources (such as knowledge, experience, reputation, proprietary services, operating procedures and know-how about key performance outcomes such as innovation, efficiency and customer centricity)?
- Is it a focal point for dispersed capabilities that can be used to leverage pockets of expertise inside the organization effectively as a source of competitive advantage only through co-ordinated management, i.e., it is a focal point for knowledge development that serves other people or units with related skills or disciplines?
- Is it a conduit for the dissemination of knowledge within the organization?
- Is it a problem-solving unit that provides advice and can be seen to foster new competences within the organization?

Performance: have we really got the qualities necessary to qualify the unit as a Center of Excellence?

- Has it really only been established on the basis of there being substantial strategic importance or pay-off (rather than as a mechanism to make some functions feel they are important)?
- How is it focused on the resources and performance outcomes that are the most valuable to the business model?
- Is it only specialized in its own knowledge base (i.e., does it simply equate to existing functions inside an organization)? If so, it is just a focal point for functional expertise? Functions are about operational know-how, not strategic mandate.
- Does it have the capability to create *and* maintain one, or several, critical fields of knowledge – knowledge that has a long-term impact on the development of activity in the other functions and units of the organization?

Prosper and survive: what are the factors necessary to ensure its continued endurance?

In order to survive and endure – and the evidence is that it is not only in the HR function that Centers of Excellence often have a tough time of it – any Center of Excellence must be able to get involved in progressive levels of knowledge transfer. So, again:

- Has it taken on a strategic role in the organization that reaches beyond operational undertakings?
- Is it tightly integrated with its surrounding technical or professional communities (internal and externally networked)?
- Does it have both high competence *and* high use of its competence throughout surrounding units?
- Has it got a definite life cycle? When would you dismantle it or let its purpose expire to prevent it from becoming an overhead?

On this basis, not surprisingly, we would argue, based on the insights revealed throughout this book, that rather than focus on its own HR processes, HR needs to contribute to the building of centers around the fundamental strategic capabilities that we have discussed – i.e., innovation, customer centricity or consumer insight, or productivity and lean management, and cross-organization delivery (which therefore might require the building of expertise around the different choices being pursued such as supply chain or joint ventures). The kinds of issues that the line find important are more cross-functional and less HR process-based. For example, with the productivity challenge, HR Directors need to be able to say how HRM influences both the internal (organizational) and external (national) challenge, understand the implications of both of these for future resource demands, and know what policy agendas the pursuit of a productivity focus will trigger.

Only once you are sure that the 4P questions have been answered should you challenge the function and ask what are the real questions that your expertise should really be addressing, then move on to the more bottom-line and pragmatic questions.

Can it reduce cost?
Can it increase revenue?
Can it reduce risk?

Can it reduce capital?
Does the customer expect it?
Do the competition offer it?
Will the customer pay more for it?
Will the customer miss it not being there?

8.2.2 The "diffusion" of HR into new non-functional structures

We think that this will inevitably lead to many strategically important and interesting areas of HR diffusing more and more activity into non-functional structures. The good news for HR from this book is that on nearly every business issue, other management functions are now framing the problems in ways that recognize the centrality of people management issues to the solution. The bad news for HR from this book is that on nearly every business issue, other management functions are now framing the problems in ways that recognize the centrality of people management issues to the solution! In other words, general management will encroach on HR's aspired turf. They will take responsibility for many of these issues themselves. Manufacturing Directors see themselves as Engagement Directors, as might the Employee Advocacy and brand people. Chief Operating Officers see themselves as Talent Directors. Business Intelligence functions and Big Data analyzers will see HR analytics as an offshoot of their own world.

We have long argued that HR reverse engineers itself into the business. Well, the business is reverse engineering itself into HR.

As a "customer" of the organization, it is a matter of supreme indifference who owns these new value-adding but cross-functional areas of activity. Whether activity is ceded to HR, or to contiguous functions, is not the issue. It is more important that the transfers take place as part of a broader business logic rather than as a consequence of successful HR Director politics.

8.2.3 Constellations of activity

Again, although we apply our theory of value next just to talent management, we believe that the same process could be used to think about what we call "Constellations" of activity. It is not just parts of HR functions that might start to break up and diffuse into new cross-functional structures – parts of other functions too will begin to coagulate together.

We use the notion of constellations of Centers of Excellence – or ecosystems – to explain the dominant patterns, or combinations, that should best exist between various HR activities. In trying to achieve this more holistic HR management, we explore the nature of the different constellations of functions that are being woven together in new and novel ways as a means of navigating towards more holistic HR management. We use the analogy of a "constellation" to signal the growing importance of some new interfaces between previously separate Centers of Excellence and functions. The word constellation means different things. In astronomy it is a formation, or a configuration, of stars or planets by which we may navigate. In common parlance it is a group of ideas felt to be related, a fixed pattern of individual elements functioning in a related way, a gathering of brilliant or famous people or ideas with similar eccentricities, attitudes and inclinations. Under a constellations model, HR functions may not end up being dismantled as such, but instead *being reconfigured*, because people will start to see different ways of joining them up and different ways of managing that joining-up process. Finally, we signal two important points about constellations which we might eventually decide to navigate by:

1. There are rarely single integrating logics at play, but rather competing logics that HR needs to work through.
2. The closer HR gets to the business (or the closer the business gets into people), the more the logic of the business and the culture of its operating core serves to highlight which functions should best be aligned with each other, and what the bottom line consequence of aligning them this way or not might be.

8.3 Four value-driven processes within a talent management architecture

Beyond these obvious battle lines, there is a second major challenge that we have alluded to in this book. This is that both within a major HR process – and in the last chapter and in this chapter we use the example of talent management as such a process – and most certainly when looking across these processes (for example, looking at the interfaces between activities such as Talent Management, Learning and Development, and Organizational Effectiveness), it seems that line managers are looking for a much more joined-up, integrated and flexible way of linking to the HR support. Now, there are two solutions to this:

1. come up with some kind of "mix and match" flexible resource allocation model, then workload allocation, model through which expertise in HR can be assigned to project and programme-based activities, i.e., "reachback" into the existing Centers to pull out resources and combine them into suitable "packages" for the internal client business units (reachback is a term used in various cross-organization business contracts to cover arrangements

whereby one organization must have contractual access to people or skills that might formally exist within another); or

2. think more strategically about how best to combine the activities in the first place, i.e. think about the organizational design and how it creates new more powerful Centers.

We prefer the latter option. But we need to suggest a way in which HR should think about "breaking up" and "re-combining" its expertise. We think the best way of doing this is to go back to theory, as it were, and to ask "how does this activity (or function or process) add value?"

To help suggest a way of doing this, throughout the rest of this chapter we outline what we see as four crucial value-driven processes. We work these four processes through just one important area of HR – that of talent management. We use this one area for a number of reasons: first, because of its relevance and centrality to all of the performance challenges that we have discussed throughout the book; and, second, because, as will become clear throughout the rest of the chapter, once you start to ask questions about strategic value, you very quickly have to get into quite fine-grain detail and specifics. It would simply be too complex and too distracting to try to generalize our answers across each and every activity stream that HR might be called upon to get involved in.

However, it is very important that we stress that the same principles that we now lay out in relation to talent management– the same sets of questions about value and the same thought processes – can and should now be applied across all the activities of HR.

We also hope that by asking some of the more difficult questions about strategic value and then trying to answer them, it becomes much clearer as to what is being done effectively by HR and what pieces of the jigsaw might still be missing. So, many of the questions we have raised earlier in the chapter about how best to reconfigure the expertise that HR has and how to build more flexible constellations of activity that truly have value for the organization can be thought about by analyzing the value, or otherwise, that lies in the current systems and functions.

So let's begin with our worked example. What must result from talent management for it to be seen as truly valuable? We believe it must deliver value through four processes: creating value, capturing that value once created, leveraging that value, and then protecting and preserving it. There are three implications of this:

- If you were to design a valuable talent management function from scratch, you would combine all four of the processes we are about to lay out and manage them within a single architecture.

- If you are reconfiguring your talent management function based on existing activities, you should combine activities that forge connections between the four.
- If you are thinking about metrics and analytics, think more broadly.

In the previous chapter we laid out four different ways to think about what talent management is, or should be, i.e. key people, key positions, key practices and key strategic pools. By now it should be evident that:

- the various talent philosophies that exist are not competing and alternative approaches, but reflect different and alternative dimensions of a more strategic approach to talent management;
- each approach makes different contributions and creates value in different ways;
- they are in need of a more balanced application.

However, we are still using a number of terms and concepts, such as value creation, capture, leverage and protection, rather loosely. We need to provide more clarity around this terminology and explain the contributions that the strategy literature can make in helping HR professionals answer the following question: *what is the value of talent management*?

A QUICK PRIMER ON THE RESOURCE-BASED VIEW

From this perspective, "human capital" is one set of resources open to the firm, and this refers to the knowledge, skills, capabilities, intelligence, relationships and experience of the firm's employees.[5] Such resources need to be implemented in ways dictated by a prior value-creating strategy. In order to support such value creation and act as a source of competitive advantage, these resources must:

- vary across competing firms (called being heterogeneous); and
- be difficult to transfer from one firm to another (called being immobile).

Hence the mantra that they must be valuable, rare, imperfectly imitable and unsubstitutable. In an HRM context, "value" refers to the potential of the human capital at hand to contribute to its organization's core competence and enhance its competitive advantage. In thinking about how talent management may create value for the organization, a distinction is made between: the definition of *valuable talent* that is used; and the *process of creating such value* through the talent management system and architecture that is adopted. However, three things become important:

1. Talent resources are strategic assets that have the potential to create and capture value and execute business strategies.
2. Organizations must have in place talent management strategies, systems and practices that identify, develop and retain talent resources.
3. Sustained competitive advantage is only realized when a firm succeeds in organizing its internal processes, policies and procedures to exploit the potential of its valuable, rare and inimitable resources (be that elite or collective capital).[6]

The most valuable "rents" that talent can create – through superior management skills and expertise – are firm-specific skills in the form of developed knowledge and relationships with customers, suppliers and critical employees, and a deep understanding of internal technologies.[7]

We draw upon the general management literature to lay out a theory of value that clarifies four ways in which talent management can be valuable to the organization (see Figure 8.1). We explain how each process should be assumed to operate, and use this insight to suggest a series of design principles – and ways of thinking about the return on investment argument. Talent specialists should use these conclusions to help sharpen the design and integration of their talent management systems. HR Directors should generalize the ideas into the design of the broader HR function.

8.4 How is value created through talent management?

If we bring what we know about strategic value creation to bear on talent management, what are the critical tests that should guide the design of our talent systems? In this and the subsequent sections, we lay out a series of design principles that should be used to guide the design and evaluate the value of a talent management system.

To understand the strategic value of assets, we need to first ask what is value, how is it created and who captures it?[8] There is still disagreement about what value creation actually is within the general management literature, let alone

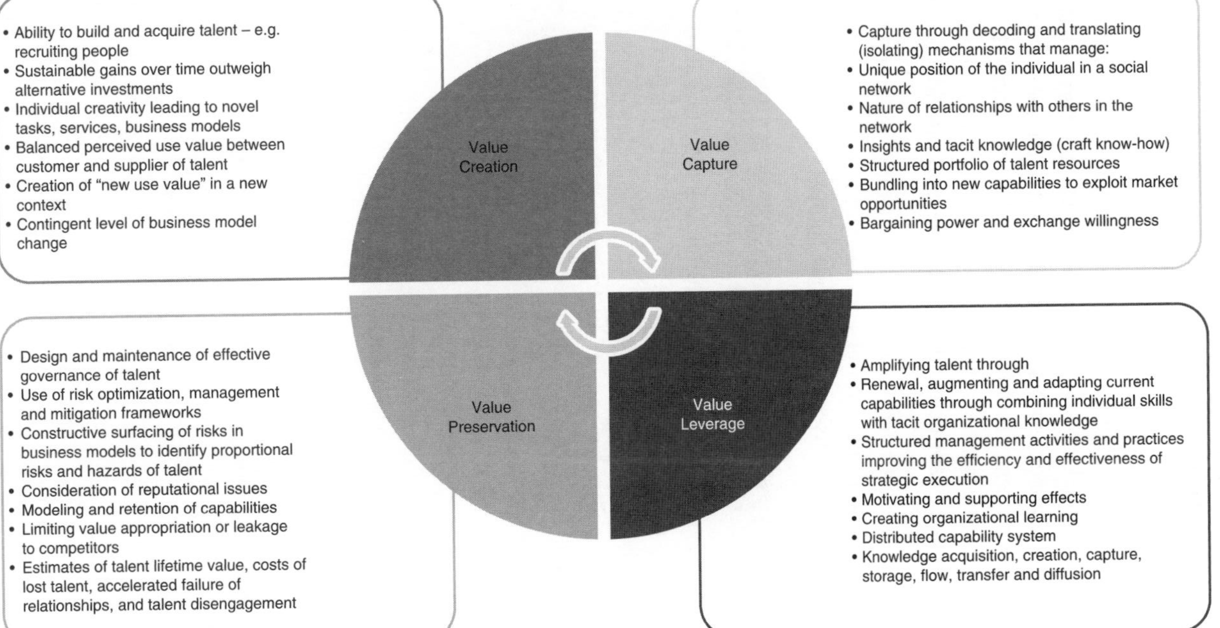

FIG 8.1 Four value-driven processes within a talent management architecture

in relation to talent management.[9] However, it is useful to think about the question of "value" in three ways:

1. by looking at the *content* of talent management (what is valuable, who values what and where the value resides);
2. by thinking about the *different targets for whom value is being created* by talent management (business owners, organizations, stakeholders such as society or nation states, customers, employees or important employee segments); or
3. by looking at the *processes by which value is created or generated* by talent management (the mechanisms that allow value, once created by the talent system, to actually be captured and exploited beyond the individual).

Individuals – star or expert talent - can be value-creating "by acting creatively to make their job/service more novel and appropriate in the eyes of their employer or some other end user in a particular context."[10]

THE MYTH OF TALENT MANAGEMENT?

Strategists believe the view that it is individual talent or stars who are value-creating is misleading. They call it the myth of talent management and argue that human capital is better understood as the broader "collective capital" of the firm.[11] This capital is not something that can easily be transferred or embedded in other organizations because:

- the knowledge that resides within stars represents only the starting point;
- a deeper organizational capability (and hence value) is only created once this knowledge has been internalized within the organization and supported by all of the supporting systems, structures and processes;
- this is the result more of the collective interactions and interconnections between talent than what is in the mind of any one individual;
- it is more easily built rather than bought, because such insight is very difficult to export or re-create from one organization to another.

The myth that it is individuals or stars who create the value – and the potential advantage that their intellective capacity and insight into new value-creating possibilities represents – is actually a danger or a risk.

In practice, star talent is only really likely to be able to add value when the level of flux in business models is low – when there is strategic stability. In such a situation, the links between the sorts of knowledge that are needed have been learned and are more obvious and easier to explain – and therefore to codify in the talent system and the decisions it makes about selection and promotion. Only in low business model change environments does it become easier to:

- predict who will be successful;
- figure out what constitutes being talented (to pursue a people approach with a degree of validity); and
- to hone and improve specific talent practices that form part of the talent system accordingly.

Too much importance is given to the notion of general management potential, underplaying the value of expert knowledge. The competitive advantage of organizations in high-talent industries is increasingly rooted both in the stock of experts they can access and also in the organizational capabilities that such talent can harness. As we saw in Chapter 7, there are risks involved in relying on a particular talented individual. As Chapter 6 reminded us, if the exchange value is somehow felt to be unduly weighted, then deep questions about fairness might be created.

So, one way of thinking about the value of your talent management systems is to consider the extent to which they enable you to manage (broadly in the organization's favour) what is called *use value* and *exchange value*.

THINKING ABOUT THE USE VALUE AND THE EXCHANGE VALUE OF STAR TALENT

When strategists think about resources or assets and how they create value at the organizational level, they differentiate two types of value:[12]

- *use value*; and
- *exchange value*.

Use value refers to the specific quality of a new job, task, product or service as perceived by users in relation to their needs. How might we think about the use value of either procured valuable (star) talent or the ability of the broader talent management system as a whole to generate value? Use value requires an assessment of the novelty and usefulness of star talent, which assumes that users of the talent possess specialized knowledge, so they can evaluate the knowledge of new talent. Much acquired and potentially useful talent gets rejected very quickly after it has joined the organization. The perceived use value of talent management is also directly related to senior executives' perceptions of the value they expect by investing in talent management strategies, and these perceptions vary from one organization to another. The monetarization of this perceived "use value" is determined mainly at the point of purchase, and this reflects the price that the customer (purchasing organization) is willing to pay for such talent, minus the opportunity costs.[13]

Exchange value, on the other hand, refers to either the monetary amount realized at a certain point in time, when the exchange of the new task, good, service, or product takes place, or the amount paid by the user to the seller for the use value of this. In terms of *exchange value*, for an individual to be value-creating, there are two pre-conditions that must be created:[14]

1. The monetary amount exchanged must exceed the producer's costs (costs may be measured in terms of money, time, effort or joy).
2. The perceived performance difference is that between the new value that is created and the closest alternative that existed (current tasks, products or services).

It is not easy for an organization's talent system to create this more sustainable "new use value," nor does elite talent automatically have the ability to create such new use value. Elite talent have to demonstrate how their own unique insights can be worked by others in ways that ultimately create sustained value. They require two types of knowledge about business models:[15]

1. knowledge of the business model's parts rather than the whole (called component knowledge); and
2. a shared understanding of the interconnection of all the components, or how things must fit together, in order to deliver effective performance (called architectural knowledge).

The understanding of how these two sorts of knowledge combine is what was earlier referred to in Chapter 7 as an intellective capability.[16] People whose talent suits a particular business model know how to combine both types of knowledge. Business model change, then, alters the strategic value that is attached to particular types of knowledge and the way that different types of knowledge have to relate to each other.

Following a similar logic, another way is to look at how good your organization is at transferring and internalizing valuable people. Strategists have also analyzed how value is created when a strategic asset – any strategic asset – is transferred from Organization A to Organization B.

What does a talent system have to do to ensure use value? When strategists look at the transfer of strategic assets, they also make a distinction between what they call "initial use value" and "new use value." It works like this:

- use value is created in Organization A;
- that value is then exchanged between Organizations A and B;
- a monetarized exchange value is realized;
- then the use value of the asset has to be "transformed" so that it creates the same or additional use in Organization B;
- the true value of this "new use value" is only clear once that strategic asset is lost or moves on again voluntarily to Organization C.

Valuable talent acquired externally can only be expected to create what is called an "initial use value." A more sustainable, and valuable, "new use value" (for the acquiring organization) is only created if the talent system goes on to make a further transformation. New use value is:

> created by the actions of organizational members, who combine to transform the use values that the organization has acquired.[17]

Put simply, the onus is on the receiving organization to know how to translate the potential use value talent has into useful value in the new organization context – strategists never assume that use value automatically exports.

FIVE CRITICAL DESIGN PRINCIPLES FOR VALUE CREATION

The first five of our design principles for a talent management system if it is to claim that it creates value are as follows:

1. Additional value is only created by "stars" if it outweighs the value that is shared with them (salaries, bonuses and share rights), provides sustainable gains over time and outweighs the efforts to manage such talent or lost productivity (through lost effort) of the alternative people who might otherwise have been invested in.
2. Individual stars can create value only through their individual creativity, i.e., to the extent that they can create novel tasks,

services and business models that could not have been arrived at through alternative investments. For value to be created, the investment in stars has to outperform similar investment in existing resources and skill base.

3. The greater the gap between the price the customer is willing to pay and the price the supplier (star talent) has the power to extract (i.e., the less monopoly power the supplier has), the higher the perceived "value for money" (use value).
4. In acquiring a strategic talent asset, value is only created when organizations can put the assumed use value to work and create "new use value" in a new context, and organizations need "decoding and translating mechanisms" for this "different use value" to yield added exchange value.
5. The ability of elite talent to create new use value is likely to be contingent upon the level of business model change and to be higher only where there are relatively stable and incremental levels of change.

What are the tools, policies and practices that would help your talent system to measure up to the above?

8.5 How is value captured by talent management?

Talent systems need to ensure that the organization has viable options in any negotiations that take place between actors in the talent system. Organizations need mechanisms to capture, assimilate and re-create captured know-how – and to commoditize that know-how – if they are not to be overly dependent on the provider of talent.

Following our theory of value, and thinking about the successful transfer of strategic assets, strategists go on to argue that to focus simply on value creation is not sufficient;[18] they prefer the concept of value capture. However, the source that creates value in some way (the talent system) may or may not be able to "capture" the value for the organization once it has been created. You need separate and additional processes to ensure this happens:[19]

1. Artful procurement (of talent that has "use value") has to be supplemented with processes that ensure that the value they have the potential to create is actually captured.

2. Organizations need what strategists call "isolating mechanisms" that enable them to actually capture this value. These mechanisms help *decode* and *translate* what it is that is making the individual have talent so that it can be applied more widely.

Those who believe that human capital is central to value generation obscure the importance of knowledge production – and this knowledge is only really captured through relationships. The ability of organizations and their talent architectures to capture value depends on other factors. In addition to being able to decode and translate the value that talent brings, the following must exist:[20]

- Organizations need additional processes to "capture" that value once they have created the transferable "new use value."
- Talent, whilst having the potential to deliver use value to the organization, might choose not to hand it over.
- The capture of value is therefore a function of the bargaining process between the actors involved (be they customers, employees or suppliers).
- The economic basis of these power relationships is a function of the organization's perceived dependence.

CAPTURING THE VALUE OF TALENT: LESSONS FROM ECONOMICS

From an economic perspective, star talent are actors who have "value creating advantages, capabilities and action potential." [21] To capture these, organizations need systems that can motivate and capture co-created value. Strategists draw upon the economic notion of "incomplete links" and "frictions" between buyers and sellers that limit the abilities of buyers to find alternatives. They use coalitional game theory to argue that:[22]

- Organizations in effect are selling their resources to valuable talent, in the hope of capturing value from that talent.
- That value is only captured when there are freeform exchanges.
- The value offered by one coalition partner can only be decoded and captured when the resources and capabilities of all the players involved are equal.

For a talent management architecture to be effective:

- it has to entice talent to actually give of their talent;

- but then reduce the dependence of the organization on such talent (akin to the battles between regulators and investment bankers in the financial services sector).

If we bring what we know about strategic value capture to bear on talent management, what are the critical tests that should guide the design – and evaluation – of our talent systems?

THREE CRITICAL DESIGN PRINCIPLES FOR VALUE CAPTURE

There are three more design principles that a talent management system must have if it is to claim that it captures value from talent:

1. Even where a particular employee or group of employees have high exchange value and may be seen as a vital element in a business model once they are provided with access to the organization's resources, the organization (as sellers of these resources) may only capture minuscule amounts of exchange value where they have weak bargaining power.
2. In order to capture the value from talent at the individual level, organizations (and their talent management architecture) need decoding and translation mechanisms that exploit: the unique position of the individual in a social network; the nature of their relationship with others in the network; and their insights into otherwise tacit knowledge associated with the performance of a new task, service or business model (craft know-how).
3. In order to capture the value from talent at the organizational level, organizations (and their talent management architecture) need isolating mechanisms that structure the portfolio of talent resources, bundle these resources together in ways that builds new capabilities, and leverage these new capabilities to exploit market opportunities. Think of a soccer team flexing stars between a 4-4-2 or 3-5-2-1 formation, or an R&D manager generating innovations by mixing key scientists across different disciplines and networks. It is the conversations and interactions that talent has that helps capture value and needs managing.

What are the tools, policies and practices that would help your talent system to measure up to the above?

8.6 How is talent amplified or leveraged by talent management?

Leveraging refers to the successful application of a firm's capabilities through the processes of learning, mobilization, co-ordinating and deploying.

Our theory of value argues that the next thing to do is to amplify the value that has been captured – make it even more impactful – so that it can be more widely leveraged across the organization.[23] Insight into the ways in which talent management can do this come from studies that have looked at the:

- utility of resourcing practices;[24]
- economic benefit created by the intellectual capabilities, knowledge and social capital of talent in the professional services sector;[25]
- importance of organizational learning and high-level or meta-learning;[26]
- management of intangible assets;[27]
- evaluation of the efficiency and effectiveness of practices needed for the implementation of organizational strategies;[28] and
- analysis of how firms build global capabilities and transfer knowledge.[29]

Insights into how best to argue that there is a return on investment from a leveraging perspective come from five sources: studies that look at the development and aggregation of the whole system;[30] studies that examine the effects that human capital has on the firm performance;[31] consideration of the role of intellectual capital;[32] the identification of financial and non-financial value-based measures;[33] and international HRM research that looks at how organizational capabilities have to be leveraged across different geographical markets[34] and how talent management forms the art of a capabilities-building and knowledge-transfer strategy. Much of this can only come about through the integration of learning and development and talent management Centers of Expertise.

WAYS OF THINKING ABOUT THE LEVERAGING CONTRIBUTION OF TALENT MANAGEMENT

From all of these perspectives, the following lessons can be drawn:

- Those HR processes (typically around recruitment, selection, training and career development) that reduce the cost of providing employees with relevant information, assess the "whole person" beyond just the immediate task performance needs or increase the speed to competence (improve efficiency) all free up existing resources. They leverage investment by enabling more to be done for the same spend.

- Those intra-person (within the person) talent management practices that enable an individual to be the best they can, serving to optimize and amplify their performance, also leverage the initial investments made in that person.[35]
- There is often a U-shaped effect, where only at a certain point does the leveraging of human capital have a positive and increasing effect, e.g., firms typically pay more to employees in their early career (invest in development) on the assumption that they will recoup investment and leverage future productivity.[36]
- Processes are needed to combine individual skills with tacit organizational knowledge in ways that lead to novel and valuable outcomes, creating greater human capital for the serving of customers, e.g., the assignment of young talent to strategically important projects and clients, mentoring and exploitation of networks.[37]
- Processes are needed to extract the "value components" and "drivers" associated with an organization's strategy (such as customers, competitors, employees, information, partners, processes, services and technology) and help identify the performance-based activities that leverage these drivers, e.g., the generation of new ideas that improve skills and services; structuring of resources to capture, transfer and share knowledge and interactions between such resources; and cultural reinforcers of collaboration, creativity, communication and trust.
- A set of "intangible" value drivers serve to leverage firm and market-level financial outcomes, including activities associated with customer satisfaction, brand equity, patents and processes that focus attention on things like total quality management, business process engineering, customer relationship management and teamworking.
- More collective processes of knowledge generation and talent management are needed. These more collective processes can serve to improve a number of things. They build the ability of important social networks to conduct conversations and

have a much higher-quality dialogue about the strategy. They also help build the organization's capacity to combine and exchange knowledge, and to agree on which practices it needs to acquire, integrate or reconfigure.

- From a knowledge management perspective, investments in talent can also be "leveraged" through devices that tie people together more flexibly, across markets and geographies, or the deployment of what are seen as a series of "knowledge integration mechanisms"[38] such as Centers of Excellence, expatriate advice networks and transnational teams; a more proactive role of international mobility functions in creating social capital; and the active management of global expertise networks, based on communities of practice and social communities.

If we bring what we know about the leveraging of value to bear on talent management, what are the critical tests that should guide the design – and evaluation – of our talent systems?

THREE CRITICAL DESIGN PRINCIPLES FOR VALUE LEVERAGING

There are three design principles for a talent management system to enable the leveraging of value from talent:

1. In order for organizations to renew, augment and adapt their current capabilities, they need to build processes into their talent management architecture that combine individual skills with tacit organizational knowledge in ways that lead to novel and valuable outcomes.
2. A series of talent management activities and practices are capable of being structured in ways that will leverage value by improving the efficiency and effectiveness of strategic execution. They must improve the quality of this execution through their motivational, learning and supporting effects.
3. Organizations need to position talent management as part of a broader knowledge and capability strategy, and build a distributed capability system that combines the acquisition, creation, capture and storage of knowledge, through activities that ensure its subsequent flow, transfer and diffusion.

What are the tools, policies and practices that would help your talent system to measure up to the above?

8.7 How can value be protected, preserved and retained by talent management?

For once, HRM and strategy experts agree. HRM specialists argue the importance of ensuring that value, once created and captured, is not lost. Strategists and economists argue that an organization can only preserve value – stop it from being captured by others – through a series of "isolating mechanisms" that stop rival firms from acquiring or replicating a desired bundle of resources. The value of any strategic asset – including talent – has to be protected.

Finally, we consider the fourth value-adding process in the theory of value, which is that of retention, protection and preservation. Our final suggestions come from a number of perspectives that have helped to articulate what is involved in this final value-generating (more accurately preserving) process. All the judgments below of course map over into the value of talent and talent management architectures. Imagine co-opting specialists with these insights into your talent function.

THE ISSUE OF PROTECTION COMES FROM A VARIETY OF STUDIES AND DISCIPLINES

- Human capital metrics that look at the value and utility of human resource interventions, such as salary growth and promotions on job turnover.[39]
- Avoiding dysfunctional high-performance employee turnover through organizational practices that influence the performance distribution of leavers.[40]
- The organizational benefits of retaining top talent by demonstrating that top talent produces a disproportionately large amount of output.
- The retention of top managers and other value-creating human capital in mergers based on the creation of governance arrangements that provide credible commitments and maintenance of managerial discretion.[41]

- Intellectual property rights, which identify how intellectual property has to be managed across a value chain. This value chain requires that the organization understands what is involved in the generation, protection, utilization and finally the appropriation of intellectual property. All four sets of activities have to be brought together if the organization is to ever really get a return on investment. Having captured intellectual property, it then has to protect it from the forces of competition.[42]
- Guarding against the threats of value leakage caused by the spread of competitive intelligence incursions and the passing of information through a supply chain or within knowledge-sharing networks,[43] i.e., more knowledge, in more heads, under less control problem.
- The question of customer value, with value models that contain ideas that can be mapped over to talent. These look at the perceptions needed in order for a customer to buy (such as wants or esteem value, worth or exchange value, and needs or utility value) or benefits-costs ratio models (which look at perceptions of customer value based on the benefits received versus the sacrifices made).[44]
- Marketing research gives attention to customer acquisition and customer expansion through cross-selling. At the heart of these two processes is the challenge of customer retention and the subsequent development of customer lifetime value.[45]

Investments in talent may be viewed in all these ways, with ideas about customer lifetime value being particularly relevant. Value exists in customer relationships over their whole life cycle (value is defined as the present value of all the future profits obtained from a customer over the life of their relationship with the organization). Small increases in customer retention, and the avoidance of customer defections to competitors, can lead to large increases in net present value profits under certain conditions.

Given the curvilinear relationship between human capital and return on investment mentioned in the previous section, talent management likely operates on the same basis as customers, with increases in retention having considerable benefit. This requires arguments to be developed about preserving and protecting prior investments in talent by giving value to the intensity or longevity of the relationship that the talent management architecture creates. How might this be done?

Customer retention models estimate the value of a range of outcomes:

- lost for good and brand-switching customers (talent that leaves);
- customers' loyalty and remaining alive and repeat buying (for companies, talent being engaged or disengaged); and
- the cost of accelerated failure of a relationship, or the proportional risks or hazards (see the discussion in the previous chapter of risk optimization and mitigation in talent management).

We believe that all of these constructs can be mapped over to the field of talent management. They are judgments that can be used to evaluate the consequences of talent management systems, their practices and the talent they spawn.

If we bring what know about the protection of value to bear on talent management, what are the critical tests that should guide the design – and evaluation – of our talent systems?

THREE CRITICAL DESIGN PRINCIPLES FOR VALUE PROTECTION

Three final design principles for a talent management system are as follows:

1. The protection of prior talent investments requires a talent management architecture built around processes of: design and maintenance of effective governance of talent; the use of risk optimization, management and mitigation frameworks; constructive surfacing of risks in business models; and consideration of reputational issues.
2. Talent architectures need to include processes that enable the modeling and retention of the best capabilities by limiting levels of value appropriation or leakage to competitors.
3. The utility of talent protection strategies may be captured through estimates of talent lifetime value, which includes the proportional risks, hazards and costs of lost for good talent, the accelerated failure of talent relationships, and talent disengagement.

What are the tools, policies and practices that would help your talent system to measure up to the above?

8.8 Conclusions

In the previous chapter we revealed the assumptions made by four different talent management philosophies – talent management as a categorization of people, the presence of key HRM practices, the identification of pivotal positions, and human capital planning and management around strategically important internal talent pools. In doing this, we showed that each perspective brings with it implicit claims about the value of talent management. However, most of these claims are in the main still untested.

Hopefully, as this chapter demonstrates, as the field matures, we can now adopt a broader and more strategic set of frameworks in order to consider how individual talent, and the broader talent management architecture, is of value to the organization. If we are to attempt to argue a return on investment from HR, then we need to design more strategic HR systems, and to do this we need to co-opt the language and thinking of other management fields, such as strategy.

In this chapter we have used ideas about value generation, value capture, value leverage and value protection to think more broadly. We have used this framework specifically around one narrow question – how we might evaluate what it is that talent is supposed to be doing, the value of this activity and its contribution to the underlying strategic purpose of the organization? In using talent management as one example of how important it is to think this way, and in looking at the way in which we must try to answer these more challenging questions, it is clear that the value of each and every activity that HR might be involved in – be it their talent systems or the way they align their offerings to the challenges of innovation, customer centricity, lean management or collaborative business models – now needs to be thought about in the same way. If we are to answer the question "Do We Need HR?" we need to develop arguments and evidence the answers both in the context of the underlying strategic performance challenges analyzed throughout this book and in the context of the new cross-functional sets of activities that HR functions find themselves a part of. We hope we have made three contributions:

- First, to identify the different types of value that should be provided by either the pursuit of specific performance outcomes such as innovation, customer centricity, lean management and collaborative business models, or the broader HRM architecture and system. The incorporation of the broader and non-HR literatures into our framework leads to the identification of a series of processes that must be central to any contribution that HR makes,

which we call value creation, value capture, value leverage (or amplification) and value protection (retention and preservation).
- Second, to explain how each type of value is delivered in general terms, and therefore what the contribution and scope of a good HR function should be if it is really to be effective or of value to the organization.
- Third, by thinking this way, it becomes possible to organize and position many of the debates and criticisms about whether or not we need HR, and whether should still be organized along traditional functional lines, by linking these debates to the broader question of value.

Whilst it is legitimate to ask "Do we need HR?" and to "Reposition people management for success," it is equally as legitimate to ask the same questions about the way that all of the current functional directorates inside organizations operate. Hence, this book should be of relevance to any people-minded business leader.

Notes

Chapter 1

1. Sparrow, P.R., Hird, M., Hesketh, A. and Cooper, C. (2010) *Leading HR*. Basingstoke: Palgrave Macmillan.
2. Hodgkinson, G. and Sparrow, P.R (2002) *The Competent Organization: A Psychological Analysis of the Strategic Management Process*. Buckingham: Open University Press.
3. Gartner Inc. (2014) *The Gartner CEO and Senior Executive Survey 2014 – "Risk-On" Attitudes Will Accelerate Digital Business*. Stamford, CT.
4. PricewaterhouseCoopers (2014) "17th Annual CEO Survey," www.pwc.com/usceo survey (date accessed May 15, 2014).
5. Sparrow, P.R. (1986) "The erosion of employment in the UK: the need for a new response." *New Technology, Work and Employment*, 1(2): 101–12.
6. OECD (2014) *Focus on Top Incomes and Taxation in OECD Countries: Was the Crisis a Game Changer?* Directorate for Employment, Labour and Social Affairs.
7. See www.ioe.ac.uk/newsEvents/86758.html (date accessed May 15, 2014).
8. Sparrow, P.R. and Pettigrew, A. (1987) "Britain's training problems: the search for a strategic human resources management approach." *Human Resource Management*, 26: 109–27, p. 118.
9. Hendry, C., Pettigrew, A. and Sparrow, P.R. (1988) "Changing patterns of human resource management." *Personnel Management*, 20(11): 37–41.
10. Flood, P.C., Gannon, M.J. and Paauwe, J. (1996) *Managing without Traditional Methods: International Innovations in Human Resource Management*. Wokingham: Addison-Wesley.
11. Flood, P.C., Gannon, M.J. and Paauwe, J. (1996) "Competitive advantage through strategic innovations in human resource management." In P.C. Flood, M.J. Gannon

and J. Paauwe (eds), *Managing without Traditional Methods: International Innovations in Human Resource Management*. Wokingham: Addison-Wesley, p. 108.

Chapter 2

1. Pettigrew, A., Hendry, C. and Sparrow, P.R. (1990) *Corporate Strategy Change and Human Resource Management*. Employment Department Research and Development Report No. 63. Sheffield: Department of Employment.
2. Hamel, G. and Breen, B. (2007) *The Future of Management*. Cambridge, MA: Harvard Business School Press.
3. Sparrow, P.R. (2010) *The Innovation Imperative: Charting the Territory for HR*. Centre for Performance-led HR White Paper 10/01, Lancaster University Management School.
4. King, N. (1990) "Innovation at work: the research literature." In M. West and J.L. Farr (eds), *Innovation and Creativity at Work: Psychological and Organizational Perspectives*. Chichester: John Wiley & Sons Ltd, pp. 309–33.
5. Tidd, J., Bessant, J. and Pavitt, K. (2001) *Managing Innovation: Integrating Technological, Market and Organizational Change*, 2nd edn. Chichester: John Wiley & Sons Ltd.
6. See West, M.A. and Farr, J.L. (eds) (1990) *Innovation and Creativity at Work: Psychological and Organizational Strategies*. Chichester: John Wiley & Sons Ltd; Tushman, M.L. and O'Reilly, C.A. (1997) *Winning through Innovation*. Cambridge, MA: Harvard Business School Press; Florida, R. (2002) *The Rise of the Creative Class and How it is Transforming Work, Leisure, Community and Everyday Life*. New York: Basic Books; Hamel and Breen (2007) *The Future of Management*.
7. Damanpour, F. (1991) "Organizational innovation: a meta-analysis of effects of determinants and moderators." *Academy of Management Journal*, 34(3): 555–90.
8. Barsh, J. (2008) "Innovative management: a conversation with Gary Hamel and Lowell Bryan." *The McKinsey Quarterly*, 1: 1–10, p. 2.
9. *Ibid*.
10. Bryan, L.L. and Joyce, C.I. (2007) *Mobilizing Minds: Creating Wealth from Talent in the 21st Century Organization*. New York: McGraw-Hill.
11. Freeman, J. and Engel, J.S. (2007) "Models of innovation: start-ups and mature corporations." *California Management Review*, 50(1): 94–119.
12. Anthony, S.D., Johnson, M.W. and Sinfield, J.V. (2008) "Institutionalizing innovation." *MIT Sloan Management Review*, 4: 45–53.
13. Dobni, C.B. (2008) "The DNA of innovation." *Journal of Business Strategy*, 29(2): 43–51, p. 46
14. Christensen, C.M. (1997) *The Innovator's Dilemma: When New Technologies Cause Great Firms to Fail*. Cambridge, MA: Harvard Business School Press; Christensen, C.M., Roth, E.A. and Anthony, S.D. (2004) *Seeing What is Next:*

Using Theories of Innovation to Predict Industry Change. Cambridge, MA: Harvard Business School Press.

15. Anthony, Johnson and Sinfield (2008) "Institutionalizing innovation."
16. IBM Global Services (2006) *Business Model Innovation: The New Route to Competitive Advantage*. Somers, NY: IBM plc.
17. Powell, W.W., Koput, K.W. and Smith-Doerr, L. (1996) "Interorganizational collaboration and the locus of innovation: networks of learning in biotechnology." *Administrative Science Quarterly*, 41: 116–45.
18. Thorgren, S., Wincent, J. and Örtqvist, D. (2009) "Designing interorganizational networks for innovation: an empirical examination of network configuration formation and governance." *Journal of Engineering and Technology Management*, 26: 148–66.
19. Hewrold, D.M., Jayaraman, N. and Narayanaswamy, C.R. (2006) "What is the relationship between organizational slack and innovation?" *Journal of Managerial Issues*, 18(5): 372–92, p. 372.
20. Chesbrough, H. (2003) *Open Innovation: The New Imperative for Creating and Profiting from Technology*. Cambridge, MA: Harvard Business School Press; Chesbrough, H. (2004) "Managing open innovation." *Research Technology Management*, 47(1): 23–6.
21. Huston, L. and Sakkab, N. (2007) "Implementing open innovation." *Research Technology Management*, 50(2): 21–5; Igartua, J.I., Garrigós, J.A. and Hervas-Oliver, J.L. (2010) "How innovation management techniques support an open innovation strategy." *Research Technology Management*, 53(3): 41–52.
22. Ojasalo, J. (2008) "Management of innovation networks: a case study of different approaches." *European Journal of Innovation Management*, 11(1): 51–86; Matheus, T. (2009) "A conceptual model and illustrative research framework for inter-organizational innovation." *Management Research News*, 32(3): 254–71.
23. Jüttner, U. and Schlange, L.E. (1996) "A network approach to strategy." *International Journal of Research in Marketing*, 13: 479–94.
24. Häkansson, H. and Ford, D. (2002) "How should companies interact in business networks?" *Journal of Business Research*, 55: 133–9.
25. Hobday, M., Rush, H., and Tidd, J. (2000) "Innovation in complex products and system." *Research Policy*, 29: 793–804; Prencipe, A. (2005) "Corporate strategy and systems integration capabilities: managing networks in complex systems industries." In A. Prencipe, A. Davies and M. Hobday (eds), *The Business of Systems Integration,* Oxford University Press, pp. 114–32.
26. Kodama, M. (2000) "Business innovation through strategic community management: a case study of NTT's digital network revolution." *Strategic Change*, 9(3): 177–96.
27. Von Hippel, E. (1988) *The Sources of Innovation*. New York: Oxford University Press; Sanchez, R. (1996) "Strategic product creation: managing new interactions of technology, markets, and organizations." *European Management Journal*, 14(2): 121–38; Sanchez, R. (1997) "Managing articulated knowledge in competence-based competition." In R. Sanchez and A. Heene (eds), *Strategic Learning and Knowledge Management*. Chichester: John Wiley & Sons, pp. 163–87; Garud,

R. (1997) "On the distinction between know-how, know-what and know-why." In J.P. Walsh, A.S. Huff, P. Shrivastava and J. Dutton (eds), *Advances in Strategic Management*. Greenwich, CT: JAI Press, pp. 81–101; Ritter, T. (1999) "The networking company: antecedents for coping with relationships and networks effectively." *Industrial Marketing Management*, 28(5): 467–79.

28. Ragatz, G., Handfield, R. and Scannell, T. (1997) "Success factors for integrating suppliers into new product development." *Journal of Product Innovation Management*, 14(3): 190–202; Dyer, J.H. and Nobeoka, K. (2000) "Creating and managing a high-performance knowledge sharing network: the Toyota case." *Strategic Management Journal*, 21(3): 344–68; Ritter, T. and Gemünden, H.G. (2003) "Network competence: its impact on innovation success and its antecedents." *Journal of Business Research*, 56: 745–55.
29. Hafkesbrink, J. and Schroll, M. (2011) "Innovation 3.0: embedding into community knowledge – collaborative organizational learning beyond open innovation." *Journal of Innovation Economics*, 1(7): 55–92.
30. *Ibid*.
31. Kanter, R.M. (1989) *When Giants Learn to Dance*, New York: Simon & Schuster.
32. Iyer, B. and Davenport, T.H. (2008) "Reverse engineering Google's innovation machine." *Harvard Business Review*, 86(4): 59–68.
33. *Ibid*., p. 61.
34. *Ibid*., p. 62.
35. Scharmer, C.O. (2009) *Theory U: Leading from the Future as it Emerges*. San Francisco, CA: Berrett-Koehler Publishers Inc.
36. De Rond, M. and Thiétart, R.A. (2004) "Chance, choice and determinism in strategy." *Cambridge Business School Working Paper 05/2004*. Judge Institute of Management, University of Cambridge, p. 17.
37. Byrne, C.L., Mumford, M.D., Barrett, J.D. and Vessay, W.B. (2009) "Examining the leaders of creative efforts: what do they do, and what do they think about?" *Creativity and Innovation Management*, 18(4): 256–68, p. 256.
38. West, M.A. (2000) "State of the art: creativity and innovation at work." *The Psychologist*, 13(9): 460–4.
39. Hamel and Breen (2007) *The Future of Management* .
40. Barsh (2008) "Innovative management," p. 9.
41. West, M.A. (2002) "Sparkling fountains or stagnant ponds: an integrative model of creativity and innovation implementation in work groups." *Applied Psychology: An International Review*, 51: 355–87.
42. Unsworth, K.L. and Clegg, C.W. (2010) "Why do employees undertake creative action?" *Journal of Occupational and Organizational Psychology*, 83: 77–99, p.77.
43. Sternberg, R.J. (ed.) (1999) *Handbook of Creativity*. New York: Cambridge University Press.
44. Patterson F. (2002) "Great minds don't think alike? Person-level predictors of innovation at work." *International Review of Industrial and Organizational Psychology*, 17: 115–44.

45. *Ibid.*
46. Weisberg, R.W. (1999) "Creativity and knowledge: a challenge to theories." In Sternberg (ed.), *Handbook of Creativity*, pp. 226–50.
47. Jack, S., Rose, M. and Johnston, L. (2010) "Tracing the historical foundations of social networks in entrepreneurship research." *Institute for Entrepreneurship and Enterprise Development Research Paper*, Lancaster University Management School, p. 1
48. Mumford, M.D., Baughman, W.A. and Sager, C.E. (2003) "Picking the right material: cognitive processing skills and their role in creative thought." In M.A. Runco (ed.), *Critical and Creative Thinking*. Creskill, NJ: Hampton. pp. 19–68
49. Byrne *et al.* (2009) "Examining the leaders of creative efforts," p. 257.
50. Sternberg (ed.), *Handbook of Creativity*.
51. Patterson F. (2002) "Great minds don't think alike?"
52. Barsh (2008) "Innovative management," p. 4.
53. Smith, M., Bush, M., Ball, P. and Van der Meer, R. (2008) "Factors influencing an organization's ability to manage innovation: a structured literature review and conceptual model." *International Journal of Innovation Management*, 12(4): 655–76.

Chapter 3

1. Sparrow, P.R., Hird, M., Hesketh, A. and Cooper, C.L. (eds) (2010) *Leading HR*. Basingstoke: Palgrave Macmillan.
2. See, for example, Heskett, J.L., Sasser, W.E. and Schlesinger, I.A. (1997) *The Service Profit Chain*. New York: Free Press; Ruci, A.J., Kim, S.P. and Quinn, R.T (1998) "The employee-customer-profit chain at Sears." *Harvard Business Review*, 76(1): 82–97; Wiley, J.W. and Brooks, S.M. (2000) "The high-performance organizational culture." In N.M. Ashkanasy, C.P.M. Wilderom and M.F. Peterson (eds), *Handbook of Organizational Culture and Climate*. Thousand Oaks, CA: Sage, pp. 177–91.
3. Schneider, B., Bowen, D.E., Ehrhart, M.G. and Holcombe, K.M. (2000) "The climate for service." In N.M. Ashkanasy, C.P.M. Wilderom and M.F. Peterson (eds), *Handbook of Organizational Culture and Climate*. Thousand Oaks, CA: Sage, pp. 1–36.
4. Koys, D.J. (2001) "The effects of employee satisfaction, organizational citizenship behaviour and turnover on organizational effectiveness: a unit-level, longitudinal study." *Personnel Psychology*, 54: 101–14.
5. See, for example, Schneider, B., White, A. and Paul, M. (1998) "Linking service climate and customer perceptions of service quality: test of a causal model." *Journal of Applied Psychology*, 83: 150–63; Schmit, M.J. and Allscheid, S.P. (1995) "Employee attitudes and customer satisfaction: making theoretical and empirical connections." *Personnel Psychology*, 48: 521–35; Johnson, J.W. (1996) "Linking employee perceptions of service climate to customer satisfaction." *Personnel Psychology*, 49: 831–51.
6. See, for example, Gunter, B. and Furnham, A. (1996) "Biographical and climate predictors of job satisfaction and pride in organization." *Journal of Psychology*,

130: 192–208; Johnson, J.J. and McIntyre, C.L. (1998) "Organizational culture and climate correlates of job satisfaction." *Psychological Reports*, 82: 843–50; Ostroff, C., Klinicki, A.J. and Clark, M.A. (2002) "Substantive and operational issues of response bias across levels of analysis: an example of climate-satisfaction relationships." *Journal of Applied Psychology*, 87: 355–68.

7. See, for example, Mittal, V., Kumar, P. and Tsiros, M. (1999) "Attribute-level performance, satisfaction and behaviuoral intentions over time: a consumption system approach." *Journal of Marketing*, 63: 88–101; Zeithaml, V.A., Berry, L.L. and Parasuraman, A. (1996) "The behavioural consequences of service quality." *Journal of Marketing*, 60: 31–46.
8. See, for example, Bolton, R.N. (1998) "A dynamic model of the duration of the customer's relationship with a continuous service provider: the role of satisfaction." *Marketing Science*, 17: 45–65; Bolton, R.N. and Lemon, K.N. (1999) "A dynamic model of customers' usage of services: usage as an antecedent and consequence of satisfaction." *Journal of Marketing Research*, 36: 171–86.
9. Hennig-Thurau, T. and Klee, A. (1997) "The impact of customer satisfaction and relationship quality on customer retention: a critical reassessment and model development." *Psychology and Marketing*, 14: 737–64; Verhoef, P.C., Franses, P.H. and Hoekstra, J. (2002) "The effect of relational constructs on customer referrals and number of services purchased from a multi-service provider: does age of relationship matter?' *Journal of the Academy of Marketing Science*, 30: 202–16.
10. Ruci, Kim and Quinn (1998) "The employee-customer-profit chain at Sears."
11. Sparrow, P.R., Balain, S. and Fairhurst, D. (2010) "McDonald's UK: from corporate reputation to trust-based HR." In P.R. Sparrow, M. Hird, A. Hesketh and C. Cooper (eds), *Leading HR*. Basingstoke: Palgrave Macmillan pp. 209–30.
12. Toffler, A. (1980) *The Third Wave*. New York: Bantam, p. 274.
13. Scott, D. (2010) *American Heritage Dictionary of Business Terms*. Boston, MA: Houghton Mifflin Harcourt.
14. Meredith, R., Remington, S., O'Donnell, P. and Sharma, N. (2012) "Organizational transformation through Business Intelligence: theory, the vendor perspective and a research agenda." *Journal of Decision Systems*, 31(3): 187–201.
15. www.takepart.com/article/2014/03/04/what-mcdonalds-future-looks (date accessed May 10, 2014).
16. http://blog.kobie.com/2013/07/qsrs-turning-the-data-deluge-into-actionable-insights/ (date accessed May 10, 2014).
17. www.fastcodesign.com/3023505/4-ways-to-fix-the-fast-food-industry (date accessed May 10, 2014).
18. Marsh, C., Sparrow, P.R. and Hird, M. (2010) *Is Customer Centricity a Movement or a Myth? Opening The Debate For HR.* Centre for Performance-led HR White Paper 10/03, Lancaster University Management School.
19. Carlzon, J. (1987) *Moments of Truth: New Strategies for Today's Customer-Driven Economy*. New York: HarperCollins.

20. Gummesson, E. (2008) "Customer centricity: reality or a wild goose chase?' *European Business Review*, 20(4): 315–30, p. 316.
21. Heskett, J.L., Jones, T.O., Loveman, G.W, Sasser, W.E. and Schlesinger, L.A. (2008) "Putting the service-profit chain to work." *Harvard Business Review*, 86(7/8): 118–29.
22. Sheth, J.N., Sisodia, R.S. and Sharma, A. (2000) "The antecedents and consequences of customer-centric marketing." *Journal of the Academy of Marketing Science*, 28(1): 55–66.
23. Peppers, D. and Rogers, M. (1993) *The One to One Future: Building Relationships One Customer at a Time*. New York: Currency Books.
24. Oliver, R.L. (1999) "Whence customer loyalty?' *Journal of Marketing*, 63: 33–44.
25. Parasuraman, A. and Grewal, D. (2000) "The impact of technology on the quality-value-loyalty chain: a research agenda." *Academy of Marketing Science Journal*, 28(1): 168–74.
26. Reichheld, F.F. (2001) *The Loyalty Effect: The Hidden Force behind Growth, Profits and Lasting Value*. Boston, MA: Harvard Business School Press; Kumar, V. and Shah, D. (2004) "Building and sustaining profitable customer loyalty for the 21st century." *Journal of Retailing*, 80(4): 317–29.
27. Boulding, W., Kalra, A., Staelin, R. and Zeithaml, V.A. (1993) "A dynamic process model of service quality: from expectations to behavioural intentions." *Journal of Marketing Research*, 30(1): 7–27; Rust, R.T., Moorman, C. and Dickson, P.R. (2002) "Getting return on quality: revenue expansion, cost reduction, or both?" *Journal of Marketing*, 66(4): 7–24.
28. Day, G.S. (1999) *The Market-Driven Organization*. New York: Free Press.
29. Vorhies, D.W. and Morgan, N.A. (2005) "Benchmarking marketing capabilities and sustainable competitive advantage." *Journal of Marketing*, 69 (1): 80–94.
30. Vargo, S.L. and Lusch, R.F. (2004) "Evolving to a new dominant logic for marketing." *Journal of Marketing*, 68(1): 1–21.
31. See Edvardsson, B., Gustafsson, A., Kristensson, P., Magnusson, P. and Matthing, J. (eds) (2006) *Involving Customers in New Service Development*. London: Imperial College Press; Engeseth, S. (2006) *One: A Consumer Revolution for Business*, London: Marshall Cavendish.
32. Nicholls, R. (2005) *Interactions between Service Customers*. Poznan: Poznan University of Economics.
33. Shah, D., Rust, R.T., Parasuraman, A., Staelin, R. and Day, G.S. (2006) "The path to customer centricity." *Journal of Service Research*, 9(2): 113–24.
34. *Ibid.*, p. 115.
35. Porter, M.E. (1985) *Competitive Advantage*. New York: Free Press.
36. *Ibid.*, p. 56.
37. Gummesson (2008) "Customer centricity," p. 323.
38. Boulding, W., Staelin, R., Ehret, M. and Johnson, W. (2005) "A customer relationship roadmap: what is known, potential pitfalls, where to go." *Journal of Marketing*, 60(4): 155–66.

39. Coverage can be found at: www.customerthink.com/blog/observing_customer_centricity_from_an_outside_perspective (date accessed May 10, 2014).
40. Paternoster, J. (2007) "Excellent airport customer service meets successful branding strategy." *Airport Management*, 2(3): 218–26. p. 219,
41. We have based this suite of solutions on a web search on 29 November 2010 of consulting offerings on "customer centricity" and "airlines." This search reveals offerings from consulting firms that include mainline consulting firms and specialist houses. It also reveals case studies on airlines such as Delta and South West Airlines, reports on a number of airline mergers, a magazine and newsletters on the topic and various surveys measuring centricity.
42. See Erat, P. and Zorzi, O. (2007) "Organizing for networked healthcare: towards future organizational models." *Journal of Medical Marketing*, 7: 6–17; Burmann, C., Meurer, J., and Kanitz, C. (2011) "Customer centricity as a key to success in pharma." *Journal of Medical Marketing*, 11: 49–59.
43. See Gummesson (2008) "Customer centricity"; Gummesson, E. (2008) "Extending the service-dominant logic: from customer centricity to balanced centricity." *Journal of the Academy of Marketing Science*, 36: 15–17.
44. Gummesson (2008) "Customer centricity," p. 317.
45. Coverage can be found at: www.customerthink.com/article/customer_centricity_movement_or_myth (date accessed May 10, 2014).
46. Tseng, M.M. and Piller, F.T. (2003) *The Customer-Centric Enterprise: Advances in Mass Customization and Personalization*. New York: Springer Verlag.
47. *Ibid.*, p. 5.
48. Galbraith, J.R. (2005) *Designing the Customer-Centric Organization: A Guide to Strategy, Structure and Process*. New York: Wiley.
49. Coverage can be found at: http://the56group.typepad.com/pgreenblog/2009/07/time-to-put-a-stake-in-the-ground-on-social-crm.html (date accessed May 10, 2014).
50. Coverage can be found at: http://blogs.gartner.com/michael_maoz/2009/05/07/why-your-twitter-and-social-crm-efforts-will-fail (date accessed May 10, 2014).
51. Coverage can be found at: www.radian6.com/blog/2009/06/the-rockstars-of-social-crm (date accessed May 10, 2014).
52. Stone, M. (2009) "Staying customer-focused and trusted: Web 2.0 and Customer 2.0 in financial services." *Journal of Database Marketing & Customer Strategy Management*, 16: 101–31.
53. Kates, A. and Galbraith, J. (2007) *Designing Your Organization: Using the Star Model to Solve Five Critical Design Challenges*. San Francisco: Jossey Bass.
54. *Ibid.*, p. 22.
55. Bernoff, J. and Schadler, T. (2010) "Empowered." *Harvard Business Review*, 88(7/8): 94–101.
56. Rafiq, M.A. and Ahmed, P.K. (1998) "Customer-oriented framework for empowering service employees." *Journal of Services Marketing*, 12(5): 379–96.
57. Coverage can be found at: www.slideshare.net/martinwalsh/social-crm-definition-by-martin-walsh (date accessed May 10, 2014), p. 6.

58. Coverage can be found at: www.slideshare.net/martinwalsh/social-crm-definition-by-martin-walsh (date accessed May 10, 2014).
59. *Ibid.*, p. 23.
60. Coverage can be found at: www.altimetergroup.com/2010/03/altimeter-report-the-18-use-cases-of-social-crm-the-new-rules-of-relationship-management.html (date accessed May 10, 2014).
61. *The Economist* (2010) "Untangling the social web." *The Economist Technology Quarterly*, 4 September, p. 12.

Chapter 4

1. Larman, C. and Vodde, B. (2009) *Lean Primer.* Available at: www.leanprimer.com (date accessed June 30, 2014), p. 3.
2. Womack, J., Jones, D.T. and Roos, D. (1990) *The Machine that Changed the World*. New York: Harper Perennial.
3. Womack, J. and Jones, D.T. (1996) *Lean Thinking*. New York: Free Press.
4. De Menezes, L.M., Wood, S. and Gelade, G. (2010) "The integration of human resource and operation management practices and its link with performance: a longitudinal latent class study." *Journal of Operations Management*, 28: 455–71, p. 455.
5. Pepper, M.P.J. and Spedding, T.A. (2010) "The evolution of lean Six Sigma." *International Journal of Quality and Reliability Management*, 27(2): 138–55.
6. Holweg, M. (2006) "The genealogy of lean production." *Journal of Operations Management*, 25: 420–37, p. 430.
7. See Womack, J.P. and Jones, D. (1996) *Lean Thinking*. New York: Simon & Schuster; Murman, E., Allen, T., Bozdogan, K., Cutcher-Gershenfeld, J., McManus, H., Nightingale, D., Rebentisch, E., Shields, T., Stahl, F., Walton, M., Warmkessel, J., Weiss, S. and Widnall, S. (2002). *Lean Enterprise Value: Insights from MIT's Lean Aerospace Initiative.* New York: Palgrave; Scherrer-Rathje, M., Boyle, T.A. and Deflorin, P. (2009) "Lean, take two! Reflections from the second attempt at lean implementation." *Business Horizons*, 52(1): 79–88.
8. See Womack, Jones and Roos (1990) *The Machine that Changed the World*; Womack, J.P. and Jones, D. (1994) "From lean production to the lean enterprise." *Harvard Business Review*, 72: 93–103; Womack, J.P. and Jones, D. (1996) *Lean Thinking*. New York: Simon & Schuster.
9. Gershon, M. (2010) "Choosing which process improvement methodology to implement." *Journal of Applied Business and Economics*, 10(5): 61–70.
10. Antony, J. (2011) "Six Sigma versus lean: some perspectives from leading academics and practitioners." *International Journal of Productivity and Performance Management*, 60(2): 185–90.
11. Quote cited by Larman and Vodde (2009) *Lean Primer*, as coming from Liker, J. and Hoseus, M. (2008) *Toyota Culture: The Heart and Soul of the Toyota Way*. New York: McGraw-Hill.

12. Pande, P., Neumann, R. and Cavanagh, R. (2000) *The Six Sigma Way: How GE, Motorola and Other Top Companies are Honing their Performance*. New York: McGraw-Hill.
13. Antony, J. (2004) "Six Sigma in the UK service organizations: results from a pilot survey." *Managerial Auditing Journal*, 19(8): 1006–13, p. 1008.
14. See, for example, Bendell, T. (2006) "A review and comparison of six sigma and the lean organisations." *The TQM Magazine*, 18(3): 255–62; Pepper and Spedding (2010) "The evolution of lean Six Sigma."
15. Womack and Jones (1994) "From lean production to the lean enterprise."
16. Jina, J., Bhattacharya, A.K. and Walton, A.D.W. (1997) "Applying lean principles for high product variety and low volumes: some issues and propositions." *Logistics Information Management*, 10(1): 5–13.
17. Larman and Vodde (2009) *Lean Primer*.
18. See, for example, Sprigg, C.A. and Jackson, P.R. (2006) "Call centers as lean service environments: job-related strain and the mediating role of work design." *Journal of Occupational Health Psychology*, 11: 197–212; McAdam, R., Davies, J., Keogh, B. and Finnegan, A. (2008) "Customer-oriented Six Sigma in call centre performance measurement." *International Journal of Quality & Reliability Management*, 26(6): 516–645; Piercy, N. and Rich, N. (2009) "Lean transformation in the pure service environment: the case of the call service centre." *International Journal of Operations and Production Management*, 29(1): 54–76; Laureani, A. and Antony, J. (2010) "Reducing employees' turnover in transactional services: a lean Six Sigma case study." *International Journal of Productivity and Performance Management*, 59(7): 699–700; and Teehan, R. and Tucker, W. (2010) "A simplified lean method to capture customer voice." *International Journal of Quality and Service Sciences*, 2(2): 175–88.
19. See, for example, Kollberg, B., Dahlgaard, J.J., and Brehmer, P. (2006) "Measuring lean initiatives in health care services: issues and findings." *International Journal of Productivity and Performance Management*, 56: 7–24; Collins, K. and Muthusamy, S. (2007) "Applying the Toyota Production System to a healthcare organization: a case study on a rural community healthcare provider." *Quality Management Journal*, 14(4): 41–52; and Fillingham, D. (2007) "Can lean save lives?" *Leadership in Health Services*, 20(4): 231–41.
20. Staats, B.R., Brunner, D.J. and Upton, D.M. (2011) "Lean principles, learning and knowledge work: evidence from a software services provider." *Journal of Operations Management*, 29: 376–90.
21. See, for example, Furterer, S. and Elshennawy, A. (2005) "Implementation of TQM and Lean Six Sigma tools in local government: a framework and a case study." *Total Quality Management*, 16(10): 1179–91; Bhatia, N. and Drew, J. (2006) "Applying lean production to the public sector." *The McKinsey Quarterly*, 3: 97–8; Krings, D., Levine, D. and Wall, T. (2006) "The use of lean in local government." *Public Management*, 88(8): 12–17; Radnor, Z. and Bucci, G. (2007) *Evaluation of Pacesetter, Lean, Senior Leadership and Operational Management within HMRC*

Processing. London: HMRC; Radnor, Z. (2010) "Transferring lean into government." *Journal of Manufacturing Technology*, 21(3): 411–28.

22. See, for example, Delgado, C., Ferreira, M. and Branco, M.C. (2010) "The implementation of lean Six Sigma in financial service organizations." *Journal of Manufacturing Technology Management*, 21(4): 512–23; Heckl, D., Moormann, J. and Rosemann, M. (2010) "Uptake and success factors of Six Sigma in the financial services industry." *Business Process Management Journal*, 16 (3): 436–72.
23. See, for example, Laureani, A., and Antony, J. (2010) "Reducing employees' turnover in transactional services: a Lean Six Sigma case study." *International Journal of Productivity and Performance Management*, 59(7): 699–700; Suárez-Barraza, M.F. and Ramis-Pujol, J. (2010) "Implementation of lean-Kaizen in the human resource service process: a case study in a Mexican public service organization." *Journal of Manufacturing Technology Management*, 21(3): 388–410.
24. Levitt, T. (1976) "The industrialization of service." *Harvard Business Review*, 54 (5): 32–43.
25. See, for example, Wright, C., and Mechling, G. (2002) "The importance of operations management problems in service organizations." *Omega*, 30(2): 77–87; Antony (2004) "Six Sigma in the UK service organizations"; Abdi, F., Shavarini, S. and Hoseini, S. (2006) "Glean lean: how to use lean approach in services industries." *Journal of Services Research*, 6: 191–206; Prajego, D. (2006) "The implementation of operations management techniques in service organizations: an Australian perspective." *International Journal of Operations and Production Management*, 26(12): 1374–90; and Maleyeff, J. (2006) "Exploration of internal service systems using lean principles." *Management Decision*, 44(5): 674–89.
26. Antony (2004) "Six Sigma in the UK service organizations."
27. Radnor (2010) "Transferring lean into government," p. 422.
28. Gummesson, E. (2008) "Extending the service-dominant logic: from customer centricity to balanced centricity." *Journal of the Academy of Marketing Science*, 36: 15–17.
29. Hino, S. (2006) *Inside the Mind of Toyota: Management Principles for Enduring Growth*. New York: Productivity Press
30. Larman, C. and Vodde, B. (2009) *Scaling Lean and Agile Development: Thinking and Organizational Tools for Large-Scale Scrum*. New York: Addison-Wesley.
31. Quoted in *ibid.*
32. Quoted in *ibid.*
33. Antony (2011) "Six Sigma versus lean," p. 186.
34. Aboelmaged, M.G. (2010) "Six Sigma quality: a structured review and implications for future research." *International Journal of Quality and Reliability Management*, 27(3): 269–318.
35. Fullerton, R.R. and Wempe, W.F. (2009) "Lean manufacturing, non-financial performance measures and financial performance." *International Journal of Operations and Production Management*, 29: 214–240.
36. Shook, J. (2010) "How to change a culture? Lessons from NUMMI." *Sloan Management Review*, 51(2): 63–8, p. 68.

37. See, for example, Delbridge, R., Turnbull, P. and Wilkinson, B. (1992) "Pushing back the frontiers: management control and work intensification under JIT/TQM regimes." *New Technology Work and Employment*, 7: 97–106; Anderson-Connolly, R., Grunberg, L., Greenberg, E.S. and Moore, S. (2002) "Is lean mean?: workplace transformation and employee well-being." *Work, Employment and Society*, 16: 389–413.
38. Pepper and Spedding (2010) "The evolution of lean Six Sigma," p. 141.
39. Conti, R., Angelis, J., Cooper, C., Faragher, B. and Gill, C. (2006) "The effects of lean production on worker job stress." *International Journal of Operations and Production Management*, 26(9): 1013–38.
40. Stewart, P., Danford, A., Richardson, M. and Pulignano, V. (2010) "Workers' experiences of skill, training and participation in lean and high performance workplaces in Britain and Italy." *Employee Relations*, 32(6): 606–24, p. 607.
41. *Ibid.*
42. Wood, S.J., Stride, C.B., Wall, T.D. and Clegg, C,W. (2004) "Revisiting the use and effectiveness of modern management practices." *Human Factors and Ergonomics in Manufacturing*, 14(4): 415–32; Birdi, K., Clegg, C.W., Patterson, M., Robinson, A., Stride, C,B., Wall, T.D. and Wood, S.J. (2008) "The impact of human resource and operational management practices on company productivity: a longitudinal study." *Personnel Psychology*, 61: 467–501.
43. De Menezes, L.M., Wood, S., and Gelade, G. (2010) "The integration of human resource and operation management practices and its link with performance: a longitudinal latent class study." *Journal of Operations Management*, 28: 455–71, p.456.
44. Parry, G., Mills, J. and Turner, C. (2010) "Lean competence: integration of theories in operations management practice." *Supply Chain Management: An International Journal*, 15(3): 216–26.
45. Scherrer-Rathje, M., Boyle, T.A., and Deflorin, P. (2009) "Lean, take two! Reflections from the second attempt at lean implementation." *Business Horizons*, 52(1): 79–88.
46. See, for example, Hines, P., Holweg, M. and Rich, N. (2004) "Learning to evolve: a review of contemporary lean thinking." *International Journal of Operations and Production Management*, 24(10): 994–1011; Holweg, M. (2006) "The genealogy of lean production." *Journal of Operations Management*, 25: 420–37; Hines, P., Found, P. and Harrison, R. (2008) *Staying Lean: Thriving, Not Just Surviving, Lean Enterprise Research Centre*. Cardiff University; Radnor, Z. (2010) "Transferring lean into government." *Journal of Manufacturing Technology*, 21(3): 411–28.
47. Cullinane, S.-J., Bosak, J., Flood, P. and Demerouti, E. (2012) "Job design under lean manufacturing and its impact on employee outcomes." *Organizational Psychology Review*, 3(1): 41–61.
48. De Treville, S. and Antonakis, J. (2006) "Could lean production job design be intrinsically motivating? Contextual, configurational and levels-of-analysis issues." *Journal of Operations Management*, 24: 99–123.
49. Parker, S.K. (2003) "Longitudinal effects of lean production on employee outcomes and the mediating role of work characteristics." *Journal of Applied Psychology*, 88: 620–34.

50. Antony (2011) "Six Sigma versus lean."
51. Samson, D., Sohal, A.S. and Ramsay, E. (1993) Human resource issues in manufacturing improvement initiatives: case study experiences in Australia, *The International Journal of Human Factors in Manufacturing*, 3(2): 135–52.
52. Forza, C. (1996) "Work organization in lean production and traditional plants – what are the differences?" *International Journal of Operations & Production Management*, 16(2): 42–62; Bonavia, T. and Marin-Garcia, J.A. (2011) "Integrating human resource management into lean production and their impact on organizational performance." *International Journal of Manpower*, 32(8): 923–38.
53. Sparrow, P.R., Hird, M., Hesketh, A.J. and Cooper, C.L. (eds) (2010). *Leading HR*. Basingstoke: Palgrave Macmillan.
54. Becker, B.E. and Huselid, M.A. (2006) "Strategic human resources management: where do we go from here?" *Journal of Management*, 32: 898–925.
55. Ulrich, D. (1997) *Human Resource Champions*. Cambridge, MA: Harvard Business School Press.
56. Kang, S-C., Morris, S.S. and Snell, S.A. (2007) "Relational archetypes, organizational learning and value creation: extending the human resource architecture." *Academy of Management Review*, 32(1): 236–56.
57. Henderson, R.M. and Clark, K.B. (1990) "Architectural innovation: the reconfiguration of existing product technologies and the failure of established firms." *Administrative Science Quarterly*, 35: 9–30.

Chapter 5

1. Sparrow, P.R., Hird, M., Hesketh, A. and Cooper, C. (2010) *Leading HR*. Basingstoke: Palgrave Macmillan, p. 272.
2. Sparrow, P.R. and Marchington, M. (1998) "Re-engaging the HRM function: rebuilding work, trust and voice." In P. Sparrow and M. Marchington (eds), *Human Resource Management: The New Agenda*. London: Financial Times Pitman Publishing, pp. 296–313 at pp. 308–9.
3. See Dyer, J.H. and Singh, H. (1998) "The relational view: co-operative strategy and source of interorganizational competitive advantage." *Academy of Management Review*, 23(4): 660–79; Inkpen, A.C. and Tsang, E.W.K. (2005) "Social capital, networks and knowledge transfer." *Academy of Management Review*, 30(1): 146–65; Digman, L.A. (2006) *Strategic Management: Competing in the Global Information Age*. New York: Thomson; and Barringer, B.R. and Harrison, J.S. (2000) "Walking a tightrope: creating value through interorganizational relationship." *Journal of Management*, 26(3): 367–403.
4. See Sparrow, P.R. and Miller, J. (2013) *Understanding the Business Issues in Partnering*. CIPD Research Report, August, London: Chartered Institute of Personnel and Development; Sparrow, P.R. and Miller, J. (2013) *Organising HR for*

Partnering Success. CIPD Research Report, November, London: Chartered Institute of Personnel and Development.

5. Gummesson, E. (2008) "Customer centricity: reality or a wild goose chase?" *European Business Review*, 20(4): 315–330, p. 326.
6. Nicholls, R. (2005) *Interactions between Service Customers.* Poznan: Poznan University of Economics.
7. See, for example, Wise, R. and Baumgartner, P. (1999) "Go downstream: the new profit imperative in manufacturing." *Harvard Business Review*, 7(5): 133–41; Davies, A. (2004) "Moving base into high-value integrated solutions: a value stream approach." *Industrial and Corporate Change*, 13(5): 727–56; Windahl, C. and Lakemond, N. (2006) "Developing integrated solutions: the importance of relationships within the network." *Industrial Marketing Management*, 35: 806–18; Kinnunen, R.E. and Turunen, T. (2012) "Identifying servitization capabilities of manufacturers: a conceptual model." *Journal of Applied Management and Entrepreneurship*, 17(3): 55–78; Gebauer, H., Ren, G.J., Valtakoski, A. and Reynoso, J. (2012) "Service-driven manufacturing: provision, evolution and financial impact of services in industrial firms." *Journal of Service Management*, 23(1): 120–36.
8. Gummesson (2008) "Customer centricity."
9. Gebauer, Ren, Valtakoski and Reynoso (2012) "Service-driven manufacturing."
10. This vignette draws on material from Rolls-Royce websites, the 2013 annual report, press reports and the following sources: Rolls-Royce (2010) "Supply chain management," *Nuclear Innovation and Technology Briefing*; Ryals, L. (2010) "Rolls-Royce TotalCare: meeting the needs of key customers.," *Executive briefing Number 6*, Cranfield School of Management; *Financial Times* on "The power of partnerships" and "Competing within a changed world," Times 100 Case Studies; Hares, S., Morris, I. and Galloway, I. (2011) "Through life supportability learning and development model," *UKCeB Good Practice Marketplace and Excellence Award*.
11. Fang, E., Palmatier, R.W. and Steenkamp, J. (2008) "Effect of service transition strategies on firm value." *Journal of Marketing*, 72(5): 1–14; Neely, A. (2008) "Exploring the financial consequences of the servitization of manufacturing." *Operations Management Research*, 1(2): 103–18; Brax, S. and Jonsson, K. (2009) "Developing integrated solution offerings for remote diagnostics. A comparative case of two manufacturers." *International Journal of Operations & Production Management*, 29(5): 539–60; Gebauer, H., Edvardsson, B., Gustafsson, A. and Witell, L. (2010) "Match or mismatch: strategy-structure configurations in the service business of manufacturing companies." *Journal of Service Research*, 13(2): 198–215; Martinez, V., Bastl, M., Kingston, J. and Evans, S. (2010) "Challenges in transforming manufacturing organizations into product-service providers." *Journal of Manufacturing Technology Management*, 21(4): 449–69.
12. Johnstone, S., Dainty, A. and Wilkinson, A. (2009) "Integrating products and services through life: an aerospace experience." *International Journal of Operations & Production Management*, 29(5): 520–38.

13. See: Ahuja, G. (2000) "Collaboration networks, structural holes, and innovation: a longitudinal study." *Administrative Science Quarterly*, 45(3): 425–55; Sobrero, M. and Roberts, E.B. (2001) "The trade-off between efficiency and learning in interorganizational relationships for product development." *Management Science*, 47 (4): 493–511.
14. See Ahuja (2000) "Collaboration networks"; Sobrero, M. and Roberts, E.B. (2001) "The trade-off between efficiency and learning in interorganizational relationships for product development." *Management Science*, 47(4): 493–511.
15. Pucik, V. (1988) "Strategic alliances, organizational learning, and competitive advantage: the HRM agenda." *Human Resource Management*, 27(1): 77–93, p. 77.
16. See Waddock, S.A. (1989) "Understanding social partnerships." *Administration & Society*, 21: 78–100; Selsky, J. and Parker, B. (2005) "Cross-sector partnerships to address social issues: challenges to theory and practice." *Journal of Management*, 31: 849–73; Provan, K.G., Fish, A. and Sydow, J. (2007) "Interorganizational networks at the network level. A review of the empirical literature on whole networks." *Journal of Management*, 33: 479–516; Koschmann, M.A., Kuhn, T. and Pfarrer, M.D. (2012) "A communicative framework of value in cross-sector partnerships." *Academy of Management Review*, 37(3): 332–54.
17. See, for example, Provan, K.G. and Kennis, P. (2009) "Models of network governance: structure, management and effectiveness." *Journal of Public Administration Research and Theory*, 18: 229–52.
18. Linder, S.H. (1999) "Coming to terms with the public-private partnerships: a grammar of multiple meanings." *American Behavioural Scientist*, 43: 35–51.
19. Loza, J. (2004) "Business-community partnerships: the case for community organization capacity building." *Journal of Business Ethics*, 53: 297–311.
20. Seitanidi, M and Crane, A. (2009) "Implementing CSR through partnerships: understanding the selection, design and institutionalization of nonprofit business partnerships." *Journal of Business Ethics*, 85: 413–29.
21. Arvidsson, A. (2010) "The ethical economy: new forms of value in the information society?" *Organization*, 17: 637–44; Le Ber, M.J. and Branzei, O. (2012) "Towards a critical theory of value creation in cross-sector partnerships." *Organization*, 17: 599–629.
22. Provan, K.G., Fish, A. and Sydow, J. (2007) "Interorganizational networks at the network level. A review of the empirical literature on whole networks." *Journal of Management*, 33: 479–516.
23. Bryson, J., Crosby, B. and Stone, M. (2006) "The design and implementation of cross-sector collaborations: Propositions from the literature." *Public Administration Review*, 66: 44–55.
24. Jamali, D. and Keshishian, T. (2009) "Uneasy alliances: lessons learned from partnerships between busineses and NGOs in the context of CSR." *Journal of Business Ethics*, 84: 277–85; Takahashi, I.M. and Smutny, G. (2002) "Collaborative windows and organizational governance: exploring the formation and demise of social service partnerships." *Nonprofit and Voluntary Sector Quarterly*, 31: 165–85;

Wettenhall, R. (2003) "The rhetoric and reality of public-private partnerships." *Public Organization Review*, 3: 77–107.

25. Selsky, J. and Parker, B. (2005) "Cross-sector partnerships to address social issues: challenges to theory and practice." *Journal of Management*, 31: 849–73.
26. Pouncelet, E.C. (2001) "A kiss here and a kiss there. Conflict and collaboration in environmental partnerships." *Environmental Management*, 27: 13–25.
27. Gray, B. (2000) "Assessing inter-organizational collaboration: multiple conceptions and multiple methods." In D.O. Faulkener and M. DeRond (eds), *Cooperative Strategy: Economic, Business and Organizational Issues.* Oxford University Press, pp. 243–60.
28. Koschmann, M.A., Kuhn, T. and Pfarrer, M.D. (2012) "A communicative framework of value in cross-sector partnerships." *Academy of Management Review*, 37(3): 332–54, p. 333.
29. Lawrence, T.B., Hardy, C. and Philips, N. (2002) "Institutional effects of inter-organizational collaboration: the emergence of proto-institutions." *Academy of Management Journal*, 45: 281–90; Butterfield, K.D., Reed, R. and Lemark, D.J. (2004) "An inductive model of collaboration from the stakeholder's perspective." *Business & Society*, 43: 162–95.
30. See: Gulatti, R., Nohria, N. and Zaheer, A. (2000) "Strategic networks." *Strategic Management Journal*, 21(3): 203–15; Gulatti, R. and Higgins, M.C. (2003) "Which ties matter when? The contingent effects of interorganizational partnerships on IPO success." *Strategic Management Journal*, 24(2): 127–44; and Brass, D.J., Galaskiewicz, J., Greve, H.R. and Tsai, W. (2004) "Taking stock of networks and organizations: a multilevel perspective." *Academy of Management Journal*, 47(6): 795–817.
31. See Podolny, J.M. and Page, K.L. (1998) "Network forms of organization." *Annual Review of Sociology*, 24: 57–76; Tsai, W. and Ghoshal, S. (1998) "Social capital and value creation: the role of interfirm networks." *Academy of Management Journal*, 41(4): 464–76; Williams, L.J. (2005) "Cooperative by design: structure and cooperation in interorganizational networks." *Journal of Business Research*, 58(2): 223–31; Wu, F. and Cavusgil, S.T. (2006) "Organizational learning, commitment and joint value creation in interfirm relationships." *Journal of Business Research*, 59(1): 81–9.
32. Marchington, M., Rubery, J. and Grimshaw, D. (2011) "Alignment, integration and consistency in HRM across multi-employer networks." *Human Resource Management*, 50(3): 313–39.
33. See: Dyer, J.H. (1997) "Effective interfirm collaboration: how firms minimize traction costs and maximize transaction value." *Strategic Management Journal*, 18(7): 535–56; Khanna, T., Gulati, R. and Nohria, N. (1998) "The dynamics of learning alliances: competition, co-operation and relative scope." *Strategic Management Journal*, 19(3): 193–210; Dyer, J.H. and Nobeoka, K. (2000) "Creating and managing a high-performance knowledge-sharing network: the Toyota case." *Strategic Management Journal*, 21(3): 345–67; and Goerzen, A. (2005) "Managing alliance networks: emerging practices of multinational corporations." *Academy of Management Executive*, 19(2): 94–107.

34. See Rai, A., Patnayakuni, R. and Seth, N. (2006) "Firm performance impacts of digitally enabled supply chain integration capabilities." *MIS Quarterly*, 30(2): 225–46; and Takeishi, A. (2001) "Bridging inter- and intra-firm boundaries: management of supplier involvement in automobile product development." *Strategic Management Journal*, 22(5): 403–33.
35. Lomi, A. and Pattison, P. (2006) "Manufacturing relations: an empirical study of the organization of production across multiple networks." *Organization Science*, 17(3): 313–32.
36. See www.economist.com/node/21552902 (date accessed May 28, 2014).
37. Haried, P. and Ramamurthy, K. (2009) "Evaluating the success in international sourcing of information technology projects: the need for a relational client-vendor approach." *Project Management Journal*, 40(3): 56–71.
38. Harvey, M. and Novicevic, M.M. (2002) "The co-ordination of strategic initiatives within global organizations: the role of global teams." *International Journal of Human Resource Management*, 13(4): 660–76.
39. Haried and Ramamurthy (2009) "Evaluating the success in international sourcing of information technology projects."
40. Peck, H. (2005) "Drivers of supply chain vulnerability: an integrated framework." *International Journal of Physical Distribution and Logistics Management*, 35(4): 210–32.
41. Chakrabarty, S. (2006) "Making sense of the sourcing and shoring maze: various outsourcing and offshoring alternatives." In H.S. Kehal and V.A. Singh (eds), *Outsourcing and Offshoring in the 21st Century: A Socio-economic Perspective*. London: Idea Group, pp. 18–53.
42. Barthélemy, J. and Quélin, B.V. (2006) "Complexity of outsourcing contracts and ex post transaction costs: an empirical investigation." *Journal of Management Studies*, 43(8): 1775–97.
43. Anderson, M. (1995) "The role of collaborative integration in industrial organization: observations from the Canadian aerospace industry." *Economic Geography*, 71(1): 55–78.
44. Inkpen, A.C. (1998) "Learning and knowledge acquisition through international strategic alliances." *Academy of Management Executive*, 12(4): 69–81.
45. Papadopoulos, A., Cimon, Y. and Hébert, L. (2011) "Asymmetry, heterogeneity and inter-firm relationships: organizing the theoretical landscape." *International Journal of Organizational Analysis*, 16(1/2): 152–65.
46. Harrigan, K.R. (1988) "Strategic alliances and partner asymmetries." *Management International Review*, 28: 52–72.
47. Kauser, S. and Shaw, V. (2004) "The influence of behavioural and organizational characteristics on the success of international strategic alliances." *International Marketing Review*, 21(1): 17–52.
48. Bruce, M., Daly, L. and Towers, N. (2004) "Lean or agile: a solution for supply chain management in the textiles and clothing industry?" *International Journal of Operations & Production Management*, 24 (1/2): 151–70.

49. Hendricks, K.B. and Singhal, V.R. (2003) "The effect of supply chain glitches on shareholder value." *Journal of Operations Management*, 21(5): 501–22; Hendricks, K.B. and Singhal, V.R. (2005) "An empirical analysis of the effects of supply chain disruption on long-run stock price performance and equity risk of the firm." *Production and Operations Management*, 14(1): 35–52.
50. Halldorsson, A., Kotzab, H., Mikkola, J.H. and Skjott-Larsen, T. (2007) "Complementary theories to supply chain management." *Supply Chain Management: An International Journal*, 12(4): 284–96, p. 284.
51. Madhok, A. (2002) "Reassessing the fundamentals and beyond: Ronald Coase, the transaction cost and resource based theories of the firm and the institutional structure of production." *Strategic Management Journal*, 23: 535–50; Skjoett-Larsen, T. (2000) "Third party logistics – from an interorganizational point of view." *International Journal of Physical Distribution & Logistics Management*, 30(2): 112–27.
52. Halldorsson, Kotzab, Mikkola and Skjott-Larsen (2007) "Complementary theories to supply chain management."
53. Cavinato, J.L. (2004) "Supply chain logistics risks: from the back room to the board room." *International Journal Physical Distribution and Logistic Management*, 35(4): 383–7; Chopra, S. and Sodhi, M.S. (2004) "Managing risk to avoid supply-chain breakdown." *MIT Sloan Management Review*, 46(1): 53–61; Lewis, M. (2003) "Cause, consequence and control: towards a theoretical and practical model of operational risk." *Journal of Operations Management*, 21(2): 205–24; Ritchie, B. and Brindley, C. (2007) "An emergent framework for supply chain risk management and performance measurement." *Journal of the Operational Research Society*, 58: 1398–411.
54. MacCrimon, K.R. and Wehrung, D.A. (1986) *Taking Risks: The Management of Uncertainty*. New York: Free Press.
55. Sitkin S.B. and Pablo, A.L. (1992) "Reconceptualizing the determinants of risk behaviour." *Academy of Management Review*, 17(1): 9–38, p. 9.
56. Sinha, P.R., Whitman, L.E. and Malzahn, D. (2004) "Methodology to mitigate supplier risk in an aerospace supply chain." *Supply Chain Management*, 9(2): 154–68.
57. Ritchie and Brindley (2007) An emergent framework for supply chain risk management and performance measurement."
58. Sparrow and Miller (2013) *Understanding the Business Issues in Partnering.*
59. Alberts, D. and Hayes, R. (2007) *Planning: Complex Endeavors*. Washington, DC: DoD Command and Control Research Program.
60. Chen, R., Sharman, R., Rao, R. and Upadhyaya, S. (2008) "Coordination in emergency response management." *Communications of the ACM*, 51(5): 66–73; Comfort, L. and Kapucu, N. (2006) "Inter-organizational coordination in extreme events: the World Trade Center attacks, September 11, 2001." *Natural Hazards*, 39(2): 309–27; National Research Council (2007) *Improving Disaster Management: The Role of IT in Mitigation, Preparedness, Response and Recovery*. Washington, DC: National Academic.

61. Cheng, J.-H., Yeh, C.-H. and Tu, C.-W. (2008) "Trust and knowledge sharing in green supply chains." *Supply Chain Management: An International Journal*, 11 (4): 283–95; Hernández-Espallardo, M., Rodríguez-Orejuela, A. and Sánchez-Pérez, M. (2010) "Inter-organizational governance, learning and performance in supply chains." *Supply Chain Management: An International Journal*, 15(2): 101–14.
62. Weber, L. and Mayer, K.J. (2011) "Designing effective contracts: exploring the influence of framing and expectations." *Academy of Management Review*, 36(1): 53–75.
63. Puranam, P. and Vanneste, B.S. (2009) "Trust and governance: untangling a tangled web." *Academy of Management Review*, 34(1): 11–31.
64. Faems, D., Janssens, M., Madhok, A. and Van Looy, B. (2009) "Toward an integrative perspective on alliance governance: connecting contract design, trust dynamics, and contract application." *Academy of Management Journal*, 51(6): 1053–78.
65. Sampson, R.C. (2004) "Organizational choice in R&D alliances: knowledge-based and transaction cost perspectives." *Managerial and Decision Economics*, 25: 421–36.
66. Hennart, J.F. (2006) "Alliance research: less is more." *Journal of Management Studies*, 43: 1621–8.
67. Hoetker, G. and Mellewigt, T. (2009) "Choice and performance of governance mechanisms: matching alliance governance to asset type." *Strategic Management Journal*, 30: 1025–44.
68. Barthélemy, J. and Quélin, B.V. (2006) "Complexity of outsourcing contracts and ex post transaction costs: an empirical investigation." *Journal of Management Studies*, 43(8): 1775–97.
69. Bettancourt, B.A., Dill, K.E., Greathouse, S.A., Charlton, K. and Mulholland, A. (1997) "Evaluation of ingroup and outgroup members: the role of cateogory-based expectancy violation." *Journal of Experimental and Social Psychology*, 33: 244–75.
70. Vanneste, B.S. and Puranam, P. (2010) "Repeated interaction and contractual detail: examining the learning effect." *Organization Science*, 21: 186–201.
71. Mayer, K.J. and Argyres, N. (2004) "Learning to contract: evidence from the personal computer industry." *Organization Science*, 15: 394–410.
72. Weber and Mayer (2011) "Designing effective contracts," p. 53.
73. *Ibid.*, p. 60.
74. Luo, Y. (2002) "Contract, co-operation and performance in international joint ventures." *Strategic Management Journal*, 23: 903–19.
75. Malhotra, D. and Murnighan, J. (2002) "The effects of contracts on interpersonal trust." *Administrative Science Quarterly*, 47: 534–60.
76. See Rousseau, D.M., Sitkin, S.B., Burt, R.S. and Camerer, C. (1998) "Not so different after all: a cross-discipline view of trust." *Academy of Management Review*, 23: 393–404; and Das, T.K. and Teng, B.-S. (1998) "Between trust and control: developing confidence in partner co-operation in alliances." *Academy of Management Review*, 23: 491–512.
77. Dyer, J.H. and Chu, W. (2000) "The determinants of trust in supplier-automaker relationships in the U.S., Japan, and Korea." *Journal of International Business*

Studies, 31(2): 259–85; Helper, S. and Sako, M. (1995) "Supplier relations in Japan and the United States: are they converging?" *Sloan Management Review*, 36(3): 77–84; Nishiguchi, T. (1994) *Strategic Industrial Sourcing: The Japanese Advantage*. New York: Oxford University Press; Smitka, M. (1991) *Competitive Ties: Subcontracting in the Japanese Automotive Industry*. New York: Columbia University Press; and Zaheer, A., McEvily, B. and Perrone, V. (1998) "Does trust matter? Exploring the effects of interorganizational and interpersonal trust on performance." *Organization Science*, 9(2): 141–59.

78. MacDuffie, J.P. (2011) "Inter-organizational trust and the dynamics of distrust." *Journal of International Business Studies*, 42: 35–47.
79. Salk, J.E. (2005) "Often called but rarely chosen: alliance research that directly studies process." *European Management Review*, 2(2): 117–22.
80. Ring, P.S. and Van de Ven, A.H. (1994) "Developmental processes of cooperative interorganizational relationships." *Academy of Management Review*, 19: 90–118.
81. Salk, J.E. (2005) "Often called but rarely chosen: alliance research that directly studies process." *European Management Review*, 2(2): 117–22.
82. Faems, Janssens, Madhok and Van Looy (2009) "Toward an integrative perspective on alliance governance."
83. Esposito, E. and Raffa, L. (2007) "Global reorganization in a high-technology industry: the aircraft industry." *International Journal of Globalization and Small Business*, 2(2): 166–84.
84. Corallo, A., Lazoi, M., Marcherita, A. and Scalvenzi, M. (2010) "Optimizing Competence Management Processes. A Case in the Aerospace." *Business Process Management Journal*, 16(2): 297–314.
85. De Vries, J. and Huijsman, R. (2011) Supply chain management in health services: an overview. *Supply Chain Management: An International Journal*. 16 (3); 159-165.
86. O'Reilly, C. and Tushman, M.L. (2008) "Ambidexterity as a dynamic capability, resolving the innovator's dilemma." *Research in Organizational Behavior*, 28: 185–206.

Chapter 6

1. Weinberg, A. and Cooper, C.L. (2012) *Stress in Turbulent Times*. Basingstoke: Palgrave Macmillan.
2. Bowles, D. and Cooper, C.L. (2012) *The High Engagement Work Culture*. Basingstoke: Palgrave Macmillan.
3. Sparrow, P.R. (2014) "Engagement and performance." In P. Flood and Y. Freeney (eds), *Wiley Encyclopedia of Management, Volume 11 Organizational Behavior*. Chichester: Wiley.
4. Maslach, C., Schaufelli, W.B. and Leiter, M.P. (2001) "Job burnout." *Annual Review of Psychology*, 52: 397–422.
5. Robinson, D., Perryman, S. and Hayday, S. (2004) *The Drivers of Employee Engagement*. Institute of Employment Studies Report No. 408. Brighton: IES, p. 2.

6. Viljevac, A., Cooper-Thomas, H.D. and Saks, A.M. (2012) "An investigation into the validity of two measures of work engagement." *International Journal of Human Resource Management*, 23: 3692–709.
7. Saks, A.M. (2006) "Antecedents and consequences of employee engagement." *Journal of Managerial Psychology*, 21: 600–19.
8. Kahn, W.A. (1990) "Psychological conditions of personal engagement and disengagement at work." *Academy of Management Journal*, 33: 692–724; Rich, B.L., LePine, J.A. and Crawford, E.R. (2010) "Job engagement: antecedents and effects on job performance." *Academy of Management Journal*, 53: 617–35.
9. See Harter, J.K., Schmidt, F.L. and Hayes, T.L. (2002) "Business-unit level relationship between employee satisfaction, employee engagement, and business outcomes: a meta-analysis." *Journal of Applied Psychology*, 87: 268–79; Riketta, M. (2008) "The causal relation between job attitudes and performance: a meta-analysis of panel studies." *Journal of Applied Psychology*, 93: 472–81; Winkler, S., König, C.J. and Kleinmann, M. (2012) "New insights into an old debate: investigating the temporal sequence of commitment and performance at the business unit level." *Journal of Occupational and Organizational Psychology*, 85: 503–22.
10. Schneider, B., Hanges, P.J., Smith, D.B. and Salvaggio, A.N. (2003) "Which comes first: employee attitudes or organizational financial and market performance?" *Journal of Applied Psychology*, 88: 836–51; Schneider, B., Ehrhart, M.G., Mayer, D.M., Saltz, J.L. and Niles-Jolly, K. (2005) "Understanding organization-customer links in service settings." *Academy of Management Journal*, 48: 1017–32; Van Veldhoven, M. (2005) "Financial performance and the long-term link with HR practices, work climate and job stress." *Human Resource Management Journal*, 15: 30–53.
11. Harter, Schmidt and Hayes (2002) "Business-unit level relationship between employee satisfaction, employee engagement, and business outcomes."
12. Centre for the Modern Family (2012) *Family Resilience*. London: Centre for the Modern Family.
13. See: www.osha.europa.eu.
14. Jane-Llopis, E., Anderson, P. and Cooper, C.L. (2012) "Well-being in the global agenda. *Stress & Health*, 28: 89–90.
15. Stiglitz, J.E., Sen, A. and Fitoussi, J.-P (2009) *Report by the Commission on the Measurement of Economic Performance and Social Progress*. Available at: www.stiglitz-sen-fitoussi.fr (date accessed July 1, 2014).
16. Jane-Llopis, E. and Cooper, C.L. (2012) "Mental health and well-being in the workplace." *Public Mental Health*, 136–44.
17. Bloom, D.E., Cafiero, ET., Jane-Llopis, E., Abrahams-Gessel, S., Bloom, L.R., Fathima, S. and Weinstein, C. (2011) *The Global Economic Burden of Non-communicable Diseases*. Geneva: World Economic Forum.
18. OECD (2011) *Sick on the Job? Myths and Realities about Mental Health and Work, Mental Health and Work*. Paris: OECD Publishing. Available at: http://dx.doi.org/10.1787/9789264124523-en (date accessed July 1, 2014).
19. Dewe, P. and Cooper, C.L. (2008) "Editorial: well-being: absenteeism, presenteeism, costs and challenges." *Occupational Medicine*, 1–3

20. Cooper, C.L., Field, J., Goswami, U., Jenkins, R and Sahakin, B. (2009) *Mental Capital and Wellbeing*. Oxford: Wiley-Blackwell.
21. Einarsen, S., Hoel, H. and Cooper, C.L. (2011) *Bullying and Harassment in the Workplace*. Boca Raton, FL: CRC Press.
22. Burke, R. and Cooper, C.L. (2008) *The Long Working Hours Culture*. Bingley: Emerald Publications.
23. PricewaterhouseCooper (2008) *The Business Case for Wellness Programmes*. London: PWC.
24. Cartwright, C. and Cooper, C.L. (1997) *Workplace Stress*. Thousand Oaks, CA: Sage.
25. Robertson, I. and Cooper, C.L. (2011) *Wellbeing: Productivity and Happiness at Work*. Basingstoke: Palgrave Macmillan.
26. Palmer, S. and Cooper, C.L. (2010) *The Science of Occupational Health*. Oxford: Wiley-Blackwell.
27. Level Playing Field Institute (2007) *The Corporate Leavers Survey: The Cost of Employee Turnover Due Solely to Unfairness in the Workplace*. San Francisco: LPFI.
28. Sparrow, P,R., Wong, W., Otaye, L. and Bevan, S. (2013) *The Changing Contours of Fairness*. CIPD Research Report, November. London: Chartered Institute of Personnel and Development and Work Foundation.
29. See: www.ioe.ac.uk/newsEvents/86758.html (date accessed July 1, 2014).
30. CIPD/Halogen (2014) *Employee Outlook Spring 2014*. London: CIPD.
31. Sparrow, Wong, Otaye and Bevan (2013) *The Changing Contours of Fairness*.
32. Otaye, L. and Wong, W. (2014) "Mapping the contours of fairness: the impact of unfairness and leadership inaction on job satisfaction, turnover intention and employer advocacy." *Journal of Organizational Effectiveness: People and Performance*, 1(2), 191–204.
33. See Adams, J. S. (1965) "Inequity in social exchange." In L. Berkowitz (ed.), *Advances in experimental social psychology*. New York: Academic Press, vol. 2, pp. 267–99; Leventhal, G.S. (1976) "The distribution of rewards and resources in groups and organizations." In L. Berkowitz and W. Walster (eds), *Advances in Experimental Social Psychology*. New York: Academic Press, vol. 9, pp. 91–131; Greenberg, J. and Colquitt, J.A. (2005) *Handbook of Organizational Justice*. Mahwah, NJ: Lawrence Erlbaum; Ambrose, M.L. and Arnaud, A. (2005). "Are procedural justice and distributive justice conceptually distinct?" In J. Greenberg and J.A. Colquitt (eds), *Handbook of Organizational Justice*. Mahwah, NJ: Lawrence Erlbaum, pp. 59–84; Poon, J.M. (2012) "Distributive justice, procedural justice, affective commitment, and turnover intention: a mediation-moderation framework." *Journal of Applied Social Psychology*, 42(6): 1505–32; and Morand, D.A. and Merriman, K.K. (2012) "'Equality theory' as a counterbalance to equity theory in Human Resource Management." *Journal of Business Ethics*, 111(1), 133–44.
34. See: Thibaut, J. W. and Walker, L. (1975) *Procedural Justice: A Psychological Perspective*. Hillsdale, NJ: Erlbaum; Leventhal, G. S. (1980) "What should be done with equity theory? New approaches to the study of fairness in social

relationships." In K. Gergen, M. Greenberg and R. Willis (eds), *Social Exchange: Advances in Theory and Research*. New York: Plenum Press, pp. 27–55; Greenberg, J. (1987) "Reactions to procedural injustice in payment distributions: do the means justify the ends?" *Journal of Applied Psychology*, 72: 55–61; Greenberg, J. (1987) "A taxonomy of organizational justice theories." *Academy of Management Review*, 12: 9–22; Greenberg, J. (1993) "The intellectual adolescence of organizational justice: you've come a long way, maybe." *Social Justice Research*, 6: 135–48; Greenberg and Colquitt (2005) *Handbook of Organizational Justice*; Blader, S.L. and Tyler, T.R. (2005) "How can theories of organizational justice explain the effects of fairness?" In Greenberg and Colquitt (eds), *Handbook of Organizational Justice*, pp. 329–54; and Nowakowski, J.M. and Conlon, D.E. (2005) "Organizational justice: looking back, looking forward." *International Journal of Conflict Management*, 16: 2–49.

35. See Bies, R.J. and Moag, J.F. (1986). "Interactional justice: communication criteria of fairness." In R.J. Lewicki, B.H. Sheppard and M.H. Bazerman (eds), *Research on Negotiations in Organizations*. Greenwich, CT: JAI Press, vol. 1, pp. 43–55; Greenberg, J. (1993) "The social side of fairness: interpersonal and informational classes of organizational justice." In R. Cropanzano (ed.), *Justice in the Workplace: Approaching Fairness in Human Resource Management*. Hillsdale, NJ: Erlbaum, pp. 79–103; Colquitt, J.A., Conlon, D.E., Wesson, M.J., Porter, C.O. and Ng, K.Y. (2001). "Justice at the millennium: a meta-analytic review of 25 years of organizational justice research." *Journal of Applied Psychology*, 86: 425–45.
36. Sparrow, Wong, Otaye and Bevan (2013) *The Changing Contours of Fairness*.
37. See Von Neumann, J. (1928) "Zurtheorie der gesellschaftsspiele." *Mathematische Annalen*, 100: 295–320, English translation Fin Tucker, A.W. and Luce, R.D. (1959) "Contributions to the Theory of Games IV." *Annals of Mathematics Studies*, 40; Von Neumann, J. and Morgenstern, O (1944) *Theory of Games and Economic Behaviour*. Princeton University Press; Nash, J.F. (1950) "The bargaining problem." Econometrica, 18: 155–62; Nash, J.F. (1951) "Non-cooperative games." *Annals of Mathematics*, 54: 286–95; Kuhn, H.W. and Tucker, A.W. (1950) "Contributions to the theory of games I." *Annals of Mathematics Studies*, 24; Kuhn, H.W. and Tucker, A.W. (1953) "Contributions to the theory of games II." *Annals of Mathematics Studies*, 28; Shapley, L.S. (1953.) "A value for *n*-person games." In A.W. Tucker and H.W. Kuhn (eds), *Contributions to the Theory of Games II*. Princeton University Press, pp. 307–17; Dimand, M.A. and Dimand, R.W. (1996) *The History of Game Theory, Volume 1: From the Beginnings to 1945*. London: Routledge.
38. See Rawls, J. (1971) *A Theory of Justice*. Cambridge. MA: Belknap Press of Harvard University Press; Rawls, J. (1985) "Justice as fairness: political not metaphysical." *Philosophy and Public Affairs*, 14(3): 223–51; Rawls, J. (2001) *Justice as Fairness: A Restatement*. Cambridge, MA: Harvard University Press; McKay, S., Murray, M. and Macintyre, S. (2012) "Justice as fairness in planning policy-making." *International Planning Studies*, 17(2): 147–62.
39. See Lazear, E.P. and Rosen, S. (1981) "Rank-order tournaments as optimum labor contracts." *Journal of Political Economy*, 89(5): 841–64; Dworkin, R. (2000)

Sovereign Virtue, Cambridge, MA: Harvard University Press; Dworkin, R. (2002) "Sovereign virtue revisited." *Ethics*, 113: 106–43; Dworkin, R. (2003) "Equality, luck and hierarchy." *Philosophy and Public Affairs*, 31: 190–8; Eriksson, T. (2009) "Tournaments." In S.N. Durlauf and L.E. Blume. (eds), *The New Palgrave Dictionary of Economics*. Online edition. Palgrave; Hutton, W (2010) *Hutton Review of Fair Pay in the Public Sector*. Interim Report.

40. See Sen, A. (1999) *Development as Freedom*. New York: Alfred A. Knopf; Nussbaum, M.C. (2000) *Women and Human Development: The Capabilities Approach*. Cambridge University Press; Robeyns, I. (2005) "The capability approach: a theoretical survey." *Journal of Human Development*, 6(1): 93–114; Carpenter, M. (2009) "The capabilities approach and critical social policy: lessons from the majority world?" *Critical Social Policy*, 29(3): 351–73.
41. See March, J.G. and Olsen, J.P. (1989) *Rediscovering Institutions: The Organizational Basis of Politics*. New York: Free Press; Kontogianni, A.D., Skourtos, M.S. and Papandreou, A.A. (2006) "Shared waters – shared responsibility. Application of the principles of fairness for burden sharing in the Mediterranean." *International Environmental Agreements*, 6: 209–230; Brätland, J. (2007) "Rawlsian investment rules for 'intergenerational equity': breaches of method and ethics." *Journal of Libertarian Studies*, 21(4): 69–100.
42. Terkel, S. (1972) *Working*. New York: Avon Books.
43. Kennedy, R. (1968) Quote from Speech at the University of Kansas on 18 March.

Chapter 7

1. American Productivity and Quality Center (2004) *Talent Management: From Competencies to Organizational Performance. Final Report*. Houston, TX: American Productivity and Quality Center.
2. Avendon, M.J. and Scholes, G. (2010) "Building competitive advantage through integrated talent management." In R. Silzer and B.E. Dowell (eds), *Strategy-Driven Talent Management: A Leadership Imperative*. San Francisco: Jossey-Bass-Society for Industrial and Organizational Psychology, pp. 73–122.
3. Silzer, R. and Dowell, B.E. (2010) "Strategic talent management matters." In Silzer and Dowell (eds), *Strategy-Driven Talent Management*, pp. 3–72.
4. Sparrow, P.R., Hird, M. and Balain, S. (2011) *Talent Management: Time to Question the Tablets of Stone?* Centre for Performance-led HR White Paper 11/01, Lancaster University Management School.
5. See Scullion, H., Collings, D.G. and Caligiuri, P. (2010) "Global talent management." *Journal of World Business*, 45(2): 105–8; Collings, D.G., Scullion, H. and Vaiman, V. (2011) "European perspectives on talent management." *European Journal of International Management*, 5(5): 453–62; McDonnell, A., Collings, D.G. and Burgess, J. (2012) "Asia Pacific perspectives on talent management." *Asia*

Pacific Journal of Human Resources, 50(4): 391–8; Vaiman, V. and Collings, D.G. (2013) "Talent management: advancing the field." *International Journal of Human Resource Management*, 24(9): 1737–43; and Al Ariss, A., Cascio, W.F. and Paauwe, J. (2014) "Talent management: current theories and future research directions." *Journal of World Business*, 49(2): 173–9.

6. This argument has been made from the mid-2000s up until today. See Lewis, R.E. and Heckman, R.J. (2006) "Talent management: a critical review." *Human Resource Management Review*, 16: 139–54; Collings, D.G. and Mellahi, K. (2009) "Strategic talent management: a review and research agenda." *Human Resource Management Review*, 19(4): 304–13; Iles, P., Chuai, X. and Preece, D. (2010) "Talent management and HRM in multinational companies in Beijing: definitions, differences and drivers." *Journal of World Business*, 45(2): 179–89; Tarique, I. and Schuler, R.S. (2010) "Global talent management: literature review, integrative framework, and suggestions for further research." *Journal of World Business*, 45(2): 122–33; and Garavan, T.N., Carbery, R. and Rock, A. (2012) "Managing talent development: definition, scope and architecture." *European Journal of Training and Development*, 36(1): 5–24.
7. See Collings, Scullion and Vaiman (2011) "European perspectives on talent management"; Sparrow, P.R., Scullion, H. and Tarique, I. (2014) "Multiple lenses on talent management: definitions and contours of the field." In P.R. Sparrow, H. Scullion and I. Tarique (eds), *Strategic Talent Management: Contemporary Issues in International Context*. Cambridge University Press, pp. 36–70.
8. Scullion, H. and Collings, D.G. (eds) (2011) *Global Talent Management*. London: Routledge.
9. Stahl, G.K., Bjorkman, I., Farndale, E., Morris, S.S., Paauwe, J., Stiles, P., Trevor, J. and Wright, P. (2012) "Six principles of effective global talent management." *MIT Sloan Management Review*, 53: 25–32.
10. Al Ariss, Cascio and Paauwe (2014) "Talent management: current theories and future research directions."
11. See Vaiman and Collings (2013) "Talent management: advancing the field"; and Al Ariss, Cascio and Paauwe (2014) "Talent management: current theories and future research directions."
12. Lepak, D.P., Smith, K.G. and Taylor, S. (2007) "Value creation and value capture: a multilevel perspective." *Academy of Management Review*, 32(1): 180–94.
13. Meyers, M.C. and Van Woerkom, M, (2014) "The influence of underlying philosophies on talent management: theory, implications for practice, and research agenda." *Journal of World Business*, 49(2): 192–203.
14. Collings, D.G. and Mellahi, K. (2009) "Strategic talent management: a review and research agenda." *Human Resource Management Review*, 19(4): 304–13.
15. See Chambers, E.G., Foulon, M., Handfield-Jones, H., Hankin, S.M. and Michaels III, E.G. (1998) "The war for talent." *The McKinsey Quarterly*, 3: 44–57; Michaels, E., Handfield-Jones, H. and Axelrod, B. (2001) *The War for Talent*. Cambridge, MA:

Harvard Business School Press; Axelrod, E.L., Handfield-Jones, H. and Welsh, T.A. (2001) "The war for talent. Part 2." *The McKinsey Quarterly*, 2(5): 9–11; Axelrod, E.L., Handfield-Jones, H. and Michaels, E. (2002) "A new game plan for C players." *Harvard Business Review*, 80: 80–90; Guthridge, M., Komm, A.B. and Lawson, E. (2006) "The people problem in talent management." *The McKinsey Quarterly*, 2(1): 6–9.

16. Odiorne, G.S. (1984) *Human Resources Strategy: A Portfolio Approach*. San Francisco: Jossey-Bass Inc.
17. Sparrow, Scullion and Tarique (2014) "Multiple lenses on talent management."
18. Odiorne (1984) *Human Resources Strategy*.
19. Zuboff, S. (1988) *In the Age of the Smart Machine: The Future of Work and Power*. New York: Basic Books.
20. Lawler, E.E. (1994) "From job-based to competency-based organizations." *Journal of Organizational Behavior*, 15: 3–15.
21. Sears, D. (2003) *Successful Talent Strategies: Achieving Superior Business Results Through Market-Focused Staffing*. New York: American Management Association.
22. Nijs, S., Gallardo-Gallardo, E., Dries, N. and Sels, L. (2014) "A multidisciplinary review into the definition, operationalization and measurement of talent." *Journal of World Business*, 49(2): 180–91.
23. Stein, G. and Capape, J. (2009) *Factors of CEO Failure: Mapping the Debate*. IESE Business School Study-85. Barcelona: IESE.
24. Pfeffer, J. (2001) "Fighting the war for talent is hazardous to your organization's health." *Organizational Dynamics*, 29(4): 248–59.
25. See Sparrow, P.R. (2000) "Strategic management in a world turned upside down: the role of cognition, intuition and emotional intelligence." In P.C. Flood, T. Dromgoole, S.J. Carroll and L. Gorman (eds), *Managing Strategy Implementation*. Oxford: Blackwell; Hodgkinson, G.P. and Sparrow, P.R. (2002) *The Competent Organization: A Psychological Analysis of the Strategic Management Process*. Buckingham: Open University Press; Hodgkinson, G.P. and Healey, M.P. (2008) "Cognition in organizations." *Annual Review of Psychology*, 59: 387–417; and Hodgkinson, G.P. and Healey, M.P. (2011) "Psychological foundations of dynamic capabilities: reflexion and reflection in strategic management." *Strategic Management Journal*, 32: 1500–16.
26. Sparrow, Scullion and Tarique (2014) "Multiple lenses on talent management."
27. Lawler, E.E. (2008) *Talent: Making People Your Competitive Advantage*. San Francisco: Jossey-Bass.
28. See Collings, D.G. and Mellahi, K. (2009) "Strategic talent management: a review and research agenda." *Human Resource Management Review*, 19(4): 304–13; Schuler, R.S., Jackson, S.E. and Tarique, I. (2011) "Global talent management and global talent challenges: strategic opportunities for IHRM." *Journal of World Business*, 46: 506–16; Scullion and Collings (eds) (2011) *Global Talent Management*.
29. Meyers, M.C. and Van Woerkom, M, (2014) "The influence of underlying philosophies on talent management: theory, implications for practice, and research agenda." *Journal of World Business*, 49(2): 192–203.

30. Gubman, E.L. and Green, S. (2007) *The Four Stages of Talent Management*. San Francisco: Executive Networks; Silzer and Dowell (eds) (2010) *Strategy-Driven Talent Management: A Leadership Imperative*.
31. Becker, B.E. and Huselid, M.A. (2006) "Strategic Human Resources Management: where do we go from here?" *Journal of Management*, 32: 898–925.
32. Lepak, D.P. and Snell, S.A. (1999) "The human resource architecture: toward a theory of human capital allocation and development." *Academy of Management Review*, 24: 31–48.
33. Fernández-Aráoz, C., Graysberg, B. and Nohria, N. (2011) "How to hang on to your high potentials." *Harvard Business Review*, 69(10): 69–83.
34. Sparrow, P.R. and Balain, S. (2008) "Talent proofing the organization." In C.L. Cooper and R. Burke (eds), *The Peak Performing Organization*, London: Routledge, pp. 108–28.
35. Al Ariss, Cascio and Paauwe (2014) "Talent management: current theories and future research directions."
36. Sparrow, Scullion and Tarique (2014) "Multiple lenses on talent management."
37. Martin, G. and Cerdin, J.-L. (2014) "Employer branding and career theory: new directions for research." In Sparrow, Scullion and Tarique (eds), *Strategic Talent Management: Contemporary Issues in International Context*, pp. 151–76; Martin, G. and Groen-in't Woud, S. (2011) "Employer branding and corporate reputation management in global companies." In Scullion and Collings (eds), *Global Talent Management*, pp. 87–110; and Martin, G., Gollan, P. and Grigg, K. (2011) "Is there a bigger and better future for employer branding? Facing up to innovation, corporate reputations and wicked problems in SHRM." *International Journal of Human Resource Management*, 22(17): 3618–37.
38. Huselid, M.A., Beatty, R.W. and Becker, B.E. (2005) "'A players' or 'A positions?' The strategic logic of workforce management." *Harvard Business Review*, 83(12): 110–17.
39. Collings, D.G. and Mellahi, K. (2009) "Strategic talent management: a review and research agenda." *Human Resource Management Review*, 19(4): 304–13.
40. Sparrow, Scullion and Tarique (2014) "Multiple lenses on talent management."
41. Sparrow, P.R., Hird, M., Hesketh, A. and Cooper, C.L. (2010) *Leading HR*. Basingstoke: Palgrave Macmillan.
42. See Boudreau, J.W. and Ramstad. P.M. (2005) "Talentship and the evolution of human resource management: from 'professional practices' to 'strategic talent decision science'." *Human Resource Planning*, 28(2): 17–26; Boudreau, J.W. and Ramstad, P.M. (2006) "Talentship and HR measurement and analysis: from ROI to strategic, human resource planning." *Human Resource Planning*, 29(1): 25–33; Boudreau, J.W. and Ramstad, P.M. (2007) *Beyond HR: The New Science Of Human Capital*. Cambridge, MA: Harvard Business School Press; Ingham, J. (2007) *Strategic Human Capital Management: Creating Value through People*. London: Butterworth-Heinemann; Cappelli, P. (2008) *Talent on Demand: Managing Talent in an Age of Uncertainty*. Cambridge, MA: Harvard Business School Press;

Boudreau, J.W. (2010) *Retooling HR: Using Proven Business Tools to Make Better Decisions about Talent*. Cambridge, MA: Harvard Business School Press; Boudreau, J.W. and Jesuthasan, R. (2011) *Transformative HR: How Great Companies Use Evidence-Based Change for Sustainable Advantage*. San Francisco: Jossey-Bass; Nahapiet, J. (2011) "A social perspective: exploring the links between human capital and social capital." In A. Burton-Jones and J.-C. Spender (eds), *The Oxford Handbook Of Human Capital*. Oxford University Press, pp. 71–95.

43. See: Bhattacharya, M. and Wright, P.M. (2005) "Managing human assets in an uncertain world: Applying real option theory to HRM." *International Journal of Human Resource Management*, 16(6): 929–48; Sparrow, P.R. and Balain, S. (2008) "Talent proofing the organization." In Cooper and Burke (eds), *The Peak Performing Organization*, pp. 108–28.
44. Fitz-enz, J. (2000) *The Return on Investment of Human Capital: Measuring the Economic Value of Employee Performance*. New York: American Management Association.
45. Cappelli (2008) *Talent on Demand*.
46. See: Cappelli (2008) *Talent on Demand*; Keller, J.R. and Cappelli, P. (2014) "A supply chain approach to talent management." In Sparrow, Scullion and Tarique (eds), *Strategic Talent Management: Contemporary Issues in International Context*, pp. 117–50.
47. Boudreau, J.W. and Ramstad. P.M. (2005) "Talentship and the evolution of human resource management: from 'professional practices' to 'strategic talent decision science'." *Human Resource Planning*, 28(2): 17–26; Boudreau, J.W. and Ramstad, P.M. (2006) "Talentship and HR measurement and analysis: from ROI to strategic, human resource planning." *Human Resource Planning*, 29(1): 25–33; Boudreau, J.W. and Ramstad, P.M. (2007) *Beyond HR: The New Science Of Human Capital*. Cambridge, MA: Harvard Business School Press.
48. See Cascio, W.F. and Boudreau, J.W. (2010) *Investing in People: Financial Impact of Human Resource Initiatives.* New York: Financial Times Press; Cascio, W.F. and Boudreau, J.W. (2012) *A Short Introduction to Strategic Human Resource Management.* Cambridge University Press; Cascio, W.F. and Boudreau, J.W. (2014) "HR strategy: optimizing risks, optimizing rewards." *Journal of Organizational Effectiveness: People and* Performance, 1(1): 77–97.
49. Boudreau, J.W. and Jesuthasan, R. (2011) *Transformative HR: How Great Companies Use Evidence-Based Change for Sustainable Advantage*. San Francisco: Jossey-Bass.
50. Vaiman, V. and Collings, D.G. (2013) "Talent management: advancing the field." *International Journal of Human Resource Management*, 24(9): 1737–43.
51. Mäkela, K., Björkman, I. and Ehrnrooth, M. (2010) "How do MNCs establish their talent pools? Influences on individuals' likelihood of being labelled as talent." *Journal of World Business*, 45(2): 134–42.
52. Fernández-Aráoz, C., Graysberg, B. and Nohria, N. (2011) "How to hang on to your high potentials." *Harvard Business Review*, 69(10): 69–83.

53. *Ibid.*, p. 79.
54. Davies, J. and Kourdi, J. (2010) *The Truth about Talent*. Chichester: Wiley, p. 3.
55. Sparrow, Hird and Balain (2011) *Talent Management*.
56. Bowman, C. and Ambrosini, V. (2000) "Value creation versus value capture: towards a coherent definition of value in strategy." *British Journal of Management*, 11: 1–15.

Chapter 8

1. Bowman, C. and Ambrosini, V. (2000) "Value creation versus value capture: towards a coherent definition of value in strategy." *British Journal of Management*, 11: 1–15.
2. Frost, A., Birkinshaw, J.M. and Prescott, C.E. (2002) "Centers of excellence in multinational corporations." *Strategic Management Journal*, 23(11): 997–1018.
3. Moore, K. and Birkinshaw, J.M. (1998) "Managing knowledge in global service firms: centers of excellence." *Academy of Management Executive*, 12(4): 81–92, p. 81.
4. Holm, U.I.F. and Pedersen, T. (2000) *The Emergence and Impact of MNC Centres of Excellence*. London: Macmillan.
5. Barney, J.B. (1991) "Firm resources and sustained competitive advantage." *Journal of Management*, 17(1): 99–120.
6. Rumelt, R. (1984) "Toward a strategic theory of the firm." In R. Lamb (ed.), *Competitive Strategic Management*. Englewood Cliffs, NJ: Prentice Hall, pp. 556–70.
7. Castanias, R.P. and Helfat, C.E. (2001) "The managerial rents model: theory and empirical analysis." *Journal of Management*, 27(6): 661–78.
8. Bowman and Ambrosini (2000) "Value creation versus value capture."
9. Lepak, D.P. and Snell, S.A. (1999) "The human resource architecture: toward a theory of human capital allocation and development." *Academy of Management Review*, 24: 31–48.
10. Lepak, D.P., Smith, K.G. and Taylor, S. (2007) "Value creation and value capture: a multilevel perspective." *Academy of Management Review*, 32(1): 180–94, p. 184.
11. Barney, J.B. and Clark, D.N. (2007) *Resource-Based theory: Creating and Sustaining Competitive Advantage*. Oxford University Press.
12. Bowman and Ambrosini (2000) "Value creation versus value capture."
13. See Peteraf, M.A. and Barney, J.B. (2003) "Unraveling the resource-based tangle." *Managerial and Decision Economics*, 24: 309–24; Helfat, C., Finkelstein, S., Mitchell, W., Peteraf, M., Singh, H., Teece, D. and Winter, S. (2007) *Dynamic Capabilities: Understanding Strategic Change in Organizations*. Oxford: Blackwell; Pitelis, C.N. (2009) "The co-evolution of organizational value capture, value creation and sustainable advantage." *Organization Studies*, 30: 1115–39.

14. Lepak, Smith and Taylor (2007) "Value creation and value capture."
15. Henderson, R.M. and Clark, K.B. (1990) "Architectural innovation: the reconfiguration of existing product technologies and the failure of established firms." *Administrative Science Quarterly*, 35(1): 9–30; Kang, S.-C., Morris, S. and Snell, S.A. (2007) "Relational archetypes, organizational learning and value creation: extending the human resource architecture." *Academy of Management Review*, 32(1): 236–56.
16. Zuboff, S. (1988) *In the Age of the Smart Machine: The Future of Work and Power*. New York: Basic Books.
17. Bowman and Ambrosini (2000) "Value creation versus value capture," p. 5.
18. See: Barney, J.B. (1991) "Firm resources and sustained competitive advantage." *Journal of Management*, 17(1): 99–120; Collis, D.J. and Montgomery, C. (1995) "Competing on resources." *Harvard Business Review*, 73(4): 118–28; Makadok, R. and Coff, R. (2002) "The theory of value and the value of theory: breaking new ground versus reinventing the wheel." *Academy of Management Review*, 27(1): 10–13; and Peteraf and Barney (2003) "Unraveling the resource-based tangle."
19. Lepak, Smith and Taylor (2007) "Value creation and value capture."
20. Bowman and Ambrosini (2000) "Value creation versus value capture"; Bowman, C. and Swart, J. (2007) "Whose human capital? The challenge of value capture when capital is embedded." *Journal of Management Studies*, 44(4): 488–505.
21. Pitelis, C.N. (2009) "The co-evolution of organizational value capture, value creation and sustainable advantage." *Organization Studies*, 30: 1115–39, p. 1115.
22. See Brandenburger, A. and Nalebuff, B.J. (1995) "The right game: use game theory to shape strategy." *Harvard Business Review*, 73(4): 57–71; Stirling, W.C. (2011) *Theory of Conditional Games*. Cambridge University Press.
23. Sirmon, D.G., Hitt, M.A. and Ireland, R.D. (2007) "Managing firm resources in dynamic environments to create value: looking inside the black box." *Academy of Management Review*, 32(1): 273–92.
24. O'Leary, B., Lindholm, M.L., Whitford, R.A. and Freeman, S.E. (2002) "Selecting the best and the brightest: leveraging human capital." *Human Resource Management*, 41(3): 325–40.
25. Hitt, M.A., Bierman, L., Shimizu, K. and Kichhar, R. (2000) "Direct and moderating effects of human capital on strategy and performance in professional service firms: a resource-based perspective." *Academy of Management Journal*, 44(1): 13–28.
26. Sirmon, Hitt and Ireland (2007) "Managing firm resources in dynamic environments to create value."
27. Andreou, A.N., Green, A. and Stankowsky, M. (2007) "A framework of intangible valuation areas and antecedents." *Journal of Intellectual Capital*, 8(1): 52–75.
28. Ashton, R.H. (2005) "Intellectual capital and value creation: a review." *Journal of Accounting Literature*, 24: 53–134.
29. See Sparrow, P.R. (2006) "Knowledge management in global organisations." In G. Stahl and I. Björkman (eds), *Handbook of Research into International HRM*. Cheltenham: Edward Elgar, pp. 113–38; Adenfelt, M. and Lagerström, K. (2008)

"The development and sharing of knowledge by centres of excellence and transnational teams: a conceptual framework." *Management International Review*, 48(3): 319–38; Lewin, A.Y., Massini, S. and Peeters, C. (2009) "Why are companies offshoring innovation? The emerging global race for talent." *Journal of International Business Studies*, 40: 901–25; Meyskens, M., Von Glinow, M.A., Werther, W.B. and Clarke, L. (2009) "The paradox of international talent: alternative forms of international assignments." *International Journal of Human Resource Management*, 20(6): 1439–50; Michailova, S. and Mustaffa, Z. (2011) "Subsidiary knowledge flows in multinational corporations: research accomplishments, gaps, and opportunities." *Journal of World Business*, 47(3): 383–96; and Sparrow, P.R., Scullion, H. and Farndale, E. (2011) "Global talent management: new roles for the corporate HR function." In Scullion, H. and Collings, D. (ed.), *Global Talent Management*. London: Routledge, pp. 39–55.

30. O'Leary, Lindholm, Whitford and Freeman (2002) "Selecting the best and the brightest," p. 325.
31. Hitt, Bierman, Shimizu, and Kichhar (2000) "Direct and moderating effects of human capital on strategy and performance in professional service firms."
32. Andreou, A.N., Green, A. and Stankowsky, M. (2007) "A framework of intangible valuation areas and antecedents." *Journal of Intellectual Capital*, 8(1): 52–75.
33. Ashton (2005) "Intellectual capital and value creation: a review."
34. Teece, D.J., Pisano, G. and Shuen, A. (1997) "Dynamic capabilities and strategic management." *Strategic Management Journal*, 18: 509–33.
35. Fernández-Aráoz, C., Graysberg, B. and Nohria, N. (2011) "How to hang on to your high potentials." *Harvard Business Review*, 69(10): 69–83.
36. Hitt, Bierman, Shimizu, and Kichhar (2000) "Direct and moderating effects of human capital on strategy and performance in professional service firms," p. 15.
37. *Ibid*., p. 16.
38. See Sparrow (2006) "Knowledge management in global organisations"; Sparrow, P.R. (2012) "Global knowledge management and international HRM." In G. Stahl, I. Björkman and S. Morris (eds), *Handbook of Research into International HRM*, 2nd edn. Cheltenham: Edward Elgar, pp. 117–41.
39. See Trevor, C.O., Gerhart, B. and Boubreau, J.W. (1997) "Voluntary turnover and job performance: curvilinearity and the moderating influences of salary growth and promotions." *Journal of Applied Psychology*, 82: 44–61; Sturman, M.C. (2000) "Implications of utility analysis adjustments for estimates of human resource intervention value." *Journal of Management*, 26: 281–99.
40. Sturman, M.C., Trevor, C.O., Boudreau, J.W. and Gerhart, B. (2003) "Is it worth it to win the war for talent? Evaluating the utility of performance-related pay." *Personnel Psychology*, 56(4): 997–1035.
41. See Bargeron, L.L., Schlingemann, F.P., Stulz, R. and Zutter, C.J. (2009) Do target CEOs sell out their shareholders to keep their job in a merger? *NBER Working Paper 14724*, National Bureau of Economic Research, Cambridge, MA; Wulf, J. and Singh, H. (2011) "How do acquirers retain successful target CEOs? The role of governance." *Management Science*, 57(12): 2101–14.

42. See Reitzig, M. (2004) "Strategic management of intellectual property." *Sloan Management Review*, 45(3): 35–40; Reitzig, M. and Puranam, P. (2009) "Value appropriation as an organizational capability: the case of IP protection through patents." *Strategic Management Journal*, 30: 765–89.
43. Erickson, G.S., Rothberg, H.N. and Carr, C.A. (2003) "Knowledge sharing in value chain networks: certifying collaborators for effective protection purposes." *Advances in Competitiveness Research*, 11(1): 152–64.
44. Khalifa, A.S. (2004) "Customer value: a review of recent literature and an integrative configuration." *Management Decision*, 52(5/6): 645–66.
45. Gupta, S., Hanssens, D., Hardie, B., Kahn, W., Kumar, V., Lin, N., Ravishanker, N. and Sriram, S. (2006) "Modeling customer lifetime value." *Journal of Service Research*, 9(2): 139–55.

Index

Note: page numbers in **bold** refer to figures, page numbers in *italic* refer to tables.

Printed and bound by CPI Group (UK) Ltd, Croydon, CR0 4YY